Come Hell
or
High Water

Come Hell or High Water

A Lively History of Steamboating
on the
Mississippi and Ohio Rivers

by

Michael Gillespie

HERITAGE PRESS
Rt. 1, Stoddard, WI 54658
www.greatriver.com

Published by
Great River Publishing
Heritage Press
Rt. 1, Stoddard, WI 54658
608-457-2734

On the Internet, visit **www.greatriver.com**

ISBN 978-0-9620823-2-0

Library of Congress Control Number: 2001 131697

09   10 9 8 7 6 5

Designed by Sue Knopf, Graffolio, La Crosse, Wisconsin

Printed in the United States of America

Permissions

Excerpts from *Travels on the Lower Mississippi, 1879-1880: A Memoir by Ernst von Hesse-Wartegg,* edited and translated by Frederic Trautmann, are reprinted by permission of the University of Missouri Press. Copyright © 1990 by the Curators of the University of Missouri.

Excerpts from *Journey to New Switzerland: Travel Account of the Koepfli and Suppinger Family to St. Louis on the Mississippi River and the Founding of New Switzerland in the State of Illinois,* translated by Raymond Spahn and edited by John C. Abbott, are copyright © 1987 by the Friends of Lovejoy Library of Southern Illinois University in Edwardsville, Illinois. Used by permission.

Cover painting: "Moonlight Encounter on the Mississippi" by John Stobart. Image courtesy of Maritime Heritage Prints, 23 Union Wharf, Boston, MA 02109. 617-227-0112.

To my wife — Ginger.

Remember that ride
on the Julia Belle Swain *in 1972?*
Did you ever think it would lead to this?

Contents

Introduction

The Western Rivers

Lake Superior

MINNESOTA

St. Croix R.

MICHIGAN

St. Paul
Stillwater
Prescott

Mississippi R.

WISCONSIN

La Crosse

Lake Michigan

Pittsburgh

Allegheny R.

Monongahela R.

IOWA

Davenport
Rock Island

OHIO

Wheeling

Muskingum R.

Marietta

Ohio R.

Missouri R.

Keokuk

Peoria

Illinois R.

INDIANA

Cincinnati

Quincy

Hannibal

ILLINOIS

Alton

Wabash R.

Jefferson ville

Ohio R.

KENTUCKY

Louisville

St. Louis

Chester

Henderson
Shawneetown

MISSOURI

Cape Girardeau

Cairo

Cumberland R.

New Madrid

Hickman

Tennessee R.

Nashville

ARKANSAS

Mississippi R.

TENNESSEE

Arkansas R.

Memphis

Little Rock
Helena

Pine Bluff

Napoleon

Arkansas City
Shreveport

Greenville

ALABAMA

Lake Providence

Yazoo R.

Waterproof

Vicksburg

Red R.

MISSISSIPPI

Natchez

Baton Rouge

LOUISIANA

New Orleans

The Marvelous Steamboat

For one brief moment in our nation's history it was possible to slide down a muddy bank, board a steamboat, and travel anywhere within a *16,000-mile* system of inland waterways known as the Western Rivers. These Western Rivers consisted of all the navigable streams of the Central Basin of the United States—from the Appalachians to the Rockies. They included well-known rivers—the mighty and incomparable Mississippi, the wild and muddy Missouri, the placid and scenic Ohio—as well as a score of lesser tributaries. All of these waterways were singular in their characteristics, and all of them once hosted that wonder of nineteenth century ingenuity: the steamboat.

Western River steamboats were a marvel. Intellect conceived them; necessity molded them. They were unique to their region and their time. Their means of propulsion, the shape of their hull, and the layout of their superstructure evolved specifically to suit the variegated nature of the rivers they traveled and the tonnage they hauled. In the simplest of terms, Western River steamboats were built to run in shallow depths and in narrow confines on waterways devoid of swells. They carried freight by the hundreds of tons and passengers by the score. They were propelled by paddlewheels and they literally could lift themselves over shoals and reefs.

These great craft were known by the names boldly emblazoned on their sides—names like *Time and Tide*, *City of Baton Rouge*, *Thompson Dean*, *Sucker*

State, J.M. White, and *Car of Commerce.* (Despite the persistence of movies and television, not a single steamboat on the Western Rivers operated under the generic name of *River Queen.*) They stopped at well-known cities and towns, and at hundreds of diminutive landings that no one off the river ever had heard of—clearings such as Homeplace, Hog Point, Fish Pond, Ollie, Zebra, Gold Dust, Happy Jack, Mhoon, Bull Pen, and Waterproof (which wasn't).

These smoking, puffing works of carpenter Gothic usually wore themselves out or sank to the bottom within five years of their launching. The prospect of suddenly being hurled skyward in a horrific boiler explosion or washed into icy waters from the deck of a sinking packet loomed as very real possibilities for the average steamboat passenger. The explosion and fire that killed 1,547 passengers and crew onboard the steamboat *Sultana* on April 26, 1865, remains to this day the deadliest transportation catastrophe in United States history. A traveler in the 1830s caught the essence and danger of steamboating when he wrote:

> *The New Orleans steamboats are a very different description of vessels to any I had yet seen. They are of great size, and the object being to carry as large a cargo as possible; the whole vessel, properly so called, is devoted to this purpose, and the cabins for the passengers are raised in successive tiers above the main deck. The engines are generally constructed on the high-pressure principle, and one or two generally blow up every season, sending a score or two of parboiled passengers to an inconvenient altitude in the atmosphere.[1]*

In essence, this book is an anthology of nineteenth century steamboat experiences, with emphasis on the Mississippi and Ohio Rivers. Passengers, crewmen, or newspapermen wrote most of the accounts. Some of the material was intended for publication, especially in Europe, where travel accounts of American river journeys enjoyed something of a vogue among Victorian readers. A number of episodes quoted in this book were penned as private letters and diaries. While these may be coarser of style, they often are more revealing in content. Included also are a few "stretchers" of Mark Twainian proportions. They have a basis in fact but the particulars are far out of size and season. The rivermen knew them well and could steer around them; the landsman might follow one clear out of the river.

The punctuation and spelling of the quoted material in this work requires an explanation. Typically, nineteenth century writing featured lengthy, compounded sentences laced with subordinate clauses. Commas were overused. Spelling often was quite original. This creates a dilemma: historians and serious students expect quotes to reflect the original construction, but general readers of history find the archaic styles distracting. I leaned toward the general reader in this regard. Rather than fill each page with the ubiquitous "sic," I have modified without notice the punctuation and spelling—and infrequently altered a word or phrase. The modifications and alterations are minor, and never were done if the change brought the original meaning into doubt. But for the sake of historians and students I have included precise references to the original documents. The trained historian and the conscientious student will review those documents as a normal course of research.

This book is based on the recorded impressions of those who knew steamboating from a personal point of view. Given the imprecise knowledge of the day, and the quaint romanticism of the age, one may come to wonder how our ancestors ever managed to conceive and build the Western River steamboat. But invent it, build it, and use it to their advantage, they most certainly did—come hell or high water.

1   Thomas Hamilton, *Men and Manners in America*, 2 vols. (Edinburgh: William Blackwood, 1833; reprint ed., New York: A.M. Kelley, 1968), pp. 2:195-96.

PART 1

Vessels *and* Navigation

Early Steamboats

> **"Name the greatest of all inventors. Accidents."**
> *—Mark Twain*

As with so many other useful creations, credit for inventing the steamboat did not go to the man who first conceived of it, nor to those who expended their talents to perfect it. The credit went to the last man in line—the man who made a commercial success of it. To be a success on the Western Rivers, a steamboat had to make money for its owners.

False Starts

Perhaps because it was revolutionary by nature, the idea of a steamboat found its roots in the minds of eccentric men. The merit of their innovation was judged accordingly. In 1707 a Frenchman named Denis Papin unveiled the first steam-powered boat and demonstrated his marvel on German waters. Papin reasonably expected fortune and fame; he did not get it. Instead, he aroused the anger of sailors and boatmen who feared his contraption would eliminate their jobs. A mob destroyed the boat and chased the hapless inventor out of town. A generation later, Jonathan Hulls produced his version of a steamboat in England. For his efforts, Hulls was ridiculed to the point of exile. He starved to death while in seclusion. In America, erstwhile clockmaker and inventor John Fitch began tinkering

Fig. 71.—John Fitch, 1796.

American John Fitch built this boat in 1796 and demonstrated it on a pond in New York City. His earlier boats had featured oar-like paddle mechanisms instead of the screw propeller shown here. (Thurston, *A History of the Growth of the Steam-Engine.*)

with steamboats in 1785. Over the next twelve years he built three working steamboats and staged successful demonstrations in Philadelphia and New York City. Influential men watched his demonstrations, but they were put off by Fitch's unkempt appearance and erratic mannerisms. No one offered financial backing. Impoverished and disgusted, Fitch fled to Bardstown, Kentucky, in 1798, where he found solace, and death, in a mixture of opium and whiskey.

Other inventors took their turn. Virginian James Rumsey built a working model of a jet propelled steamboat, but died in 1792 before he could perfect the thing. In that same year, Elija Ormsbee, of Rhode Island, demonstrated his concept of a steamboat. It utilized paddles—as opposed to paddlewheels. Ormsbee cast about for financial backers, but none came forward, and the project languished. Elsewhere, a gentleman named William Longstreet launched a primitive steamboat on the Savannah River in Georgia. It worked reasonably well, but apparently that small satisfaction was enough for Longstreet. He pursued the quest no further.

In the meantime, the development of the steam engine moved ahead. In the 1790s Nicholas J. Roosevelt built an engine factory in New Jersey. Roosevelt's steam engines were close copies of the dependable Boulton and Watt engines, which had enjoyed great success in England. They were low-pressure, condensing engines—designed to pump water from mine shafts and wells. In 1797 Robert R. Livingston, noted diplomat and financier, exchanged ideas with Roosevelt concerning the feasibility of a steam-powered boat. Their correspondence developed into an agreement to design and build a prototype steam vessel. But the plans were doomed to failure when Livingston insisted on propelling the boat with a horizontally-mounted paddlewheel. Roosevelt's engineers warned that the arrangement would overtax the engine, and Roosevelt suggested an alternative—a vertical paddlewheel, which he believed would require less power. Livingston, however, would have none of it. The boat was tested in 1798—with predictable results—and led to dissolution of the partnership.[1]

During the first decade of the 1800s Oliver Evans and his son, George, were building steam engines for milling and manufacturing plants in Philadelphia and Pittsburgh. Theirs were high-pressure engines, unencumbered by the complicated condensing apparatus of low-pressure designs, and much more powerful. Addressing the obvious concern, Oliver Evans had convinced business owners that high-pressure boilers were safe because their riveted seams would bleed off excess pressure rather than explode. (Experience would prove him wrong.) Evans also planned to install one of his engines in a boat then under construction at New Orleans. He estimated that his engine, with a three-foot stroke and nine-inch cylinder, was ten times more powerful than low-pressure devices of equal dimensions. "I believe my principle is the only one suitable for propelling boats up the Mississippi," he wrote. In all likelihood the Evans high-pressure engine would have worked wonderfully in the venture, but before it could be installed high water and storms swept away the boat hull. The project was abandoned and the engine sold to a sawmill to satisfy debts.[2]

Fulton Steamboats

The man credited with developing the first successful steamboat was Robert Fulton. A man of many interests and talents, Fulton had gone to France from Philadelphia in 1801, and there supported himself as a portrait artist while he tried to interest the French government in his design for a submarine vessel. While in Paris he met Robert Livingston, who was serving as the United States minister to France. Conversations between the two Americans eventually centered on their mutual interest in steam-powered vessels. Fulton mentioned that he had built a steamboat model a few years earlier, but was frustrated in his attempts to design a paddle mechanism. Livingston suggested the vertical paddlewheel design advocated by Nicholas Roosevelt. Livingston also gave Fulton a copy of John Fitch's drawings, which the inventor had entrusted to Livingston some ten years earlier. After studying the drawings and considering the use of a paddlewheel, Fulton asserted that he could adapt a combination of fea-

Robert Fulton. Though hailed as the inventor of the steamboat, Fulton's vessels were poorly suited to the rivers of the Mississippi Valley. (Thurston, *A History of the Growth of the Steam-Engine.*)

tures to create a successful steamboat. This was sweet music to Livingston's ears, for the financier had secured an agreement with the state of New York that would give him a steamboat monopoly if he could produce an efficient boat. The two men formed a partnership with Livingston bankrolling Fulton's design.

The first boat of this joint effort was built in Paris. It was slow, but Fulton had intended it only as an experiment to test his ideas. The side-mounted paddlewheels were an improvement over other motive designs and he felt sure that a better engine would increase the speed. With Livingston anxious to secure an American monopoly, Fulton agreed to build the next boat in New York. He placed an order for a Boulton and Watt engine, to be shipped to the United States, and returned to America late in 1806. After a century of experimentation, the pieces were about to fit together, once and for all.

The result of Fulton's work was the *Clermont*, a 150-foot long side-wheeler. *Clermont* made her maiden voyage on the Hudson River in August, 1807. She averaged just under 5 miles per hour during her 150-mile run. That was sufficient for her purposes. Touted as the first steamboat, she was in fact only the first to operate on a commercial basis. There was nothing truly original about the *Clermont*. Fulton all but admitted the same when he later wrote: "Every artist who invents a new and useful machine must compose it of known parts of other machines."[3]

Fulton would have gotten no argument out of Nicholas Roosevelt. The engine builder was quite sure Fulton had used "known parts," because the

Clermont featured those same vertical paddlewheels that Roosevelt had proposed nine years earlier. This was enough for Roosevelt—he threatened to bring suit against Livingston and Fulton. The matter was settled through an intermediary who saw that there were bigger prizes ahead—steam navigation of the Mississippi and Ohio Rivers. Perhaps, suggested the intermediary, Livingston and Fulton might consider a partnership with Roosevelt in a steamboat venture on those rivers. Thus the Mississippi Steamboat Navigation Company came into being in 1809. Livingston would provide the funds, Fulton would draw up the designs, and Roosevelt would supply the engine and study the navigation.[4]

Work began on the Livingston-Fulton-Roosevelt steam vessel at Pittsburgh in 1810. Apparently the boat* was 148 feet long by thirty-two feet wide. She cost the then enormous sum of $38,000. Her blue-painted hull extended four feet below the water line and eight feet above it. She was schooner-rigged with two masts and a bowsprit. Never mind that this boat did not sail; old habits died hard. A helmsman steered the vessel by means of a tiller located at the stern; the pilot positioned himself at the bow and directed the helmsman with hand signals.

The engine, an American copy of the Boulton and Watt model, was mounted vertically in the hold. It utilized low-pressure steam and an exhaust-cooling condenser. Ten to twenty pounds of steam pressure on one side of the piston stroke, enhanced by a partial vacuum on the other, provided power for perhaps twenty revolutions per minute. The piston rod extended upward, straight through the main deck, where it connected to a heavy fulcrum, known as a walking beam. Another rod, on the opposite end of the beam, reached down to a horizontal crankshaft and converted the up-and-down movements of the walking beam into the circular motions of the shaft. Both ends of the crankshaft extended outboard of the hull, where the arms of the 16-foot diameter paddlewheels radiated outward. The paddles, known as buckets, dug into and out of the water, thus propelling the craft.

The boiler, which provided steam, or "elastic vapor," was simply an upright cylinder perched atop a brick-lined firebox. A tall iron chimney

---

* The term "ship" did not apply to the Western Rivers. All powered river craft, without regard to size, were called "boats."

carried away the smoke and hot gases, and thus created a draft over the fire. A safety valve, held down by weights, rose above the boiler. The machinery and a fuel bin for wood were located amidships in the hold.

Cabins and berths occupied the middle deck. The ladies' cabin, aft, featured carpets, mirrors, windows, and four berths. Forward, in the larger gentlemen's cabin, curtains screened a dozen or more bunk beds, and a long dining table occupied the center of the room. The gentlemen's cabin adjoined the galley and pantry, and farther forward were small staterooms for the boat's officers. The vessel could carry seventy-five passengers.

Although constructed at Pittsburgh, the owners never intended for this steamboat to operate on the Ohio. The major cities of the Ohio—mere towns really—were all on the upper river, and the boat drew too much water to stay off the bottom in most places and seasons. In order to make money, this boat would go south to run in regular service on the Mississippi between New Orleans and Natchez. To make that point clear, she was christened New Orleans. The only obstacle in the way was two thousand miles of obscure channel. While Fulton oversaw the actual construction, Roosevelt traveled down the Ohio and Mississippi in a flatboat to survey the difficulties. When the time came, he would command the New Orleans.

> *The boat made Henderson, Kentucky, by December 16, and so did the opening shocks of the New Madrid earthquake. Two hundred miles below, the Mississippi rolled and churned and reversed itself as it tumbled into great chasms in the earth.*

The voyage began on October 20, 1811, with well-wishers and naysayers looking on. Many of the raftsmen and keelboatmen on hand were sure the New Orleans would blow up or sink. Yet Roosevelt had brought along his wife and daughter, and his wife was expecting another child. There were also two female servants on board, a waiter, a cook, six deckhands, a pilot, and an engineer.

Under the Great Comet of 1811, the New Orleans splashed her way down the Ohio. She lost nearly six weeks tarrying between Louisville and Cincinnati, waiting for the river to rise. During that delay Mrs. Roosevelt brought a son into the world—the first birth on a steamboat. The boat made Henderson, Kentucky, by December 16, and so did the opening shocks of the New Madrid earthquake. Two hundred miles below, the Mississippi rolled and churned and reversed itself as it tumbled into great chasms in the earth. The superstitious would say the river was angry at humans for insulting it with this puffing interloper. A day or two after leaving Henderson, the *New Orleans* outran hostile Indians. Then came a fire on board that gutted the gentlemen's cabin, and easily could have destroyed the boat. The shaken crew kept going and arrived at Natchez on December 30. A curious scene followed, for coinciding with the congratulations and celebrations—and adding nicely to it—a wedding took place, right there on the main deck. The groom was the engineer of the *New Orleans* and the bride was the boat's maid; a minister from Natchez did the honors. After all of that, the remaining 300 miles to New Orleans were understandably anticlimactic. The boat arrived on January 10, 1812.

The voyage of the *New Orleans* was not the ringing success that her proponents had hoped for—she was underpowered and scarcely could stem the current when she turned upstream. This did not deter the Livingston-Fulton-Roosevelt consortium from building two more similar boats: the *Vesuvius* and the *Aetna*. The company planned to set up a relay operation on the river; *New Orleans* would run from her namesake city to Natchez, *Vesuvius* would ply between Natchez and Louisville, and *Aetna* would steam from Louisville to Pittsburgh. That was the plan; the reality was something quite different. None of these boats had sufficient power for their assignments, and all were patterned after ocean vessels in the design of their hulls. The fate of *Vesuvius* was typical: she spent most of her useful life grounded on sandbars and shoals.[5] A true *river*-boat would require radically different features—and no one understood that more than Henry M. Shreve.

Shreve Steamboats

As captain of a keelboat, Henry Shreve had made many long, arduous trips between Pittsburgh and New Orleans and knew all too well the difficulties of navigating the Mississippi and Ohio. He believed in the feasibility of river steamboats but he had no faith in the Fulton designs. Shreve was much more interested in a boat produced by Daniel French at Pittsburgh. French's boat, the *Comet*, though too small to make money, featured some new and intriguing concepts. For one, French had eliminated the heavy and cumbersome walking beam. In its place, French developed an oscillating steam piston, which permitted the piston rod to connect directly with the paddlewheel crank. Too, French used a moderately high-pressure, non-condensing engine, more closely patterned after the Evans' engines. The *Comet* made at least two good trips between Pittsburgh and Louisville before departing for New Orleans in 1814. Ultimately, the *Comet* would break down on her return trip, but Shreve— who chanced upon the crippled vessel while piloting his keelboat—was convinced that inexperience more than flawed design accounted for *Comet's* misfortune.[6]

Not surprisingly, Shreve engaged French in a partnership to build a new steamboat, the *Enterprise*. Completed in 1814, she was a sternwheeler, 80 feet long, with a cargo capacity of 75 tons. She left Pittsburgh, bound for New Orleans, on December 1, 1814. The United States was then at war with Great Britain and *Enterprise's* cargo consisted of munitions for General Andrew Jackson's army. She made the trip in 14 days and then spent the next few weeks shuttling supplies and troops to various locations near New Orleans. At one point during these errands *Enterprise* was fired upon by British shore batteries, but suffered no material damage. After the January 8, 1815, Battle of New Orleans, *Enterprise* began an ascent of the Mississippi and Ohio Rivers, and arrived at Louisville on May 31, 1815, and at Pittsburgh in the later part of June. "She is the first steamboat that ever made the voyage to the mouth of the Mississippi and back," proclaimed a Pennsylvania newspaper. "…She was only thirty-four days in actual service in making her voyage, which our readers will remember must be performed against powerful currents, and is upwards of 2,200 miles in length."[7] The Baltimore-based publication, *Niles' Weekly Register*, waxed eloquence in its coverage of the successful voyage: "How do the rivers and canals of the old world dwindle into insignificance compared with this, and what a prospect of commerce is held out to the immense regions of the West by the means of these boats."[8]

Shreve was not a party to this self-congratulating, for he believed that the *Enterprise* had succeeded only because the Mississippi was above flood stage at the time of his ascent and he had taken advantage of slack water in the overflowed areas. In his opinion the *Enterprise* could not repeat the performance in normal river stages. So while the *Enterprise* made regular

trips on the Upper Ohio under another captain, Shreve labored over plans
for his next boat, the *Washington*.

In terms of structural layout and mechanical innovation, the *Washington*
truly was the original Western River steamboat. All that came before her
were experimental and short-lived, while the *Washington* featured innovations that set the standard for future boat building. To begin with, the
boat's engines were placed on the main deck, not in the hold. The boilers
developed high-pressure steam—about 100 pounds per
square inch—and they were laid horizontally. So, too,
was the piston cylinder, with its six-foot stroke. The
cylinder no longer oscillated; its connecting rod, called
the "pitman," pivoted on a wrist pin. Shreve devised a
"cam cutoff" that would close the steam intake valve
about half-way through the piston stroke and thus save
three-fifths of the fuel. The now-empty hold was
reserved for small freight; larger items could be placed
on the main deck. Passenger accommodations were on
a new, upper deck—the boiler deck. "She is furnished

> ∞
> *How do the*
> *rivers and canals*
> *of the old world*
> *dwindle into*
> *insignificance*
> *compared with*
> *this . . .*
> ∞

and equipped in a very superior style," bragged *Niles' Weekly Register*.
"Gentlemen from New York who have been on board of her assert that her
accommodations exceed anything they have seen on the [Hudson] River."[9]
The boat looked top-heavy, but in fact the bulk of her weight was on the
main deck. She was a sidewheeler, 148 feet long and 25 feet in beam. She
could carry 400 tons of cargo. And she was the first Western River steamboat to blow up.

The explosion took place just below Marietta, Ohio, on July 9, 1816. This
was to have been *Washington's* maiden voyage to New Orleans. The boat
had just gotten underway when she lost steerageway in the current. To
keep her from running aground, the crew threw out an anchor. The boat
listed, which apparently caused a safety valve weight to slide out of position. The steam pressure rose dramatically and one of the boilers blew
apart. At least ten were killed in the accident, and several more injured—
including Shreve. The boat itself was not destroyed. Though much affected
by the several deaths, Shreve arranged to have the *Washington* floated down
to Louisville for repairs. It would take two months to install a new boiler
and make modifications to the safety valves. At last, the scarred *Washington*

passed below Louisville on September 24, 1816, to continue her voyage and usher in the true beginning of the packet steamboat era.[10]

Lawsuits over patents and navigation rights would hinder the development of the river steamboat. Only 18 Western River steamers were built by 1817—the year the first one reached St. Louis—and it was 1823 before steamboats traversed the entire length of the Mississippi. These early boats were dangerous, unreliable, and inefficient. (In varying degrees, the same argument would hold true for the entire steamboating era.) In fact, they were often more trouble than they were worth.[11]

Voyage of the Western Engineer

By far the oddest looking of the early-day steamers made her appearance in 1819. She was the *Western Engineer*, one of six boats assigned to support an exploring and scientific expedition in the West. On board the *Western Engineer* was assistant naturalist, Titian Ramsay Peale, the twenty-year-old son of noted portrait painter and naturalist, Charles Willson Peale. Titian Peale kept a journal of his steamboat travels and begins with his description of the *Western Engineer* as the expedition prepared to leave Pittsburgh:

> *May 3, 1819. Our boat is built in the most convenient manner for the purpose. She draws about two feet and a half water, the [paddle] wheels placed in the stern in order to avoid trees, snags and sawyers, etc. On the quarter deck there is a bullet proof house for the steersman. On the right hand wheel is* James Monroe *in capitals, and on the left,* J.C. Calhoun, *they being the two propelling powers of the expedition. She has a mast to ship and unship at pleasure, which carries a square and topsail, on the bow is carved the figure of a large serpent, through the gapping mouth of which the waste steam issues. It will give, no doubt, to the Indians an idea that the boat is pulled along by this monster.*
>
> *4th. Tuesday Morning. We tried the stream and took a few turns in the river, and were visited by Mr. Evans and a few other gentlemen who advised many alterations, but we will content ourselves with covering the boilers with wool phlox, and loading the wheel with lead in place of a fly wheel for the present.*
>
> *5th. Wednesday. Having completed all alterations and taken all stores aboard at ½ past 4 in the afternoon we bid adieu to Pittsburgh and descended rapidly down the Ohio. At about fourteen miles below*

the town we saw a steamboat grounded. We received and returned her salute as we passed by. Our boat seems to attract universal attention, the people stopping all along the shore to gaze at us as we pass by.

9th. Sunday. Stopped for wood this morning about 5 miles above Maysville, Kentucky. Last night we experienced a tremendous thunderstorm with very heavy rain, in which we were blown ashore but received no injury but the loss of our flag staff with a signal lantern which was attached to it. Arrived at Cincinnati, Ohio, between ten and eleven at night.

19th. Kept under way all last night. Arrived at Louisville, Kentucky, at ½ past 2 o'clock. After taking in wood and procuring a pilot, we crossed the falls. They are not so difficult to navigate as expected. What are called the falls are two miles in length and in that distance the water falls 22 feet over flat rocks of limestone which are filled with organic remains. The water boils and splashes about in a most violent manner, and in one place resembles exactly the surf of the sea. The town of Shippingport stands directly at the foot of the falls. At this place most of the steam and other boats load and unload their cargo, for unless the water is in the highest stage large boats cannot ascend. It is in contemplation to make a canal around the falls, which I think is of first importance to the vast extent of country about. Steam navigation from here is progressing in a most astonishing manner. A few days ago, there were no less than twenty steamboats unloading here, most of them in the New Orleans trade. . . . When the obstructions are removed from the rivers, and canals made in some places, the interior navigation of this extensive country will be superior to any in the world.*

24th. Continued down the river under a pressure of upwards of 100 pounds of steam to the square inch, which carried us at the rate of some ten miles per hour.

28th. Left Shawnee Town [Illinois] at 12 o'clock, and stopped 2 miles below to take in wood. Proceeded at 2. At about 4 went aground on a sandbar 7 miles above Cave-in-Rock, or House of Nature. By

---

* The Falls of the Ohio were bypassed in 1830 with the completion of the Louisville and Portland Canal.

dint of anchor, setting poles, steam, and all the men in the water prying her, we got off just at dark, and ran down hill until we were opposite the Cave-in-Rock where we laid to for the night.

30th. Got under way early and came to for wood at 8 o'clock at a place laid out for a town called America, about as ridiculous a name as they could find for any town at present. There is only a little clearing and no houses. It stands nine miles from the mouth of the Ohio on the right side going down. The wind being strong ahead we did not reach the Mississippi until afternoon. The Indian name for it is Misachipi (Father of Waters).

31st. Finding it necessary to repack the pistons of our engine, went on shore to hunt but returned unsuccessful, having seen several deer and turkeys, but the mosquitoes and nettles preventing the necessary precaution to approach them. Started at 2 o'clock. The current of the Mississippi is astonishingly rapid and muddy and much intercepted with snags and sawyers. Came to at dark after having made 18 miles.

5th [of June]. Struck on a snag which jarred the boat considerable and soon after we discovered that the water was nearly up to the cabin floor. Set all hands to pumping and came to at dusk, on the western side, the hands at the pump all night.

6th. Sunday. Discovered the leak to be in the stern just below the water mark; having lightened her we erected a pair of shears and raised her stern sufficiently to get at the leak and caulk it.

7th. After taking in wood at Herculaneum [Missouri], started up the river. After proceeding some distance on coming to rapid part of river found that we could not raise steam enough to ascend owing to the quantity of mud deposited in the boilers from the water of the Mississippi. We accordingly anchored 2 miles above the mouth of the Meramec River to have them cleaned. The contrast between the waters of the Mississippi and Meramec River is astonishing. The one is clear and transparent and the other thick with yellow mud, though very rapid. At the junction it is very striking to a person seeing it for the first time.

9th. Arrived at St. Louis about 11 o'clock, were received with a salute from a 6-pounder [cannon] on the bank and from several steamboats along the town.[12]

The *Western Engineer* eventually would ascend the Missouri River to near present-day Council Bluffs, Iowa. Peale continued his work as a naturalist and explorer until 1849, when he became an examiner in the U.S. Patent Office.

1   Florence L. Dorsey, *Master of the Mississippi: Henry Shreve and the Conquest of the Mississippi* (Boston: Houghton Mifflin, 1941), pp. 70-73; Edith McCall, *Conquering the Rivers: Henry Miller Shreve and the Navigation of America's Inland Waterways* (Baton Rouge: Louisiana State University Press, 1984), pp. 52-89.
2   E.W. Gould, *Fifty Years on the Mississippi; or, Gould's History of River Navigation* (St. Louis: Nixon-Jones Printing Co., 1889; reprint ed., Columbus, Ohio: Long's College Book Co., 1951), p. 150; Dorsey, p. 73; McCall, pp. 88-89.
3   Dorsey, pp. 78, 84, 109.
4   McCall, pp. 82-83. A complete story of the *New Orleans'* first voyage is found in Mary H. Dohan, *Mr. Roosevelt's Steamboat* (New York: Dodd, Mead & Co., 1981).
5   Dorsey, pp. 82, 89; McCall, pp. 102-108.
6   *Ibid.*, pp. 98-98, 104-109.
7   Quoted in McCall, p. 134.
8   *Niles' Weekly Register*, 1 July 1815.
9   *Ibid.*, 20 July 1816.
10 Dorsey, pp. 111-14; McCall, pp. 144-46.
11 Walter Havinghurst, *Voices on the River* (New York: Macmillan, 1964), pp. 59-60; Louis C. Hunter, *Steamboats on the Western Rivers: An Economic and Technological History* (Cambridge, Mass.: Harvard University Press, 1949), pp. 75-76; Norbury Wayman, *Life on the River* (New York: Bonanza, 1971), p. 145.
12 *Titian Ramsay Peale Journals*, 1819-1842. Library of Congress Manuscript Division, Washington, D.C. See also *Account of an Expedition from Pittsburgh to the Rocky Mountains under the Command of Major Stephen H. Long*, with an Introduction by Howard R. Lamar (Barre, Mass.: Imprint Society, 1972), pp. xv-xxi.

Riverboat Architecture

Improvements in the utility and appearance of steamboats came steadily, through trial and error, over the span of two score years. From hybrid sailing vessels to graceful, ornamented sidewheelers, the fantastic Western riverboats of the nineteenth century gradually assumed their classic, multi-tiered form. Like the young nation, they tended towards the big, the bold, and the extravagant.

Cabins and Decks

Passenger accommodations underwent quite an evolutionary process. Early steamboat deck layouts varied a great deal, but generally they followed the Shreve plan of placing staterooms on the second deck so as to leave the lower deck—the main deck—open primarily for freight and machinery.

Eventually, it came about that the forward main deck, or forecastle, was set aside for the boats' implements: derricks, stage planks, capstan, hawsers, chains, anchors, spars, and related items. Farther back, but still forward of the beam, sat the boilers, flanked by their fuel—either racks of wood or bins of coal. Just aft of the beam, on sidewheel boats, came the "machinery:" shafts, pipes, valves, levers, cams, and steam cylinders—the paraphernalia of the engine room. The engine room was enclosed between the two

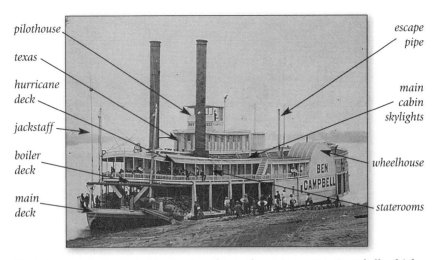

pilothouse

texas

hurricane deck

jackstaff

boiler deck

main deck

escape pipe

main cabin skylights

wheelhouse

staterooms

Deck layout of a typical sidewheeler. This is the steamer *Ben Campbell*, which operated on the Upper Mississippi during the 1850s. (Library of Congress.)

paddlewheel houses. A row of offices and storage rooms adjoined the wheel houses. The stern-most portion of the main deck was a common location for stabling livestock consignments. All other spaces on the main deck were set aside primarily for freight.

The second deck was termed the "boiler deck." It consisted of a long interior room known as the main cabin or saloon. Initially, this cabin served as both sleeping quarters and social hall, with berths cordoned off by curtains. The after-section was the "ladies' cabin," which usually was delineated by a partition. Male passengers were accomodated in the forward main cabin, where one also would find a bar, a barbershop, and the offices of the clerk and steward.[1]

By the 1840s the curtained berths of the main cabin had given way to private staterooms that now lined either side of the cabin. Staterooms featured two berths, and were further adorned with etched-glass windows, curtains, mosquito-bars, toilet stands, drawers, chairs, carpets, "and all the elegant necessaries of a cozy bedroom."[2] One stateroom door led to the interior main cabin, the other opened out onto the boiler deck. Magazine writer Julian Ralph was assigned a double stateroom during his 1892 journey to New Orleans. He was quite pleased with the room—and with the dazzling white main cabin:

I had been in my stateroom and found it the largest one that I had ever seen on a steamboat. It had a double bed in it, and there was room for another. There was a chair and a marble-topped washstand, a carpet, and there were curtains on the glazed door and the long window that formed the top of the outer wall. The supper bell rang, and I stepped into the saloon, which was a great chamber, all cream-white, touched with gold. The white ribs of the white ceiling were close together over the whole saloon's length of 250 feet, and each rib was upheld by most ornate supports, also white, but hung with gilded pendants. Colored fanlights let the light in by day, and under them other fanlights served to share the brilliant illumination in the saloon with the staterooms on either side. At the forward end of the saloon were tables spread and set for the male passengers. At the other end sat the captain and the married ladies and girls, and such men as

The main cabin. Situated on the boiler deck between the staterooms, it ran nearly two-thirds of a boat's length. The entire cabin was illuminated by dazzling colored-glass skylights. At mealtimes, the chairs and tables were rearranged to form a dining hall. (Photo courtesy Murphy Library, University of Wisconsin-La Crosse.)

*came with them. The chairs were all white, like the walls, the table-
cloths, and the aprons of the Negro servants, who stood like bronze
statues awaiting the orders of the passengers.*[3]

Another description of the main cabin comes to us from Samuel L.
Clemens—Mark Twain—during his apprenticeship as a pilot in the 1850s.
On one of his first trips on a fine Mississippi packet, Clemens noted:

*She was as clean and as dainty as a drawing-room; when I looked
down her long gilded saloon, it was like gazing through a splendid
tunnel; she had an oil picture, by some gifted sign-painter, on every
stateroom door; she glittered with no end of prism-fringed chandeliers;
the clerk's office was elegant, the bar was marvelous, and the barkeeper had been barbered and upholstered at incredible cost.*[4]

Captains did not often turn away cabin passengers, even when the staterooms were full. In such cases the staterooms went to the ladies, and the
gentlemen made do with blankets and mattresses arranged within the
main cabin, much as hotels would accommodate an overflow by placing
guests in the lobby. A magazine writer in 1857 noted an amusing incident
that arose during an overbooked run—

*It is not uncommon to accommodate the machinery of the boat, so
that some parts, such as the flywheel, work up into the cabin under
the table. Upon this table a friend had secured a bed and, laying
himself down, was congratulating himself upon his good fortune at
lying there rather than on the floor, when he heard a drawling passenger say to his companion: "See that feller there laying over the flywheel? Last week Jim Roberts went to sleep just there, and they fired
up and drove the old tub along, and the flywheel busted and sent
Jim Roberts to kingdom come in less 'n no time."*
My friend immediately moved his bed.[5]

With the cabin and staterooms situated above on the boiler deck, the
first-class passengers were spared the annoyance and odor of the cargo on
the main deck below. A professional travel writer, Ernst von Hesse-
Wartegg—the Baron de Wartegg—noted that the main deck usually was
crowded with all sorts of smelly, greasy, sticky, and oily consignments.

"Yet," he wrote, "this mess is so hidden, so separate from passengers, that one rarely suspects freight and never gets a whiff of the odors so redolent on most oceangoing steamers." The observant German wrote that the boilers could be seen in the open spaces of the main deck and that baled cotton frequently was loaded along the outer spaces of the deck, where it could be stacked without interfering with the machinery.[6] These outer deck spaces were called "guards." They extended well beyond the width of the hull, sometimes by fifteen feet or more on either side. The guards created more cargo room, but just as importantly they helped prevent the side paddle-wheels from hitting a vertical obstruction, hence their name. On the boiler deck, where the cabins were located, the outside promenade also was known as the "guard." The boiler deck guard provided ample space for sitting or strolling, with plenty of intricate carpentry work to accent the view.

The Grand Era

Eventually steamboat motif outclassed anything seen on shore. Many residents of the Valley looked upon Western River steamboats as the most beautiful of all structures; little wonder they coined the phrase "elegant as a steamboat." Newspapers announced the arrival of a spanking new boat with unparalleled enthusiasm, especially if the boat were locally owned. A St. Louis paper barely could restrain itself in describing the new steamer *Missouri* in 1846 (the first of six boats to carry the name):

> *In a walk through her spacious cabin it is hard to divest one's self of the idea that the foot is treading the hall of some regal palace, so finished is everything around—elegant carpets, splendid chandeliers, and sumptuous furniture, with all the appliances which studied attentions can devise for comfort, ease, and luxury. Her saloon, when thrown open from the office in her bow to the stern windows, is one of the most imposing on any vessel in the world. Its extreme length is three hundred and five feet, by eighteen wide and twelve high, and throughout is finished in a most superb and costly style. Seventy-three feet of this length shuts off with beautiful folding doors, separating the ladies' saloon from the gentlemen's cabin, and is furnished with an elegant piano. In this apartment Captain Twitchell has recently made a pleasing improvement: he has removed the bulkhead in the rear of*

The boiler deck guard—a breezy, comfortable place to watch the shoreline slip by. (From *Harper's New Monthly Magazine.*)

the ladies' saloon, supplied its place by curtains, and constructed large stern windows, of beautiful colored plate glass, through which a soft and mellow light falls into the ladies' apartment. When the heat is oppressive, these windows can be thrown open, leaving a free passage of air through the entire length of the cabin.

Her sleeping apartments are furnished with every comfort which can be found in the best-regulated hotels—are well ventilated and kept scrupulously neat. The cabin is divided into 54 rooms, 16 of which are intended for families—altogether capable of accommodating, comfortably, about 125 passengers with berths, and extra beds for 50 or 75 more. Bath houses for ladies and gentlemen, supplied with hot and cold water, gentlemen's barber shop, and, indeed every necessary and luxury which can tend to pleasant traveling, comfort of invalids, pleasure of the tourist, or ease of the man of leisure, is here concentrated in a floating palace.

One inconvenience generally felt by ladies on board steamboats will be obviated—the congregating of servants, black, white, and mixed, with passengers around the same fire in the ladies' cabin, there being a portion of the boat furnished expressly for them in a separate apartment.[7]

Steamboats of the 1840s and beyond not only were elegant, but also large and substantially built. The *Missouri*, for example, had a keel measuring 280 feet, with a 307-foot span of main deck, a 38-foot beam beyond which the paddlewheel houses and main deck guards extended an additional 13 feet on either side, and a 10-foot hold for additional cargo. Her bottom was 14 inches of solid oak, the main deck planking five inches thick, and her bow strengthened with seven feet of solid timber. Twenty-two tons of iron were used in her fastenings. To keep her hull from sagging under this immense weight, she was fastened fore and aft with hog chains. These sturdy links, which could be tightened or loosened with turnbuckles, passed from bow to stern over 45-foot high samson posts located amidships.

As the years progressed, steamboats developed configurations adapted to their specific use, though the unaccustomed eye seldom discerned the differences. The overall size, the draft of the hull, the shape of the bow—all told something of a boat's intended purpose. There were the "mountain boats" of the Missouri with their rounded prows, the abbreviated and unadorned light-draft vessels of the upper rivers, the stout Ohio River towboats, and the cotton transports of the Lower Mississippi with wide guards supported by truss rods.[8]

The era of the largest and fastest steamers came in the decade immediately after the War Between the States. Ironically, it was also the last hurrah for first-class steamboats; the further expansion of railroads and the introduction of Pullman sleepers soon would take away most of the long-haul river traffic. The following magazine excerpt was published in 1870—just as steamboating had reached its apex. The article praises the utility and beauty of steamboats while pointing out at the same time an unsettling reality:

This [Thompson Dean] is a noble craft which bears us safely over the turbid waters of the great river. She is some two hundred and ninety feet in length, and fifty-six in breadth. From her keel to the roof of the upper cabin she includes forty feet. Above that is the "texas," as it is called, which is an upper row of cabins where the officers' quarters are, and upon the top of which is imposed the pilothouse. The main cabin is plainly but well furnished, with large staterooms on either side. Below it is the main deck, where the big boilers and furnaces and engines are. Below this deck again there is a deep, spacious hold, where a thousand or fifteen hundred tons of freight may be stowed away. This hold is a peculiar feature of our boat. At least, with my experience, I have never seen such a space below decks.

The cabin of our boat is so large that we are able to have tables placed across as well as lengthwise. Thus, instead of three fearfully long tables, where everything is in confusion and all is in common, the passengers are divided up into parties of six and ten, to the convenience and comfort of all. The food provided is very palatable.

The staterooms, or sleeping chambers, on the boat are quite large; they have double berths, wash basins, and mirrors, and all of this is kept in good, cleanly order. Of course there is a door opening out upon the guards. This doorway has blinds, and a printed notice on the wall tells you they are very good life preservers, in the event of a burst up, or other accident. It is rather uncomfortably significant to see these means of saving life, and the constant call upon your attention, so prominent; but it is well to know that these and other means of safety, which also include cork life preservers, are at hand. By the way, if there should be an accident, I prefer, as a matter of choices, one of the blinds.

It is a question whether this steamboating is a more dangerous mode of travel than others. It had a sort of settlement the other day, at least in the mind of one of the Negroes, who exclaimed:

"If yer blowed up on de railroad, thar you is; but, good Lord, if yer blowed up on a steamboat, whar is you?"[9]

Colors, Pennants, and Distinctive Touches

When the Baron de Wartegg arrived on the river well into the heyday of steamboating, he had nothing but praise for the colossal riverboats. He informed his European readers that "Cleopatra's barge could not have been more cheerful, more luxurious, or more elegant than the Mississippi's waterborne palaces."[10] This high praise was seconded some twenty years later by a New York writer on his first Mississippi voyage:

> [Steamboats] are, so far as I remember, all painted white, and are very broad and low. Each carries two tall black funnels, capped with a bulging ornamental top, and carrying on rods swung between the funnels the trade-mark of the company cut out of sheet iron—an anchor or an initial letter, a fox or a swan, or whatever. There are three or four stories to these boats: first the open main deck for freight and for the boilers and engines; then the walled-in saloon [boiler] deck, with a row of windows and doors cut alternately close beside one another, and with profuse ornamentation by means of jigsaw work wherever it can be put; and, last of all, the "texas," or officers' quarters, and the "bureau," or Negro passengers' cabin, forming the third story.* Most of the boats have the big square pilothouse on top of the texas, but others carry it as part of the third story in front of the texas.
>
> These Mississippi packets of the first and second class are very large boats, and roominess is the most striking characteristic of every part of them. They look light, frail, and inflammable, and so they are. The upright posts that rise from the deck of such a boat to support the saloon deck are mere little sticks, and everything above them, except the funnels, is equally slender and thin. They would seem to a man from the coast not to be the handiwork of shipbuilders; indeed, there has been no apparent effort to imitate the massive beams, the peculiar "knees," the freely distributed "bright-work" of polished brass, the neat, solid joiner-work, or the thousand and one tricks of construction and ornament which distinguish the work of our coast boat builders. These riverboats—and I include all the packets that come upon the Mississippi from its tributaries—are more like the work of carpenters and house builders. It is as if their model had been slowly developed from that of a barge to that of a houseboat, or barge with a roof over it; then as if a house for passengers had been built on top of the first

---

* The "bureau" was a post-emancipation addition to some steamboats, and probably derived its name from the Freedmen's Bureau—a Federal agency created to oversee the welfare of former slaves.

roof, and the texas and bureau had followed on the second roof.

Pictures of the packets scarcely show how unlike our boats these are, the difference being in the methods of workmanship. Each story is built merely of sheathing, and in the best boats the doors and fan-lights are hung on without frames around them; all loose and thin, as if they never encountered cold weather or bad storms. All the boats that I saw are as nearly alike in all respects as if one man had built them. I was told that the great packets cost only $70,000 to $100,000, so that the mere engine in a first class Atlantic coast river or sound boat is seen to be of more value than one of these huge packets, and a prime reason for the difference in construction suggests itself. But these great, comfortable vessels serve their purpose where ours could not be used at all, and are altogether so useful and appropriate, as well as picturesque and attractive to an Eastern man, that there is not room in my mind for aught than praise of them. [11]

An occasional touch of color offered pleasant relief from the glaring white superstructure of most boats. Decks and roofs often were darkened with shades of blue. Many steamers featured a red stripe painted lengthwise on their white hulls. A few boats sported red or green hulls with a corresponding white stripe. The famous *Natchez* established a singular tradition with her trademark red chimneys. The most aesthetically pleasing opportunity for adding color to the boats' exteriors came in the design and adornment of paddlewheel housings. Here, bold and husky letters, with bright-colored shadowing, visually shouted a boat's name to all that came in view. Sometimes the name of the packet company or the points of destination would appear in an arc along the edge of the housings, and paintings frequently graced the wheelhouse sides. These works of commercial art ranged from simple sunburst patterns to intricate murals that in some way depicted or elaborated the name of the boat.

The display of banners and flags was another means of adding color and distinction. Besides the jackstaff on the bow and the verge-staff on the stern, there were flagstaffs near the wheelhouses and sometimes aft of the pilothouse. The national colors flew at the verge; brightly embellished pennants heralding the name of the boat and the principal cities it served waved from the other staffs. Etiquette suggested that the city or person for which the boat was named should donate the banners when the steamer made her first home port call. It was all very flashy, all very colorful, and of course, all intended to attract business.[12]

1   Charles J. Latrobe, *The Rambler in North America,* 2 vols. (London: Seeley & Burnside, 1836), pp. 281-82.
2   Joseph L. Cowell, *Thirty Years Passed Among the Players in England and America* (New York: Harper, 1844; reprint ed., Hamden, Conn.: Archon Books, 1979), pp. 91-92.
3   Julian Ralph, "The Old Way to Dixie," *Harper's New Monthly Magazine* 86, no. 512 (January 1893), p. 169.
4   Mark Twain, "Old Times on the Mississippi, Part 2," *The Atlantic Monthly* 35, no. 208 (February 1875): 220.
5   "Up the Mississippi," *Emerson's Magazine and Putnam's Monthly* 5 (October 1857): 455.
6   *Travels on the Lower Mississippi, 1879-1880: A Memoir by Ernst von Hesse-Wartegg,* ed. and trans. by Frederic Trautmann (Columbia: University of Missouri Press, 1990), p. 25.
7   [St. Louis] *Weekly Reveille* 1, no. 46 (25 May 1845): 362; *ibid.,* 2, no. 48 (8 June 1846): 886.
8   *Travels on the Lower Mississippi,* pp. 22-23.
9   George W. Nichols, "Down the Mississippi," *Harper's New Monthly Magazine* 41, no. 246 (November 1870): 835, 843.
10   *Travels on the Lower Mississippi,* p. 25.
11   Ralph, pp. 167-68.
12   Arthur E. Hopkins, "Steamboats at Louisville and on the Ohio and Mississippi Rivers," *The Filson Club Historical Quarterly* 17 (July 1943): 146-48.

Operations —Large & Small

Writing near the close of the steamboat era, Mississippi Valley historian John W. Monette portrayed the Western Rivers as "the great highways of nature, given for man's use."[1] Readers of the present day may tend to overlook the simple truth of his statement. As much distress as the rivers were apt to cause, they were infinitely less expensive to utilize than trails or railroads. Robert Fulton once estimated that steamboats could carry a ton of freight from Pittsburgh to New Orleans for less than it would cost to ship the same freight overland from Pittsburgh to Louisville.[2] And, unlike trails and railroads, the rivers were already in place—the Ohio an east-west route, and the Mississippi a north-south trunk line—both with dozens of feeder routes. It fell to the rivermen to develop the possibilities. The commercial operations that evolved over time ranged from the simple, to the ridiculous, to the sublime.

Rafts, Keelboats, & Flatboats

Rafts, keelboats, and flatboats were the first commercial vessels on the big rivers, and their numbers hardly diminished during the steamboat era. Rafts, which could be quite long, sometimes transported bulk items, but more often their cargo was the raft itself that would sell as lumber when it reached New Orleans. Keelboats, being more difficult to build, were far fewer in number. Although better suited to lakes and canals, keelboats remained a fixture on the rivers because the shape of their hull made it possible to work them both up and down stream. Flatboats, as the name implied, had flat bottoms with squared angles and straight sides. They were simple, sturdy craft that could carry bulk items such as coal or grain, or be configured as floating houses or stores. Flatboats typically were fifteen feet wide and at least fifty feet long. An oar, or sweep, trailed from the stern of the boat though it seldom was used except to bring the craft into a landing. Skilled craftsmen frequently traveled by flatboats from village to town and used their flats as mobile workshops. When they completed their work at one landing they drifted on to the next. An adaptation of the flatboat, known as the shanty boat, gave rise to a whole class of poor, itinerant farmers and fishermen who plied the Mississippi in search of intangible gains. Forty-five years into the steamboating era, rafts and flats still floated into New Orleans at an average rate of two per day.[3]

While steamboats and free-floating craft may have operated on the same rivers, no one claimed that they *shared* the waters. Indeed, they perpetually *competed* for space in narrow channels. When rivers were low and tempers hot, raftsmen conspired to block the flatboats, flatboaters plotted to ground the rafts, and both groups contrived to bump the steamboats into the next dry bayou. Raftsmen had the hardest time of it, for their craft were nothing more than crude masses of timber indifferently bound together and difficult to steer. Getting the rafts to New Orleans in one piece offered a challenge to the most experienced crew. In low water sandbars could break apart any raft, and at high water stage the raftsmen had their hands full trying to keep the raft from being sucked down an island chute, where the current was swift and the river narrow. Maritime law gave an edge to the rafts—since they were the least maneuverable—and nothing made their crewmen happier than a chance to flaunt the advantage by blocking the path of an up bound steamer and forcing the powered vessel to sheer off. The game went their way most of the time; if not, the survivors were free to sue.[4]

Towboats & Barges

A hybrid form of river transportation appeared on the Western Rivers beginning in the 1850s. By combining the economy of rafts and flatboats with the powered advantage of the steamboat, the concept of towing barges

Flatboat versus steamboat. Free-floating craft had the right-of-way, but raft and flatboat crewmen were notorious for not showing a warning light until a steamer was close upon them. Then the air would fill with a cacophony of engine bells and hard swearing as the steamboat pilot frantically tried to avoid a collision. (From *Harper's New Monthly Magazine*.)

made its debut. The term "towing" mislead those not familiar with the river. From a practical standpoint, a barge could not be towed, or pulled, on the moving currents of the Western Rivers—the barge would tend to swing from side to side, or else ram the back of the towing vessel. Instead, the term derived from the practice of lashing barges alongside a packet boat. But this had its disadvantages, for the addition of more than one barge on either side of the boat made the packet slow and difficult to control. Over time, it worked out better to push the barges ahead, *provided* they were tightly bound to one another and to the powered vessel.

While some of the original barges were nothing more than old steamboat hulls, true barges featured squared bows and sterns. Thus configured, they fit together in a solid "tow." Towboat bows were squared as well, and fitted with stout bumper posts, or "knees," to insure that the towboat did not run up under the stern of a barge. The steering requirements of pushing long strings of barges made sternwheelers the choice configuration for towboats. Towboats did not carry passengers, which meant they were rather unspectacular in design. This lack of esthetics disturbed many of the old-time packet boat pilots, who oftentimes referred to towboats, and the towing industry as a whole, in rather disparaging terms.[5] The typical steamboat passenger was less apt to ridicule them, as in this observation:

> *The tows that we saw were too peculiar to miss mention. On this [Mississippi] river the loads are "towed before" instead of behind. The principle underlying the custom is that of the wheelbarrow, and is necessitated by the curves in this, the crookedest large river in the world. The barges and flats are fastened solidly ahead of the towboat in a great fan-shaped mass, and the steamer backs and pushes and gradually turns the bulk as if it had hold of the handles of a barrow in a crooked lane. We saw a famous boat, the* Wilson, *from Pittsburgh, come along behind a low black island. It proved to be a tow of large, low, covered barges, thirty of them, each carrying 1000 tons. The work of propelling these tows is so ingenious that the pilots are handsomely paid. They cannot drive their loads; they merely guide them, and a mistake or bad judgment in a bend may cost thousands of dollars through a wreck. The barges are made of merely inch-and-a-half [planking], cost $700 each, and are seldom used twice. They are sold to wreckers.[6]*

Packet Freighting

The persistence of rafts and flats throughout the steamboating days, and the introduction of barge traffic, illustrated a basic economic law of the river: the real money lay in freight hauling. No matter how fancy a packet steamboat might appear or how well thought of by the traveling public, the conveyance of passengers alone did not make a boat profitable. The builders knew this and they designed the boats with an emphasis on cargo space. It was done so well that cabin passengers seldom were aware of the freight capacity of their floating hotels. On occasion, however, a casual comment would open up a whole new world to a wide-eyed passenger from the East. For a lesson in river cartage we again board the *Thompson Dean* as she lies at Cairo, Illinois, on a down bound trip in 1870:

> *Thousands of barrels of flour were rolled into the hold, which lies under the main deck, until it seemed as if not another stave could find place. Then the [railroad] cars came in from the north, and several hundred head of mules and horses came on board, and were put somewhere. Subsequently there came coops filled with geese, turkeys, and chickens, and the air was filled with braying, neighing, bleating, crowing, cackling, and gobbling, until one began really to believe they could appreciate the feeling of Noah when he was loading up for that little excursion he took in the ark.*
>
> *Upon the following morning, when we were once more puffing our way down the swollen river, I ventured with confidence to say to the captain: "Well, sir, we took in a big freight. Crowded full, are we not?"*
>
> *"Full? My good friend!" he answered, with a smile of pity at my ignorance. "Why, she'll take in fifteen hundred tons more!"*
>
> *I made no reply, but at the first opportunity plunged below stairs. What a sight it was, to be sure—piles of sacks of corn ten high and ten square, and I do not know how many of them running fore and aft. Piles upon piles of barrels of flour, almost filling the lower hold, which seemed to be another boat when you got down there. Out on the guards of the main decks were the four-legged animals. In the passageways and on the guards of the saloon deck above were stacks of wagons, plows, shovels, and all sorts of farming utensils. I gazed at all of this mass of merchandise, and, muttering to myself "fifteen hundred tons more," slowly and thoughtfully ascended to the ladies' cabin*

of the boat, where the passengers were occupied in reading, playing cribbage, or otherwise amusing themselves.

> *Sometimes we passed cornfields which extended continuously for miles along the river and for a long distance inland. Many of these places were situated upon the shore of some chute or side channel. All along the bank would be found piles of corn. A signal from its owner would cause our boat to swing around and take the pile of three or ten hundred sacks on board. Again and again and many times was this done, until we ceased to wonder at the receptive capacity of the vessel, and came to believe that there was no limit to her space.*

> *At Helena [Arkansas] we made quite a halt, in order to take on three hundred bales of cotton. We smiled derisively at the suggestion, but we had the pleasure of seeing them piled up twenty feet high on the forward deck.*[7]

This amazement with the freight carrying capacity of Mississippi steamboats carried all the way through to the end of the packet days. A passenger watching the loading process on the *City of Providence* at St. Louis in the 1890s recorded his stunned impression:

> *They loaded the* Providence's *lower deck inside and out; they loaded her upper deck where the chairs for the passengers had seemed to be supreme; and then they loaded the roof over that deck and the side spaces until her sides were sunk low down near the river's surface, and she bristled at every point with boxes, bales, agricultural implements, brooms, carriages, bags, and, as the captain remarked, "Heaven only knows what she ain't got aboard her." It was well said that twenty ordinary freight trains on a railroad would not carry as much freight as was stowed aboard of her, and I did not doubt the man who remarked to me that when such a boat, so laden, discharged her cargo loosely at one place, it often made a pile bigger than the boat itself.*[8]

Wharf Operations

Loading and unloading freight was a slow process, usually accomplished through brute human strength, and made all the more difficult when the landing was nothing more than a "rude bank." One passenger wrote: "I seldom looked long at such a bank that I did not see a piece of it loosen and crumble and fall into the rushing, yellow river. Sometimes it was only a ton that fell in; sometimes it was a good fraction of an acre."[9] As steamboat traffic increased, many towns sought to upgrade their primitive landing sites into some sort of permanent wharf. Improving the site was always in a town's best interest, not only for the benefit of local merchants and shippers, but also because the town could then levy a tax—a wharfage fee—on the boats that came to call.

The extreme rise and fall of the rivers made fixed piers impractical. Many towns and cities paved their landings with stone, and embedded mooring rings into the pavement. These permanent, paved wharves necessarily were long—in order to accommodate several boats—and wide—to conform to any stage of the river. They were expensive to build and maintain and quite inadvisable in areas where the shore was apt to be cut away. Wharfboats were the most practical alternative. Wharfboats were old

> *. . . we ceased to wonder at the receptive capacity of the vessel, and came to believe that there was no limit to her space.*

steamboat hulls with the machinery removed. All or part of the superstructure was remodeled to accommodate storage for perishable goods, freight consignment offices, and rooms for waiting passengers. Since they were tied to the shore, they rose and fell with the river and made excellent docks. Packet lines often would maintain wharfboats at principle stops for the convenience of passengers and shippers. Nevertheless, one observer noted that wharfboats were not the best place to pass idle time:

> About these wharfboats congregate all the idle and good-for-nothing fellows of the town who, having no steady occupation, hope to pick up some job which will keep them supplied with the two things needful—whiskey and tobacco. In the sheltered interior of the boat, it is not uncommon for the master and his friends to wile away the tedious hours of waiting (and they are many) with a social game of cards and a rousing song; sometimes, where whiskey is so plenty, mischief results, and the newspapers are supplied with a "startling occurrence" or a "shocking casualty."[10]

Frequent stops to load or discharge freight occurred throughout the day and night. The passengers gave little notice, but not so with the small town

Passengers waiting on a wharfboat. With the upper works built upon the hull of a derelict steamer, wharfboats were ideally suited as floating docks at landings where unstable banks or fluctuating river stages made permanent wharves impractical. (From *Harper's New Monthly Magazine.*)

urchins along the rivers' shores. From New Orleans to St. Paul, Pittsburgh to Cairo, wherever a steamboat landed, some slack-jawed boy stood enraptured by the sight. It made no difference to him if the boat simply were taking on a few sacks of grain, this was the stuff of dreamy adventure—and all the more romantic if at night, by the light of the crackling torch baskets that hung over the side of the boat.

When the boat came into a night landing the watchman filled one or two torch baskets with split pine and sap, lit them at the furnace door, and fixed each in its socket. The burning fuel illuminated the landing for hundreds of feet around. From time to time the watchman or an apprentice crewman would add more pinewood and rosin. At Prescott, Wisconsin, where the performance occurred almost nightly in season, a young man named George B. Merrick found inspiration in the ritual.

"The rosin would flare up with a fierce flame," he recalled many years later,

> *followed by thick clouds of black smoke, the melted tar falling in drops upon the water, to float away, burning and smoking until consumed. This addition to the other sites and sounds served more than any other thing to give this night work a wild and weird setting. We boys decided, on many a night, that we would "go on the river" and feed powdered rosin and pine kindling to torches all night long, as the coal-black and greasy but greatly envied white lamp-boy did, night after night, in front of our attic windows on the levee at Prescott.* [11]

Small Boats, Little Rivers

Not all steamboats were the huge, swift packets depicted in Currier and Ives prints. Size worked against a riverboat, for the larger craft were restricted to the main stems of the river system. With competition so keen on the big rivers, some enterprising captains found more lucrative trade on smaller streams and bayous. Of course, commanding a boat no larger than a cottage down some backwater bayou did lack a certain prestige. The diminutive size of the boat and the relative obscurity of the stream sometimes were offset by the overinflated ego of the captain, and the combination made for an interesting, if not spectacular, trip. That was the experience of Thomas Bangs Thorpe, a widely read humorist and newspaper correspondent, in a story datelined Concordia, Louisiana, February 1844:

> *The first time I found myself on one of these boats I looked about me as did Gulliver when he got in Lilliput. It seemed as if I had gotten larger, and more magnificent than an animated colossal. The machinery was tremendous, two large kettles firmly set in brick, attached to a complicated looking coffee mill, two little steam pipes, and one big one. And then, the way the big steam pipe would smoke, and the little ones let off steam was singular. Then the puffing of the little coffee mill! Why, it worked spiteful as a tomcat with his tail caught in the crack of a door. Then the engineer, to see him open the "furnace" doors and pitch in wood; and open the little stop cocks to see if the steam was not too high, all so much like a big boat. Then the name of the boat, THE U.S. MAIL, EMPEROR, the letters covering the whole side of the boat, so that it looked like a locomotive adver-*

tisement. Then the U.S. MAIL *deposited in the corner of the cabin, and two rifles standing near it, as if to guard it, said mail being in a bag that looked like a gigantic shot pouch, fastened to a padlock, and said pouch filled with three political speeches, franked by members of Congress, one letter to a man that did not live at the place of its destination, and a bundle of post office documents put in by mistake.*

The bell that rung for this boat's departure was a tremendous bell; it swung to and fro awfully; it was big enough for a cathedral, and as it rung for the twentieth last time, one passenger came on board weighing about three hundred, and the boat got under weigh. "Let go that hawser!" shouted the captain, in a voice of thunder. Our track lay for a time down the Mississippi, and we went ahead furiously, overhauled two rafts and a flatboat within two hours, and resented the appearance of a real big steamer most valiantly, by nearly shaking to pieces in its waves. Being light myself I got along very well, but whenever the fat passenger got off a line with the center of the cabin, the pilot would give the bell one tap, and the captain would bawl out: "Trim the boat!"

After an hour or so the little boat turned up a "dry outlet," which Thorpe described as "a little gutter that draws off some of the water of the Mississippi when very high." Thorpe continues:

The banks of the dry outlet were very low, very swampy, and were disfigured occasionally with wretched cabins, in which lived human beings who, the captain of the Emperor *informed me, lived—as far as he could judge—by sitting on the heads of barrels and looking out on the landscape, and at his boat as it passed; from the fact that they had not cultivable land, and looked like creatures fed on unhealthy air, we presumed that was their only occupation.*

In time we arrived at the "small village," the destination of the mail pouch, and landing, visited the town. It was one of the ruins of a great city, conceived by land speculators in "glory times." Several splendid mansions were decaying about, in the half-finished frames that were strewn upon the ground. A barrel of whiskey was rolled ashore, the mail delivered, the fat man got out, and we departed.

Thus we struggled on until, sailing up a stream with incessant labor such as we went down when we commenced our sketch, we merged into the world of water that flows into the Mississippi. Down the rapid current we gracefully went, the very astonishment of the regular inhabitants on its banks.

Again for the innumerable time, the "furnaces" consumed the wood, and as it had to be replenished, we ran alongside one of those immense woodyards, so peculiar to the Mississippi, where lay in one continuous pile thousands of cords of wood. The captain of the Emperor, as he stopped his boat before it, hallooed out from his "upper deck" in a voice of the loudest kind: "Got any wood here?"

Now the owner, who was a very rich man, and a very surly one, looked on the "heap," and said he thought it possible.

"Then," said the captain, "how do you sell it a cord?"

The wood-man eyed the boat, and its crew, and its passengers, and then said he would not sell the boat any wood, but that the crew might come ashore and get their hats full of chips for nothing.[12]

1   John W. Monette, "The Progress of Navigation and Commerce on the Waters of the Mississippi River and the Great Lakes, A.D. 1700 to 1846," *Publications of the Mississippi Historical Society* 7 (1903): 480.

2   Mark Reardon, *Big Load Afloat: The History of the Barge and Towing Industry*, vol. 1: *Early Years* (Arlington, Va.: The American Waterway Operators, 1981), p. 15.

3   Willard Glazier, *Down the Great River* (Philadelphia: Hubbard Brothers, 1892), pp. 332-33. See Ben L. Burman, *Big River to Cross: Mississippi Life Today* (New York: John Day Co., 1940), for an interesting and revealing look at shanty boat life as it existed in the early twentieth century.

4   Thomas B. Thorpe, "Remembrances of the Mississippi," *Harper's New Monthly Magazine* 12 (December 1855-May 1856): 39.

5   Reardon, p. 17; see also *Encyclopedia USA*, s.v. "Barge Lines," and "Barges," by Michael Gillespie. Mark Twain referred to towboats as "vulgar," in *Life on the Mississippi* (Boston: Osgood & Co., 1883), p. 142.

6   Ralph, p. 184.

7   Nichols, pp. 839-40, 843.

8   Ralph, p. 166.

9   *Ibid.*, p. 179.

10 "Up the Mississippi," p. 456.

11 George B. Merrick, *Old Times on the Upper Mississippi: The Recollections of a Steamboat Pilot from 1854-1863* (Cleveland: Arthur H. Clark, 1909; reprint ed., St. Paul: Minnesota Historical Society Press, 1987), pp. 34-35.

12 Thomas B. Thorpe, "The Little Steamboats of the Mississippi," [New York] *Spirit of the Times*, 9 March 1844, p. 19.

Propulsion, Engines
& Wooding

Western River steamboats bore little resemblance to coastal or open sea vessels. The disparity was even more apparent when one began to examine the inner workings of the riverboats. Their engines and propelling mechanisms were designed for shallow waterways with dangerous currents. Always in the mind of every steamboat pilot and engineer was one overriding thought: if the machinery ran afoul, the boat simply did not drift to a stop—it hit something!

Paddlewheels

Paddlewheels were the most distinctive feature of riverboats. Whether placed on the sides or at the stern, river steamers retained the paddle much longer than their oceangoing cousins—and they did so for reasons that went beyond tradition. Although screw propellers became the preferred motive device at sea, the river was by its very nature an altogether different medium. In order to produce the requisite thrust for an average steamboat, a propeller would have to measure seven or eight feet in diameter. The shallow Western Rivers did not permit that size. Steamboat hulls rarely drew more than six feet, and even then they frequently struck bottom. Furthermore, experimentation on small vessels with correspondingly smaller propellers demonstrated the vulnerability of propeller blades to driftwood and other debris. The same experiments showed that sand in the water rapidly cut away at the underwater journals.[1]

In every way paddlewheels were better suited to the river. No matter how large their diameter, they extended only two or three feet below the waterline, and they could be adjusted for less. Paddlewheels were, in effect, a simple application of the principle of gearing. The individual paddles, or buckets, struck the water at the rate of three or four hundred strokes per minute even though the wheel itself turned at a mere twelve or fifteen revolutions. The buckets were made of wood, and most boats carried spares; if a floating log broke a bucket, it could be replaced with minimal trouble. And paddlewheel bearings were located high above the waterline where normal friction was the only concern.

Paddlewheel steamboats differed principally from one another in the positioning of the paddles. They could be mounted at the sides, at the stern, or amidships. The paddlewheel amidships, or centerwheel, arrangement often was utilized on ferryboats. It was convenient for ferries to have the generous deck space afforded by a single inboard paddle; otherwise, centerwheel steamers lacked commercial speed. The Union navy implemented an adaptation of the centerwheel arrangement during the War Between the States. Seven river gunboats and an additional series of turreted vessels featured the design. The paddlewheels were set inboard just astern of the beam and encased in thick wood sheathing and iron armor. These boats were slow, but the paddlewheel was protected from damage by cannon shot.[2]

Sidewheelers were suited best to mercantile use. Unlike the single engine and common shaft arrangement of the earliest models, later sidewheelers used independent wheels with two separate engines. In a difficult navigational situation, one wheel could be set ahead, with the other running in reverse, and the boat would twist around like a pinwheel. They also handled better in tricky winds and currents. Nevertheless, sidewheelers had their own inherent faults. The paddles were unprotected by the hull and therefore subject to damage by floating logs, vibration was excessive at times, the boats were heavier and more expensive than sternwheelers of similar dimensions, and the peculiar fluid mechanics of sidewheel propulsion sometimes rendered the rudder ineffective.

Sternwheelers were considered more powerful than sidewheelers, and the hull protected the stern-mounted paddlewheel from most floating hazards. For a long time in their evolution, however, sternwheelers were plagued with a steering problem of their own. The rudder hinged aft from the stern post and extended partially below the paddlewheel. The stern rake was abrupt; the stern itself fully as wide as the beam. Water flowing along the bottom and sides of the vessel swirled and eddied as it closed around the blunt stern. The churning of the paddlewheel further agitated the water. This whirling, fluid zone acted on the surface of the rudder and greatly decreased its effectiveness; the boat tended to understeer. Placing additional rudders across the transom did little to overcome this. Then, in the 1870s, the "balance rudder" came into general use on sternwheelers. The balance rudder featured an enlarged surface area. About half of it extended in front of the stern post and under the rake of the stern—which was now modified to a more gradual slope. The larger rudder, equalized by the movement of water fore and aft of its pivot point, turned easier and produced a remarkable improvement in steering response. With the rudder problem solved, sternwheelers became the vessel of preference late in the steamboat era.[3]

Engines

Technically, the engine consisted of the steam cylinder together with its valve mechanisms. The engine connected to the paddlewheel by means of a pitman rod. It was a heavy wooden beam reinforced with stay bolts and iron plates. The engine was in a separate compartment from the boilers, which were placed in the forward half of the boat in order to offset the weight of the paddlewheel. Steamboat engines fell into two distinct categories: high- and low-pressure. The low-pressure engine, as seen on the Fulton steamboats and occasionally revived on later vessels, derived much of its power from a condenser. Water jets within the condenser cooled the steam as it exhausted from the piston cylinder, and this created a partial vacuum. Aided by this vacuum, the steam on the expansion side of the stroke entered under a pressure only moderately higher than the outside atmosphere. Boiler explosions on low-pressure engines were rare, and the traveling public knew this, but low-pressure engines were ill-suited to conditions on the Western Rivers. Pound for pound, they were not nearly as powerful as high-pressure engines, and could not respond quickly to changes in throttle settings. (On a turbid river with a swift current, pilots needed sure and immediate response from the engines to get them out of trouble.) The condensing apparatus was complicated and brittle, and the cylinders were large and heavy. If a low-pressure boat broke her machinery on the river, she might have to be towed hundreds of miles to an engine shop capable of making repairs.

High-pressure engines were characterized by their relatively small diameter and long stroke, and by venting their high-pressure exhaust directly into the atmosphere. The steam exhaust went up escape pipes, which on side-wheelers looked like two small-diameter chimneys positioned ahead of the wheelhouses. The noise they made could be annoying, or pleasant, depending on one's point of view. "It is nothing like the puff, puff, of an ordinary steam motor," wrote one passenger. "It is a deep, hollow, long-drawn, regular breathing—lazy to the last degree, like the grunt of a sleeping pig that is dreaming."[4]

In the mid-1850s, high-pressure engines became much more efficient with the advent of the "automatic variable cutoff." Sometimes also called the Corliss engine, after its inventor, George H. Corliss, this new pattern replaced the existing slide-valve arrangement and cutoff apparatus. At the heart of the improvement was the long-accepted principle that high-pressure steam entering the cylinder would continue to expand and move the piston even after the intake port had closed. This closure was called the cutoff point. On all previous high-pressure engines, the cutoff was a fixed point in the stroke cycle, regardless of the load placed upon the engine. But the load factor could vary constantly due to changes in a boat's course and trim. And the slow movement of the slide-valve led to decreased cylinder pressure and wasted power. The Corliss design improved engine operation in two ways: first, the cutoff point varied from stroke to stroke, based on the response of the governor to ever-changing load demands; and second, the

> *The noise they made could be annoying, or pleasant, depending on one's point of view. "It is nothing like the puff, puff, of an ordinary steam motor," wrote one passenger. "It is a deep, hollow, long-drawn, regular breathing—lazy to the last degree, like the grunt of a sleeping pig that is dreaming."*

reconfigured intake and exhaust valves opened and closed much more quickly and efficiently.[5] Passengers may not have noticed the new Corliss engines, but the engineers and boat owners certainly did.

Boilers

In the simplest terms, a boiler was a cylindrical tank made up of individual iron plates, riveted together. A supply pipe, with a check valve, fed water into the tank. The boiler was filled to two-thirds or three-fourths of its capacity in order to allow room for steaming. A steam pipe carried the pressurized steam from the top of the boiler to the engine. Boilers were equipped with safety valves that would open (usually) and release excess pressure at a predetermined level.

Low-pressure boilers often were simple cylinders. The heat was generated from a firebox underneath. Obviously, low-pressure boilers, operating in the range of 20 to 40 pounds per square inch were considered much safer, given the state of nineteenth century metallurgy. But since boiler water came directly from the river, the boilers were prone to clog with mud, especially those operating on the lower rivers. This only added to the general dislike among boatmen for low-pressure designs.

High-pressure boilers were much less apt to clog. A sump device known as a mud drum collected most of the sediment. Additional mud blew out the safety valve. High-pressure boilers raised steam pressure to around 100 pounds per square inch. Most were classified as "return-flue" boilers. These boilers—usually there were several arranged together—sat horizontally atop brick-lined fireboxes. The firebox doors faced forward in order to take advantage of the wind draft of a moving boat. The hot gasses from the firebox passed all the way to the rear of the boiler, then rose and passed forward *through* the boiler via dry pipes known as flues. At the front end of the boiler the gasses passed out of the flues and up into the smokestacks. Return-flues greatly added to the heating surface of the boiler—an absolute necessity to raise the required pressure—but those same flues were a contributing factor to most boiler explosions. If they became exposed inside the boiler due to low water level, they would overheat and bring about a catastrophic failure.

The water level was critical at all times. An independent engine, called the "doctor," kept water flowing into the boiler, but it was only as reliable as the check valve located just inside the boiler shell. The method of meas-

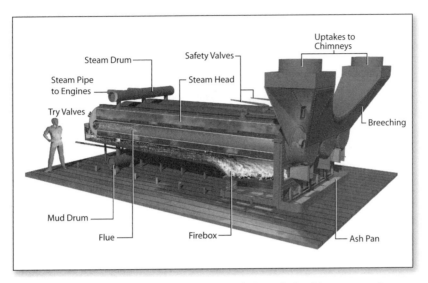

Three high-pressure boilers are arranged side by side in this cutaway drawing. Each boiler utilized two internal flues to carry the hot gases forward to the breechings. Water level within the boilers was the critical safety factor. (Illustration by Andrew Hall. Copyright © 2001 by Andrew Hall.)

uring the water level was rather crude. Three try cocks, or valves, were positioned vertically on the backhead of the boiler. Ideally, the lower cock would emit all water, the middle cock steam and water, and the upper cock all steam. To be effective the cocks had to be tested *frequently*—and foaming within the boiler could result in a false reading. Glass sight tubes gradually came into being, but the early models tended to fog up or break.[6]

Some boilers were destined to failure as a result of the manufacturing process. That process included punching the boiler plate rivet holes, rather than drilling them, then forcing the alignment of overlapping rivet holes with a tapered rod called a driftpin. The combined practices created unseen stress fractures around the holes. This was theorized as early as the 1830s, but the practice continued for decades because punching was quicker and less expensive than drilling.[7] One steamboat passenger, who probably expressed the typical sentiments of his day, acknowledged the "great danger" of high-pressure boilers, but he felt that much of the danger came not from inherent flaws in the boiler, but from "incompetent and careless persons" who attended them.[8]

A St. Louis newspaper of the mid-1840s provides a description of the engines, boilers, and paddlewheels of a typical river steamer. We have already toured the boat—it is the much-lauded *Missouri:*

> This majestic boat is propelled by two powerful high-pressure engines, each twenty-nine inch cylinder, twelve-foot stroke, and six hundred horsepower. Her steam is generated by seven boilers, 29 feet long and 42 inches in diameter; these are supplied with hot water by a separate engine built for that purpose, and also for the purpose of working a fire engine by steam, in case of necessity. There can be but little danger of fire, however, as her roof is made fireproof. She works 36-foot wheels, with 14-foot buckets, two-and-a-half feet under water, and which, if revolving eighteen times in a minute, will give her a velocity not heretofore attained on the Western waters. [9]

Murphy's Law claimed the *Missouri.* That "little danger of fire" proved her undoing; she burned to the waterline in 1851.

Wooding

As a rule, passengers did not comprehend the mechanical workings of the boat; most stayed away from the engine and boiler spaces where a disapproving stare and occasional comment from an oily engineer let them know they were not welcome. The typical passenger knew only that the boat required wood—lots of it—to keep the engines going. One passenger estimated that a large steamer would consume four or five hundred tons of wood in twenty-four hours. "Wooding up" was often the highlight of the day on an otherwise dull stretch of river. It usually took place twice a day, and might consume up to an hour. Passengers could go ashore and stretch their legs during a wooding stop, though often they preferred to line the railing to watch the spectacle. All the deckhands and roustabouts, and deck passengers who had purchased their ride for reduced fare, turned to for the heavy work of loading by hand. [10] Very often an "exciting physical contest" ensued to determine who could carry the largest pile, and the passengers cheered for their favorites. One traveler recorded that during this rush to get the wood aboard, the mate of the boat stood amongst the laboring crew, shouting: "'Oh, bring them *shavings* along! Don't go to sleep at *this* frolic,' and by swearing of such mon-

The woodyard man and his family. In antebellum days, steamboat boilers used wood for fuel and that gave rise to a flourishing cottage industry along the rivers' banks. (From *Harper's New Monthly Magazine.*)

strous proportions, that even very good men are puzzled to decide whether he is really profane or simply ridiculous."[11]

Woodyards were common along the rivers until the post-Civil War years when coal replaced wood as the preferred fuel. In antebellum days a family could scratch out a living—sometimes a very good living—by cutting and cording wood along the rivers' banks. To the well-bred, however, the life of a woodyard family was anything but idyllic, as attested to by this 1850s observation:

> *One of the unfortunate professions met with along this river is that of the woodcutter who . . . spends his time in communion with Nature, without being inspired by her to attempt an ideal life. His shanty stands on some elevated bank, above the reach of ordinary floods, surrounded with ranks of firewood, the only prospect he enjoys. A wretched specimen of maternity here drags out a sickly and tedious existence, surrounded by a drove of towheaded children, who live or*

die in ignorance and degradation. There are few exceptions to this class of "poor whites," so common along the rivers of the South.

At the bank, near the woodcutter's shanty, are tied two or more broad scows, in which the wood is piled in cords. Should the owner be away in the woods, a shingle stuck on a stick tells the price, such as $1.75 for soft wood, $2.25 for hard; and the steamboat clerk is expected to deposit the amount in some box or at the house, if any is taken. Boats coming down the river are obliged to round-to and tie up, while taking wood aboard; in going upstream, the steamer runs her nose between the two scows and, with one in tow on either side, goes steaming up, all hands working sharp to get the wood aboard, when the scows are cast off and, in charge of the owner, float down again to their station. [12]

1   *Official Records of the Union and Confederate Navies in the War of the Rebellion*, 30 vols. (Washington: GPO, 1895-1925), series I, 23:83.

2   James B. Eads, "Recollections of Foote and the Gun-Boats," in *Battles and Leaders of the Civil War*, 4 vols., eds. Clarence C. Buel and Robert U. Johnson (New York: Century, 1884), pp. 1:338-45.

3   Jerome E. Petsche, *The Steamboat Bertrand: History, Excavation, and Architecture* (Washington: GPO, 1974), pp. 83, 102; Wayman, pp. 160-62.

4   Ralph, p. 169.

5   Louis C. Hunter, *A History of Industrial Power in the United States, 1780-1930*, vol. 2: *Steam Power* (Charlottesville: University Press of Virginia, 1985), pp. 253-63.

6   *Ibid.*, pp. 327-29, 346-47.

7   *Ibid.*, pp. 314-16.

8   Latrobe, pp. 302-03.

9   *Weekly Reveille* 1, no. 46 (25 May 1845): 362; *Weekly Reveille* 2, no. 48 (8 June 1846): 886.

10   Latrobe, pp. 302-03.

11   Thorpe, "Remembrances of the Mississippi," pp. 37-38.

12   "Up the Mississippi," p. 456.

The Restless River

The Western Rivers of olden times were wide and shallow. Some of them were clogged with debris, and most were apt to change course after every rise. Under no circumstances could they be considered ideal avenues of transportation; indeed, from the standpoint of the steamboat industry the rivers were regarded as mean-spirited, moody, unforgiving, and dangerous. Engineers and rivermen of the nineteenth century proposed many plans to control the rivers, but they lacked the means of affecting any large-scale improvements. The rivers were too much for them—a force that knew no bounds. Man could tinker with the rivers, but never master them.

Bends & Eddies

The term "lazy river" doubtless took its origin from the fact that the big rivers never flowed in a straight line when a more scenic opportunity presented itself. This was nowhere more evident than on the Lower Mississippi, where great bends and loops followed one another in endless succession. Indeed, in steamboat days, the Mississippi settled upon a leisurely course of one thousand miles from Cairo to New Orleans where a more purposeful river might have accomplished the same communication in six hundred miles. Some of the Mississippi's bends added as much as forty miles between points that stood less than two miles apart in a straight line. After traveling the lower river in 1831, British author Thomas Hamilton found the broad bends so regular in frequency and size that he conceived it quite practicable to draw a "tolerably accurate sketch" of the river's course without bothering to survey it.[1]

But the Mississippi was misunderstood. It was not lazy; quite the opposite. In its passion to take the meandering route it always toiled to make its bends larger and longer. By throwing the considerable power of its moving water against the outer shore of the bends the river would eat away at the banks and hew a great, growing curve. This was an immutable law of the river and a continual process occurring at many places at the same time. It could have unexpected consequences. One captain recalled the time his boat tied up to a landing and he stood looking at a certain huge tree, located well inshore. Suddenly the land around the tree dissolved into the river. The big oak came crashing down—right on top of the steamboat![2]

The bank caving process often created backeddies along the shore, especially where the banks had recently caved in. These backeddies were obvious in the daylight, but at night they were indiscernible—as the following bit of mirth illustrates:

> *A sober passenger, who was floating down to [New Orleans] on one of that steady river craft called a flatboat, highly interested in the new scenery which met his eyes, remained on the watch quite into the night. It happened that the boat was caught in one of those wide eddies, often a half-mile or more in circuit, where she floated round and round, while he, happy man, supposed he was fast making his way to New Orleans. It happened also that a rich planter was that night celebrating his daughter's marriage with music and the dance. It was an interesting feature of our traveler's journey that every half-hour he came to a gaily-lighted house where he could hear the sounds of enchanting music and could see, through the windows, the foot of beauty tripping on its fantastic toe. He was, of course, interested and delighted; but he said to his friend in the city—"This country does beat all for dancing! There was a ball in every house; we passed twenty-two in one evening—it beats all!"*[3]

The Channel

The deepest part of the river—the channel—was an elusive ditch that coursed its way back and forth across the streambed. The channel seldom ran down the middle of the river, and any steamboat that got out of the channel, as they were often wont to do, would soon find herself hard aground, or worse.

The good water was on the outside of the bends, where centrifugal force cut a deep channel. But the river, like a serpent, always reversed itself from bend to bend so that the channel moved from one side to the other. The point at which the channel changed over—the crossing—was the least defined and shallowest portion of the stream. These were the places that aged a pilot before his time. During low water the current in the crossing could decrease to such a point that sediment would bar the way, and only a rise in the river stage would reopen it.

The surest way of locating the channel was to "sound" the river; in other words, to measure the depth with a leaded line or sounding pole. This routine function was performed several times a day when low water hampered navigation on the big rivers. On one occasion during the Civil War, a very inexperienced crew found another way to locate the channel. The improvised plan—crude, born of desperation, but effective—was recorded by a New York newspaper correspondent:

> Shortly after the occupation of Little Rock by General Steele, a dozen soldiers passed the lines, without authority, and captured a steamboat eighteen miles below the city. Steam was raised, when the men discovered they had no pilot. One of their number hit upon a plan as novel as it was successful.
>
> The Arkansas was very low, having only three feet of water in the channel. Twenty-five able-bodied Negroes were taken from a neighboring plantation, stretched in a line across the river, and ordered to wade against the current. By keeping their steamer . . . directly behind the Negro who sank the deepest, the soldiers took their prize to Little Rock without difficulty.[4]

Islands and Towheads

The Western Rivers were prodigious island builders, using whatever materials were at hand. Sand, driftwood, and organic matter, deposited together around a semi-fixed object during low water—topped off by a layer of airborne dust and seed—made for fertile ground. In one season a dense stand of willow chutes would take possession of this new property and help reinforce it against the encroachments of the river's currents. At this tenuous stage of its development the slender plot was known as a tow-head. The continued existence of the towhead depended entirely on the river. Minor rises would not harm it, but a big flood most certainly would do it in. If the river raised no objection and left the towhead to develop at a leisurely and natural pace for a few dozen years—no time at all to the river—the towhead would grow in all of its dimensions to become an *island,* a nearly-permanent fixture in the river's path. Often hundreds of acres in size, islands supported dense hardwood forests—and perhaps a farm or two for respectability.[5]

Islands and large towheads were numbered in sequential order from a common point of beginning. In his river travels, Thomas Hamilton once asked a pilot to name a certain prominent island they had passed. "The answer was five hundred and seventy-three, . . . the only name by which it was known."[6] More recent surveys listed 114 islands on the Mississippi between Cairo and Natchez, and 68 between Cairo and St. Louis. Islands below Natchez, and between Cairo and St. Louis, were named rather than numbered; then again, many islands below Cairo were named *and* numbered. Add to this the hundreds of sandbars and small towheads, and the many horseshoe-shaped bends that disguised themselves as islands, and the confusion became sublime.

Cut-offs

During high water the Lower Mississippi changed its character altogether. Dissatisfied with its long, winding path it seemed to want nothing more than to visit New Orleans in a hurry. To accomplish this it would feel for a weakness in some disfavored bend and then tear through the narrow neck of that bend with apologies to no one. The velocity and force of the rising water insured a permanent incision. Though at first shallow, this shorter course—the *cut-off*—would deepen in time and claim the navigation channel.[7]

Occasionally a political subdivision changed with a new cut-off. When a state boundary followed the river channel, and the channel moved to the cut-off, property owners along the inner bend of the old channel found themselves in a different state without having bothered to move. In a few regions this change meant the immediate loss of certain possessions. A Northern news correspondent recorded the following incident during the War Between the States:

> *Once, while passing up the Mississippi, above Cairo, a fellow passenger called my attention to a fine plantation situated on a peninsula in Missouri. The river, in its last flood, had broken across the neck of the peninsula. It was certain the next freshet would establish the channel in that locality, thus throwing the plantation into Illinois. Unless the Negroes should be removed before this event, they would become free.*
>
> *"You see, sir," said my informant, "that this great river is an Abolitionist."*[8]

Nineteenth century cut-offs usually were done by nature, but nature could get an assist. The Corps of Engineers coaxed the river through many man-made cuts. One of the more spectacular in its effect was the 1876 Centennial Cut-off, at Vicksburg, Mississippi. The one-mile cut-off eliminated a six-mile bend in front of the city, essentially retiring Vicksburg from the river and making "a country town out of it," according to Sam Clemens. After that, steamboats could get to the old town wharf only in high water.[9] Many years later, the Corps diverted the Yazoo River into the old Mississippi channel. Without moving, Vicksburg changed allegiance, and now fronts the Yazoo where the Mississippi once had flowed.

If a farmer owned property within a great bend of the Mississippi, and stood to profit by having the river change course, he needed only to carve a ditch where he wished the river to go. More often than not the river would take the cut during the next rise and abandon its former bend. This might prove injurious to the neighbors, but the river cared nothing for their loss. Those old bends were mysterious and forlorn places. The superstitious stayed away from them. Some claimed that weird sounds echoed down the dismal waters, and spectral shapes floated by in the fading light of dusk—best not to gaze too long down the old river, lest a phantom from the past make its chilling presence known. Consider the strange case of Raccourci Bend, Louisiana, where the old channel was cut-off in 1848:

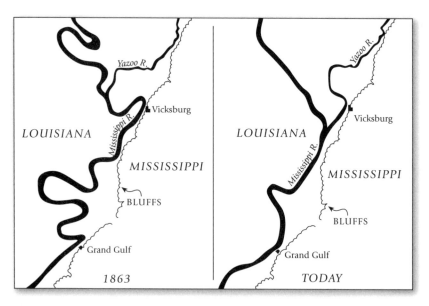

One hundred years of cut-offs and diversions have greatly altered the river course in the Vicksburg region. What had been a 135-mile stretch of river in steamboat days is now reduced to 65 miles—and the Yazoo River flows into the Mississippi's former bed.

It happened suddenly, as usual, and had not been made known to the pilots of one of the steamers of that day which was splashing and wheezing down from Vicksburg. It was night when they entered the old channel, and a gray, drizzly night at that. Presently they felt the grind of a new bar under their vessel. They cleared it, and in another minute had rammed a reef that was entirely out of place. Failing to dislodge it, they backed into a lot of snags and began to punch holes in the bottom. Nearly ready to cry at the many and uncalled for perplexities that had come into the steering business since their last trip, the pilots resorted to profanity as a relief to their own and the passengers' feelings and to the delight of that gentleman who is never far away when people go wrong. Finally one of the men at the helm roared, in a rage, that he was blessed if he didn't hope the blinkety-blanked old ark would stay right there, in the vanishing river, and never get out. He was only a fresh-water sailor and had never heard of the Flying Dutchman. *His wish was granted.*

The bend was filled up so long ago that none but the oldest men recollect when it was navigable for rowboats; yet every now and again tow captains and deckhands report a strange light in that dark and winding channel—a light as of fox-fire or phosphorus; and when the weather is not too thick, and the witnesses not too sober, they add to this tale a garnish of pale form, a phantom steamer, in short, with bell ringing funereally, engines faintly puffing, and voices using nearly forgotten "cuss words" in plaintive tones as the form bumps and staggers this way and that, ever seeking a channel that moved away for miles in a night.[10]

Floods

Whenever high water came the river surely would rearrange itself somewhere along its winding route, and high water came with the certainty and regularity of the seasons. Fed by rises out of the Missouri in late spring, and out of the Ohio in late fall, these were more than mere swellings; when the Mississippi spilled from its banks it filled a plain of fifty miles and more. Sam Clemens noted that the seasonal overflows usually opened up island chutes to steamboat passage, and treated the resident backwoodsmen to a glimpse of the passing world:

. . . There were crazy rail fences sticking a foot or two above the water, with one or two jeans-clad, chills-racked, yellow-faced male miserables roosting on the top rail, elbows on knees, jaws in hands, grinding tobacco and discharging the result at floating chips through crevices left by lost teeth; while the rest of the family and the few farm animals were huddled together in an empty wood-flat riding at her moorings close at hand. In this flatboat the family would have to cook and eat and sleep for a lesser or greater number of days (or possibly weeks), until the river should fall two or three feet and let them get back to their log cabins and their chills again—chills being a merciful provision of an all-wise Providence to enable them to take exercise without exertion. And this sort of watery camping out was a thing which these people were rather liable to be treated to a couple of times a year. . . . And yet these were kindly dispensations, for they at least

enabled the poor things to rise from the dead now and then, and look
upon life when a steamboat went by. They appreciated the blessing, too,
for they spread their mouths and eyes wide open and made the most
of these occasions. Now what could these banished creatures find to
do to keep from dying of the blues during the low water season![11]

While the stoic residents of the Valley expected the floods, endured them, and thought nothing more of them, the same could not be said for most steamboat passengers. It always seemed to catch them by surprise. With treetops swaying like bushes in the water, they sensed their vantage point to be somehow higher than it ought to be. These uninitiated tourists lined the railings to gawk at the damage brought by the awful tide upon which they rode. The spectacle inspired a passenger in 1870 to write:

It is not so much what the eye takes in upon the surface of drift-
ing trees and logs and houses, but it is the hidden force which, rush-
ing and whirling and eating underneath, undermines the giant trees
of the forest; they tumble as if smitten with the hand of death, and
plunge into the stream to be whirled and turned like twigs in a whirl-
wind. Then secret currents dig and dig at the base of some high bluff
and, in an instant, acres of rock and earth and forest sink into the
waters, and before your very eyes the solid land is engulfed and dis-
appears. As the steamboat with assured pace steams quickly past the
forest of cotton and cypress, with their solemn depth made more than
melancholy by their long draping of hanging moss, as you pass
swamps and cultivated fields, you will detect a break in the brimful
bank, and in a second the flood is upon the land, not with a rush and
a roar, giving the poor farmer with his wife and children yonder in his
cabin notice of its approach, but with silent, fatal speed it covers and
envelops field and cabin, and fortunate is its human prey should he
escape the deadly embrace.[12]

Ten years later, the well-traveled adventurer, Baron de Wartegg, sought some way to impress upon his distant readers the extent of the seasonal overflows. His effort to quantify the overflows still gives pause for thought:

Along its lower length the Mississippi annually floods to a width
of forty-seven and a half miles, and to a depth of twelve feet! This

lake of twelve billion cubic feet would require forty-eight days to drain via the normal river if not another drop arrived from the Upper Mississippi and the tributaries below Cairo. Furthermore, Mississippi Valley rainfall amounts [annually] to another lake 400 miles long, 49 feet wide, and 160 deep. In other words, enough to turn Louisiana into a sea eight feet deep. The time the Mississippi alone would need to drain this mass of water? Three years![13]

Except for the hazard of drifting logs, steamboats could operate with little hindrance during an overflow. Down bound boats, freed of their normal concern for bars and reefs, took to the middle of the river for added speed; up bound steamers hugged projecting points to find slack water and, sometimes, to catch a backeddy that would boost them upstream. Or, then again, they might choose an altogether different route. Thomas Knox, a newspaper reporter, was on hand to record one of the more original high water steamboat excursions:

During the freshet of '63, General Grant opened the levee at Providence, Louisiana, in the hope of reaching Bayou Mason, and thence taking his boats to Red River. After the levee was cut an immense volume of water rushed through the break. Anywhere else it would have been a goodly-sized river, but it was of little moment by the side of the Mississippi. A steamboat was sent to explore the flooded region. I saw its captain soon after his return.

"I took my boat through the cut," said he, "without any trouble. We drew nearly three feet, but there was plenty of water. We ran two miles over a cottonfield, and could see the stalks as our wheels tore them up. Then I struck the plank road, and found a good stage of water for four miles, until I was stopped by fallen trees, when I turned about and came back. Coming back, I tried a cornfield, but found it wasn't as good to steam in as the cottonfield."[14]

Planters, Sawyers, & Snags

The overflows filled the river with debris, especially floating logs. Every up bound boat encountered these floating forests—and the pilots did their best to thread through the bigger trees. A half-submerged log, forty feet long and four feet in diameter, hitting a wooden-hulled steamer at eight miles an hour, was going to cause some damage. It all depended on the angle of the collision. Striking a big log that had turned broadside would create enough of a jolt to turn over chairs on the boiler deck and send dishes flying from the pantry shelves. Those were the lucky hits. But more often the heavy logs came down lengthwise. If a free-floating log of substantial dimensions struck the boat end-on, in the very least it would topple those same dishes and chairs, then proceed to loosen a few hull timbers and utterly demolish a dozen or so of the paddlewheel buckets.

With its hull pierced as if by a gigantic spear, the boat would "tremble for a moment like a thing of life, when suddenly struck to its vitals, and then sink into its grave."

Some boats carried iron plating on their bows to reduce damage from drift. The real hazard came when floating tree trunks stopped moving and instead affixed themselves firmly in the riverbed; then even iron-prows were no protection. It was an unhappy phenomenon of the river that the biggest, heaviest logs eventually became waterlogged in their rooted end. Those roots anchored in the muddy bottom, with the still-buoyant top end canted upward and downriver like a lance poised to impale anything that ran upon it. These dreaded obstructions were called "planters." The danger from planters came during high water stages when their entire length was hidden and the pilot of an up bound boat had no warning, nor suspicion, of the impending collision. With its hull pierced as if by a gigantic spear, the boat would "tremble for a moment like a thing of life, when suddenly struck to its vitals, and then sink into its grave."[15]

Another type of snag was the "sawyer." Like the planter, the sawyer's rooted end embedded itself into the bottom—but not so firmly as to prevent the whole tree from bobbing up and down, occasionally breaking the surface. In 1846, Thomas Bangs Thorpe ably described the slow and dangerous movement of these frequent hazards:

> *By some elasticity of the roots they are loose enough to be affected*
> *by the strange and powerful current, which will bear them down*
> *under the surface; and the tree, by its own strength, will come grace-*
> *fully up again, to be again engulfed; and thus they wave upward and*
> *downward with a gracefulness of motion which would not disgrace a*

beau of the old school. Boats frequently pass over these sawyers, as they go downstream, pressing them under by their weight; but let some unfortunate child of the genius of Robert Fulton, as it passes upstream, be saluted by the visage of one of these polite gentry, as it rises ten or more feet in the air, and nothing short of irreparable damage or swift destruction ensues, while the cause of all this disaster, after the concussion, will rise above the ruin as if nothing had happened, shake the dripping water from its forked limbs, and sink again, as if rejoicing in its strength. [16]

In the late 1860s, government engineers conducted a careful study of the Ohio River. The study was commissioned to find ways of improving the navigation on the Ohio. In regard to snags, the following learned observations were made:

Every tree along the valley of the Lower Ohio which stands on ground not over 60 feet above low water, is naturally a prospective snag. If it blows down, or is cut down and left, it must inevitably eventually find its way into the river, whether it floats or not, where it will either float away, become a snag, or contribute to the drift pile.

Besides trees that come into the stream in this way, the river, even when within ordinary limits, is continually undermining portions of the banks, causing acres of bottomland to cave in, bringing the trees, stumps, and brushwood into the river in a wholesale manner. Immense cottonwood, sycamore, pecan, cypress, and other trees are thus continually accumulating and, as might be expected, usually settle most where the channel is otherwise impeded by sand.

A sand shoal itself usually causes no other mischief than delays, but when snags protrude themselves, they may, in addition, render a channel exceedingly dangerous, particularly so when the current is so slight as to make their presence unmarked by the usual "break."

These snags may come, as they usually do, with the first flood, and having once caught in the bottom are finally packed down with the sand, as it deposits deeper and deeper. They of course remain with the last of the sand, or as long as their foothold is secure; but what is worse, having in the meantime become thoroughly waterlogged, they often remain as permanent fixtures.

Frequently a single snag or wreck, having lodged in this way will, as the river falls, entirely change the course of the channel, which may otherwise be in a natural process of cutting through to some definite shape. One snag has been known to deflect the channel from one side of the river to the other, abruptly changing the course of the river for one thousand feet.[17]

Snags were responsible for so many steamboat accidents that the government early on established a fleet of boats that were specially designed to remove the menaces. Invented by Henry Shreve, these "snagboats" were double-hulled, double-engine sidewheelers. They carried an iron hook and heavy tackle mounted to a derrick that towered between the hulls. A single snagboat would straddle the offending log, hook onto it, and yank it out, like a dentist extracting a tooth. Then the crewmen would saw up the log and either deposit it ashore or let it harmlessly drift away. "It is said," wrote one river traveler, "that their tackle is strong enough for any snag they ever find, and that 'they could pull up the bottom of the river, if necessary.'"[18] Snagging operations worked well, but never were there enough government boats to go around. By the time a snagboat finished clearing its assigned section of channel, a new invasion of impaled trees filled the river behind it.

Newspapers sometimes carried the doings of snagboats and noted the more infamous snags they removed. This clip comes from an 1845 edition:

OLD SNAGS. The United States snagboat Gopher, *in her late descent of the Ohio, succeeded in removing the following formidable snags, viz: the snag near Brandenburg [Kentucky], on which the steamer* Dr. Watson *and another steamboat were stove; a snag at the head of Flint Island, on which the* Wm. French *was wrecked; and a snag from Shinall's Reach, by which the* Western Belle *was sunk.*[19]

Low Water Groundings

Low water was the bane of river navigation. The low stages came in mid-summer and again during the winter. Western River steamboats were phenomenal for their buoyancy; even the largest first-class packets could clear the bottom in seven feet of water. (The standard joke had it that a given boat could navigate on heavy dew!) But at times the Middle

Mississippi and several of its tributaries had no more depth than a farm pond. In very many places a man might wade all the way across the river without getting his hair wet, if the current were not there to sweep him away. Thus, when a boat ran aground—and all boats did run aground—the experienced crew knew immediately which method of several would suit best to get her off.

Towing was the simplest means. It required the presence of another boat—with an obliging captain on board. Boats routinely passed their stranded competition without stopping; there were no rules of chivalrous conduct on the river. When an offer was made to lend assistance it usually carried a steep cash price, payable in advance.

> ∞
>
> *In very many places a man might wade all the way across the river without getting his hair wet . . .*
>
> ∞

If the river showed signs of a rise, the captain of a stranded steamer might decide to save his money and let the coming flood sweep his boat off the shoal. It could take time; the captain would bear the expense of feeding the cabin passengers in the meantime, but a rise of mere inches might free the boat.

If a steamboat were not too hard aground, and rested upon a narrow shoal such as a reef, the crew could "kedge" it off. A kedge was an anchor small enough to be transported in the yawl. After securing a heavy line to the kedge, the yawl crew dropped the kedge at a point beyond the shoal; the other end of the line was wrapped around the capstan. Using the combined power of the capstan (which in later years was steam-powered) and the engines, the boat literally pulled herself over the bar or reef.

Another method consisted of lightening the boat by putting freight and sometimes passengers ashore in the yawl. This inconvenience could be eliminated in seasons of low water by towing a "lighter" alongside. A lighter was either a barge or old hull upon which a portion of the steamer's freight and fuel were carried. By thus spreading the weight between the steamer and the lighter, neither vessel drew too much water.[20]

In some instances a grounded steamer could be extracted off a sandbar by digging out the boat. The deckhands would wade into the water with shovels and attempt to excavate a trench through the bar. The sight of a dozen or more men digging in waist deep water a half mile from shore must have seemed ridiculous, even humorous, to onlookers—but it was dangerous work as attested to in the dairy of an Irish passenger on the Ohio River in 1854:

> *The rising beams of the morn's red sun were just bursting on us when I was startled from my sleep by the cries of a man in the water—the awful cry which a poor human being utters when he begins to despair of his ability to escape from death. This poor fellow was just being carried past my cabin window away with the stream when I started up and looked out. Presently the current bore him away from the vessel's side. At about 50 yards from us he sank, but presently rose again and this time upright for he could stand on the bottom and keep his head above water. But the current is too strong and he is now floundering about perhaps with the intention of walking to shore or finding a more steady footing place. Poor fellow! He is doomed never to find such in this work for now he stumbles again and again recovers himself, but once more and for the last time he goes down and now nought is to be seen but his hat and his hands thrown wildly above the surface of the water as if imploring aid from those persons who were still standing on the steamboat watching his struggles for life—and I'm sorry to have to [admit] it—many of them even laughing at his efforts to save himself.*
>
> *And 'tis only now that the conceited little clerk of the boat gets into a skiff with a boy who rows to the spot where the man went down last. Mr. Clerk gives a few prods with his little sounding stick but none of them in the proper place for the current has carried the boat down from the spot, and the puppy clerk not finding the poor fellow left him there and returned to the ship in less [than] ten minutes from his leaving it and back he comes getting aboard with an air of as little concern as though it had been a bottle of whiskey he had been seeking, and I suspect far less than if it had been.*
>
> *His only remark was: "Well 'twas the fellow's own fault for I told him not to go to the front of the vessel where the water was so deep and the current so strong."*

The diarist later learned, much to his disgust, that the officers of the boat did not wish to recover the body, for then the law required a coroner's inquest into the death, and that would delay the boat's trip. Furthermore, he was told, the boat's captain probably owed wages to the drowned man's estate. Without a body there could be no inquest, and without an inquest the man's family could not press for his unpaid wages. As soon as the boat got off the bar it moved on, and the accident conveniently was forgotten. The greatest irony of all was the name of the boat—the *Justice!*[21]

Sparring Off

One additional method of extricating a vessel from shallow water was "sparring off." Sparring was an ingenious method that only a steamboat-man could invent. To the landsman it seemed every bit as droll as digging out, but on the Missouri, the Ohio, and the Middle Mississippi sparring off was the most common exercise of freeing a stranded boat. The spars were two thick poles, about thirty feet long, that normally were suspended by derricks and booms on the left and right sides of the bow. The lower end of the spar was cut at a sharp angle; an eye-ring was attached to the upper end of each spar. A heavy pulley hung from the eye-ring, and it was connected by manila rope to a tackle block affixed on either side of the bow. The tail of the rope wound around the capstan. When the boat grounded, the crew lowered both spars into the water until the sharp ends embedded themselves into the bottom. The spars were set vertically and canted slightly upward and inward. Then, with the paddle-wheels in motion, the crew tightened the ropes around the capstan and set the capstan to turning like a winch. With lines and pulleys strained to the utmost, the bow would lift upward and the boat would move forward a few feet. The boat was then set down upon the bar and the current would wash the sand away from the hull. The whole process was repeated, sometimes for days, until the boat had been "walked" over the bar. The position of the spars and booms reminded many observers of grasshopper legs; hence the practice came to be called "grasshoppering."

The position of the spars and booms reminded many observers of grasshopper legs; hence the practice came to be called "grass-hoppering."

Sparring off a shoal worked best when the boat grounded with her head upstream. (The current usually swung the stern around on down bound vessels.) Often the engines were put in reverse during the sparring process so the paddlewheels would turn slowly against the current. This would force water to back up and lift the boat a few inches, which could mean the difference between getting off and remaining stranded. The forward pull of the spars was strong enough to overcome the slow reverse movement of the paddlewheels.[22]

Dikes, Dredges, & Rapids

Sandbars had a most perplexing habit of showing up in the worst possible places. As the result of some gradual change upstream the water in front of a city wharf would begin to shoal, and before long steamboats could not get in close enough to make a landing. More than one small town landing site went to weeds when the river played its spiteful trick. If the river threatened to close the wharf of a major city, as at St. Louis in 1837, the government responded with a few devices of its own.[23] The most common remedy was the construction of wing dikes. These were rows of stone or timber piles, like sea jetties, which extended from the shore out into the stream. A series of these built on the opposite side of the river could divert the greater flow of water to the trouble spot and wash away the sandy shoal. If this did not work, due perhaps to sustained low water, then the site might be a candidate for dredging. The process involved the scooping or suctioning of sand from the bottom. It required complicated machinery that was generally not available on the Western Rivers until late in the century. But gifted individuals saw the need and began working on dredge designs from an early date, as evidenced by this St. Louis newspaper article from December, 1842:

> REMOVING SANDBARS. Captain John Russell, commander of the U.S. snagboats, has invented a boat for plowing up and removing sandbars. We cannot pretend to give an accurate or even satisfactory description, but this much may convey some idea of its formation: two keels, drawing from 8 to 10 inches, are made fast together, leaving a space of about 10 feet between them; in this space three buckets or plows are so spaced as to drive into the sand, lift it up, and bear it off. The boat is to be worked by a double engine, one boiler on each keel, with a stern wheel. Great power is gained by this double engine. We cannot pretend to judge of the merits of the invention; but if the opinions of men familiar with the river is any criterion, it is a most valuable invention and one which the government should avail itself.[24]

There were rapids along the upper rivers. These were not the tumbling chaotic torrents of mountain streams; rather they were mildly aberrant gradients that descended over rock beds for a considerable distance. The Falls of the Ohio at Louisville, for example, dropped 22 feet in two miles. There were two other falls on the Ohio, three on the Tennessee, two on the Upper Mississippi, and several near the head of navigation on the Missouri. Most of these rapids were not even discernible in high water. There were times, however, when the current simply prevented up bound boats from making headway against them. In such a situation, the captain might decide to "warp" his boat ahead by tying a line to a stout tree above and reeling the boat forward on the capstan. In the absence of a suitable tree, he could order the crew to "plant a dead man" a few hundred feet upriver. A "dead man" was a log about the size of a railroad tie. The crew tied a heavy rope to it, dropped it into a trench on shore, staked it down, buried it, and then pulled ahead with the capstan, just as in warping.[25]

1   Hamilton, pp. 2:195-96.
2   Ralph, p. 179.
3   "Up the Mississippi," pp. 441-43.
4   Thomas W. Knox, *Camp-fire and Cotton-field: Southern Adventure in Time of War* (New York: Blelock & Co., 1865; reprint ed., New York: DaCapo Press, 1969), pp. 466-67.
5   Glazier, p. 350.
6   Hamilton, pp. 2:197-98.
7   *Ibid.*, 2:196; Thomas B. Thorpe, *The Mysteries of the Backwoods; or, Sketches of the Southwest* (Philadelphia: Carey & Hart, 1846), p. 172.
8   Knox, p. 458.
9   Twain, *Life on the Mississippi*, p. 277.
10 Charles M. Skinner, *American Myths and Legends*, 2 vols. (Philadelphia: J.B. Lippincott, 1903), pp. 2:36-39.
11 Twain, *Life on the Mississippi*, p. 95.
12 Nichols, pp. 840-43.
13 *Travels on the Lower Mississippi*, pp. 130-31.
14 Knox, pp. 462-64.
15 Hamilton, pp. 2:194-95; Thorpe, *Mysteries of the Backwoods*, pp. 173-74.
16 *Ibid.*
17 U.S., Congress, House, Letter from the Secretary of War, *Survey of the Ohio River*, Ex. Doc. 72, 41st Cong., 3d sess., 1871, p. 60.
18 Ralph, p. 180.
19 *Weekly Reveille* 2, no. 10. (15 September 1845): 490.

20   Solomon F. Smith, "Bewailings of a Barge," *ibid.*, p. 489.

21   William James Hinchey Diary, National Frontier Trails Center, Independence, Missouri.

22   Hiram M. Chittenden, *History of Early Steamboat Navigation on the Missouri River: Life and Times of Joseph LaBarge*, 2 vols. (New York: Francis P. Harper, 1903; reprint ed., Minneapolis: Ross & Haines, 1962), pp. 120-21; Joseph M. Hanson, *The Conquest of the Missouri, Being the Story of the Life of Captain Grant Marsh* (n.p.: A.C. McClurg, 1909; reprint ed., New York: Murray Hill Books, 1946), pp. 86-87; *Annual Report of the Secretary of War, 1868*, part 2: *Engineers*, p. 628.

23   See various techniques of river improvement described in Wayman, pp. 264-77.

24   [St. Louis] *Daily Missouri Republican*, 6 December 1842.

25   Chittenden, *History of Early Steamboat Navigation*, p. 121.

Winter Perils

Though moody in all seasons, the big rivers saved their meanest tricks for winter. Ice could appear anywhere above Memphis—not mere sheets, but boulders of ice capable of crushing any boat left moored in its path. Ice usually closed the upper rivers by December. Winter travel on the middle rivers—especially the Mississippi between St. Louis and Cairo, Illinois—was a chancy, sometimes dangerous undertaking. With the Upper Mississippi and the Missouri frozen or blocked by ice, the Middle Mississippi suffered from very low water. Snags and reefs choked the rivers like a spreading malignancy, awaiting their chance to kill or strand the unwary steamboat in the most hostile kind of weather.

Stranded

Ironically, winter on the open portions of the Mississippi was a season of heavy traffic in both passengers and freight. The combination of bad river and teeming business made for a miserable time afloat. The plight of one unfortunate group of passengers can be told through a series of newspaper articles from 1842. Among the many steamers that operated out of St. Louis that year was the *Alexander Scott*. She was a large boat, 266 feet long by 69 feet wide with 30-foot paddlewheels on each side. An advertisement such as this one appeared regularly in the paper:

PASSENGER STEAMER—ALEX SCOTT, FOR NEW ORLEANS. The new splendid and fast running steamboat ALEXANDER SCOTT, Captain J.C. Swon, will arrive on Thursday, the 30th instant, and will have dispatch for the above and intermediate points. [1]

In late November and early December of 1842, extremely cold weather settled over the states of Missouri and Illinois. Ice and low water forced the closing of navigation on the Upper Mississippi, the Missouri, and the Illinois Rivers. On December 2, an unusual letter, with an editorial response, appeared in the columns of the *Daily Missouri Republican*:

> *To the Editor of the Republican:*
>
> *Sir—I consider it my duty to acquaint the inhabitants of St. Louis, through the medium of your valuable journal, with the state of the passengers on board the* Alexander Scott, *as I embarked with them from New Orleans, and after laying aground, in all, six days, and being obliged to spend one night in the woods, I left them, on Friday last, without any hopes of deliverance till the water may rise. There were on board upwards of two hundred souls, principally women and children, mainly from England and Scotland, and, at the time I left, between forty and fifty destitute of food and means, and many more will soon be in the same circumstances, and about five miles from any place where they can obtain provisions (Chester [Illinois]). I mention this matter, in hopes that some means may suggest themselves to you, for relieving the wants of our suffering fellow creatures.*
>
> *I am, sir, your obedient servant,*
>
> JOHN GREENHOW
>
> *December 1, 1842*

> *MORE RIVER DISTRESS. The [above] communication was handed to us yesterday. We readily give it a place, but we confess our inability to devise a remedy for the distress. It strikes us that the most speedy and proper course of remedy to be for the owners of the* Alex. Scott *to dispatch a light-draft boat down to bring up the passengers. We do not pretend to know what may be the contract subsisting between the passengers and the* Scott; *but be it what it may, human-*

ity, if not the interest of the owners, requires that this course should be taken. We have seen several of the passengers on the Scott, *who have come up by land—it is true they speak in severe terms of their treatment, but then they probably look only to their own side of the case. We know the officers, and believe they are incapable of a willful wrong. On the other hand, it should be remembered that these persons on the* Scott *contracted to be delivered in St. Louis. They are strangers in the land, and many of them have not the means nor the physical ability to reach St. Louis by land—this is especially the case of men with families and children, and to leave their families would be useless, if not worse. The* Scott *has been reported as unable to get up several days ago, and we have been somewhat surprised that no effort has as yet been made to get up her passengers. We believe that since she was reported, a boat has been sent to the relief of another [stranded boat], and returned. We agree with the writer…that something should be done for the relief of those on board; and if a boat is not sent to their relief, the citizens should take it into hands.*[2]

The paper made no further mention of the stranding except to report—a week later—that warmer temperatures, rain, and melting ice caused the river to rise significantly. Apparently the *Scott* floated free and brought her half-starved deck passengers into St. Louis. The *Alexander Scott* remained in service for another twelve years. Captain Swon later commanded the *Aleck Scott* on which Horace Bixby and Sam Clemens served as pilot and cub. Life on the Mississippi could be brutal and uncertain.

Scalping the Indian

Charles A. Murray roamed North America for three years before returning to Britain to write of his travels. Early in December, 1835, he boarded the steamer *Far West* at St. Louis for what was advertised as a ten-day voyage to New Orleans. But it was winter and, as Murray learned, nothing could be taken for granted:

> *On the following day, December 3rd, we met with no accident; but were obliged to go very slowly, in consequence of the thick and heavy masses of ice that covered the river. On the 4th, however, our misfortunes began. We ran on a sandbar at nine o'clock, a.m., but got*

off again in an hour. We grounded again soon after dusk, and floated off about nine, without having any wood on board; and we had to drop down with the stream at considerable risk, for two or three miles, when we reached a woodyard.

5th [December]—We soon found that the pilot either knew nothing of his business, or that he ran us aground on purpose; or else that the heavy descent of ice had altered the channel, and created new banks of mud or sand. We ran on a bar at nine a.m. and remained there all day. Several boats passed us. I went on board one with our captain to request her assistance in hauling us off; her captain, however, was deaf to entreaties, and even to liberal offers of payment. To complete our ill-luck, the yawl in which we had boarded this boat (the G. Clark*) was knocked under by her wheel and swamped, not half a minute after we had jumped out of her. She was held on by the painter; but we lost all our oars and two or three of the men's jackets. We had to bail her out with buckets, and with much labor towed her, half full of water, behind the* G. Clark*'s yawl back to the* Far West. *The* G. Clark *and her obliging captain then went off, leaving us in what might be called Down East, a "particular considerable unhandsome fix."*

We contrived in a few hours to rig a couple of clumsy sweeps, baled out the yawl, and kedged our anchor, with the aid of which we hauled off the bar; and once more afloat, went down two or three miles to a woodyard, where we lay-to for the night. We now thought that our troubles were over, as we had got through the worst of the ice; but, on the following day **(the 6th)**, *at half-past eight, we ran on a bar near a place called Devil's Island. Here, I almost believed that the gentleman in black had possessed our pilot; for he ran our boat right on a sandbank, which a schoolboy might have seen and avoided, inasmuch as there was a great log of wood and a quantity of drifted ice lying upon it. We were going ten or twelve miles an hour, and the boat bounded, jumped, and made every exertion to get over but in vain; her plunging only lodged her the deeper, and we, drawing five and a half feet, lay comfortably embedded in mud and sand, with only three feet and a half of water.*

We remained here several hours; it was impossible to drag her off by her anchor, and I began to fear that her fate was sealed, and that we (the passengers) must leave her by the first boat that passed. I was really grieved at this, for our captain was a most good-natured, obliging man; it was his first trip since the complete refitting of his boat, and if she lay here long with her broadside exposed to the huge masses of ice that come down the river at this season, she must have gone to pieces in a few weeks.

After a few hours, a small steamer, named the Indian, hove in sight; we hailed her, and she came alongside. Our captain agreed to give four hundred dollars if she would take some of our freight and tow us off the bar; after much time and trouble, she did so, and as soon as we floated, she went off down the channel, expecting us to follow immediately. We endeavored to do so, but something went wrong in the machinery, and we could not make the right course; consequently we dropped down again upon the bank and became embedded as fast or faster than ever.

The little Indian, though out of sight, soon missed us and returned; and, in order to obtain her further assistance to get us off, our poor captain was obliged to give a thousand instead of four hundred dollars. Notwithstanding the united efforts of the passengers and both crews, we lay there all the next day; but about eight o'clock on the 8th instant, having put all our freight on board the Indian, which was fortunately empty, we got off and made good our passage through this difficult channel. In the course of the day we found the Indian anchored in the middle of the river, having broken her paddles and otherwise injured her machinery. We took her in tow and brought her ashore; for which I trust our captain obtained some diminution of the enormous sum which she had exacted from him. We reached the mouth of the Ohio without further accident or difficulty; but the machinery was not in perfect order, owing to the illness of the engineer, who could not leave his bed.[3]

"We Hope to Reach St. Louis"

Winter passage was hard on everyone, even the famous. In March, 1843, the naturalist John James Audubon commenced a trip to the far west in search of specimens for his third book, *The Viviparous Quadrupeds of North America.* He planned to travel by steamboat from Louisville to St. Louis, and thence up the Missouri River to the Yellowstone. We join him at Louisville on the *easy* portion of his trip:

> *Ohio River. Thursday night 23rd March 1843*
>
> *My Dearest beloved Friends —*
>
> We left Louisville this morning at 10, and are now close to Flint Island, all well and in good spirits. The table I am writing upon shakes shockingly and I fear that thou wilt have some difficulty in reading this.
>
> We were accidentally detained at Louisville from Sunday evening last to this morning for the want of a steamer bound to St. Louis. We are now on board the Gallant and such a motley of 100 passengers man never saw or can form an idea of; but we go on well and hope to be at St. Louis on Sunday morning next. The weather is remarkably cold. There is ice floating in the river and so cold was last night that ponds which were open yesterday afternoon were skated on this morning. We had yesterday afternoon as fierce a snow storm as I ever have witnessed but it lasted only 20 minutes, after which we had an equinoxial gale that amounted almost to a hurricane and lasted nearly all night.
>
> **Friday 24th.** Last night was the coldest of this winter excepting one in February. The river was this morning covered with ice, but we have proceeded on tolerably well. Our steamer is one of the filthiest I ever saw—no towels, no soap, and every one this morning dipped the water to wash from the stream! Many of the passengers slept on the floor last night. We have about 15 horses on board, wagons, carts, carriages, and furniture of all description belonging to new settlers going to the Missouri frontiers. [Edward] Harris [an amateur ornithologist from New York] and I have one stateroom. He sleeps upon 3 boards and I upon 4. Our meals are none of the best, all is greasy and nasty—a first rate initiation for the trip to the Yellowstone; for we eat famously and sleep soundly. This evening we have had a severe storm and hard wind and yet we passed and stopped at several places.
>
> **[March] 25th, Saturday.** At 9 o'clock we are proceeding up the Mississippi at a good average rate. The day is clear and cold and the

river is nearly covered with skin ice. This evening the weather has come colder and cloudy. The river is lower than the captain thought and we have grounded several times. At 8 when I was about going to rest we struck a snag that so alarmed the passengers that a rush was made for the cabin door. We all ran like mad to make ready to leap overboard; but as God would have it, our lives and the Gallant *were spared—she from sinking, and we from swimming amid rolling and crashing hard ice. The ladies screamed, the babies squalled, the dogs yelled, the steam roared, the captain (who, by the way, is a very gallant man) swore—not like an angel, but like the very devil—and all was confusion and uproar. Luckily, we had had our supper, as the thing was called on board the* Gallant, *and every man appeared to feel resolute, if not resolved to die. But it was not a serious accident and we proceeded on without leaking. By the by we passed old Cape Girardeau [Missouri].*

[March] 26th—Bright morning and cold, some snow in the night, much ice on the water, but we proceeded on at daylight. Took in many persons on board and our provisions are scanty enough. We have grounded several times. When we left Louisville, another steamer called the Cicero *started after us, but we kept considerably ahead of her until this day, as she passed us during the night when we were safely fastened to the shore. This afternoon we saw her before us, passed her, and thought no more of her until we were detained in landing some persons. She was now even with us and a race was commenced. When near Chester [Illinois] she ran her bows against ours and we then ran thus coupled for half a mile to the great danger of both boats and all on board. We landed safely, however, put out freight, horses, and people, and left her there repairing damage done to her paddlewheels by the ice. It now began to snow and one could scarcely [distinguish] the shore, we therefore made fast for the night to the great satisfaction of all on board. The* Cicero *passed us, and I now hope that she is 50 miles ahead of us.*

The snow turned into rain, and this day, **the 27th,** *it is pouring hard and constantly. Whilst at tea, a person who had ½ a cup of tea poured out to him said he wanted coffee. The waiter took the cup, threw the contents on the carpet and gave the gent his coffee. Oh* *such fare, deck dirty, &c., &c. We have no bread, but biscuit as hard as flint and scanty indeed are our meals, but we hope to reach St. Louis this coming night. We are now at Ste. Genevieve [Missouri,] 60 miles from St. Louis. Our boat leaks so from the roof that we have scarcely a dry spot to stand our feet upon! We stopped for the night about 12 miles below St. Louis in a dreadful snowstorm and very cold. This morning [**March 28**] the river is almost closed but we are within 3 miles from port. No provisions on board, therefore no break-fast here.*[4]

The *Gallant* reached St. Louis at noon of that day and Audubon found comfortable lodgings. He would remain in St. Louis for one month while awaiting navigation to open on the Missouri.

1   *Daily Missouri Republican*, 1 July 1842. Information on the *Scott* is found in Frederick Way, Jr., *Way's Packet Directory, 1848-1994*, revised ed. (Athens: Ohio University Press, 1994), pp. 9, 230; and in C. Bradford Mitchell, ed., *Merchant Steam Vessels of the United States, 1790-1868* (Staten Island, New York: Steamship Historical Society, 1975), p. 6.

2   *Daily Missouri Republican*, 2 December 1842.

3   Charles A. Murray, *Travels in North America During the Years 1834, 1835, & 1836*, 2 vols. (London: R. Bentley, 1839; reprint ed., New York: DaCapo Press, 1974), pp. 2:166-72.

4   Letter, J.J. Audubon to V.G. Audubon, 23 March 1843, in the Special Collections Department, Smithsonian Institution Libraries, Washington, D.C.; Maria R. Audubon, ed. *Audubon and His Journals*, 2 vols. (New York: Scribner's Sons, 1897), pp. 1:450-51.

Accursed Bridges

In the view of most steamboatmen, the greatest hazards on the river were bridges. Had they been built properly, or located more precisely in regard to navigation, the first bridges to span the Western Rivers might have drawn scant criticism from boatmen. Then again, perhaps not. Even the best designed and most favorably placed bridge of the day could not have escaped the condemnation of rivermen. The iron, wood, and masonry bridge structures posed a challenge both real and axiomatic to those who made their living on the water. And there was no limit to what a steamboatman might do to prove his point.

The Wheeling Bridge

The first bridge to draw the steamboatmens' ire spanned the Ohio River at Wheeling, Virginia. (This was before the creation of the state of West Virginia.) Built in 1848-49, it was an engineering marvel for its day and place. The structure was a suspension bridge. It hung from two great sweeping cables. It spanned a distance of 1,020 feet. The bridge deck arched upward to reach a maximum height of 95 feet over low water.[1] The bridge designers and promoters were pleased with their bridge, as were many shippers and businessmen from towns far off the river where reliable overland transportation took precedence over river commerce.

The second Wheeling suspension bridge. The original bridge—the subject of so much controversy—blew down in a windstorm in 1854. Nature accomplished what the Supreme Court could not do. (Courtesy Library of Congress.)

But the bridge was less than perfect in one respect. In very high water a few of the largest steamboats could not pass under it due to the height of their smokestacks. It was not such a grievous wrong, though one would have thought the river had been paved over judging from the reaction of Ohio River boatmen. They were *enraged* by this affront—this menace—this dangerous and unnecessary hindrance to their livelihood and interests! After all, argued the rivermen, they had an inherent right to *unobstructed* navigation of the rivers. They buttonholed friendly politicians and reminded them that seven daily steam packets passed between Pittsburgh and Cincinnati. Over a year those seven boats carried 35 million dollars of merchandise and freight, and 80,000 passengers.

The river politicians listened. On behalf of the steamboat interests, the state of Pennsylvania sued the stockholders of the bridge company. The case was heard by the Supreme Court, which made its ruling in February, 1850. It left no room for interpretation:

> *The Wheeling bridge is a serious obstruction to the navigation of the Ohio River, and is a public nuisance.*

> *It is clearly proved by science, and confirmed by practical skill and experience, that the present height of the packet chimneys is necessary, and that they cannot be reduced in length without serious injury to the speed and power of the vessel.*
>
> *It is proved by science, experience, and the nature of things, that the packet chimneys cannot be lowered to pass the bridge without imposing heavy expenses upon the packet and endangering the safety of the vessel and the lives of the passengers and crew.*
>
> *The defendants are required to relieve navigation from obstruction by elevating the bridge to the height of one hundred and eleven feet above low water level for the width of three hundred feet over the channel.*[2]

Now the story took an unexpected turn. There were railroads converging on Wheeling. They needed to bridge the river in order to become a viable transportation mode. Citizens of inland communities served by these railroads pressured *their* politicians to do something. Otherwise the legal precedent established in the Wheeling case could render impractical any bridge over the Ohio. The inland politicians heard the clamor and responded—and they far outnumbered the partisans of the river. Two years after the Supreme Court ruling, during which time the Wheeling bridge remained unaltered (to no one's surprise), Congress found a way to circumvent the Court's decision. It prefaced its legislation with the following report:

> *The important trial in the Supreme Court of the United States in which the question at issue was the destruction of that monument of the art and skill of modern days, the Wheeling bridge, has been unfavorably decided. That great work, the thoroughfare of commerce and information in peace and pathway for armies in war, a monument of enterprise which the whole land may regard with national pride, is to be destroyed or rendered useless by an act of selfish and legalized vandalism.*
>
> *A structure which promotes the convenience of the public cannot be a nuisance to it.*
>
> *That the Wheeling bridge, at times of great floods in the Ohio, obstructs the passage of seven or eight steamboats out of the two*

hundred and thirty navigating that river, no one will entertain a doubt; but when your committee take into consideration the fact that usually there are many months in the year in which all steamboats of the "high-pipe class" are utterly unable to navigate the Ohio in consequence of low water or ice, they believe themselves justified in declaring that this obstruction is only partial and temporary whilst, on the other hand, the trade and travel across the river, which would be obstructed and inconvenienced by the abatement of the bridge, are general and continued.

Congress thus established the Wheeling bridge as a "post route and a military road." In essence this meant it was a federal highway, necessary to the good of the country, and on an equal footing with the riverways. The

Steamboats were yesterday's news.

same law also obligated vessels with tall smokestacks to refit their stacks with folding or telescoping devices if they intended to pass under the Wheeling bridge at high water. Steamboatmen complained bitterly, but the citizens of the Upper Ohio Valley heard none of it. They were flushed by the excitement of the coming railroads. Steamboats were yesterday's news.[3]

The Effie Afton *& the Rock Island Bridge*

The next bridge controversy took place on the Mississippi River. Construction began in 1854 on a bridge connecting Rock Island, Illinois, with Davenport, Iowa. Being the first railroad bridge to cross the Mississippi, it was seen by many as the most important bridge project in the nation. Built 35 feet above mean water level, each of its white-painted wooden spans rested on stone piers. Seven of those piers were identical—35 feet long and seven feet wide at the top. The much larger eighth pier supported a swing span.

The swing span pivoted open on its center axis to allow the passage of steamboats. In the open position, aligned atop its pier, the swing span stood nearly parallel to the stream with some 120 feet of clear space on either side. The pier that supported the swing span was substantial in its size: 386 feet long by 40 feet wide. It was built at an angle of 26° to the flow of the river.[4]

The bridge company engineers maintained that the 26° angle improved the channel characteristics on the left descending side of the open draw.

Steamboat pilots and captains knew otherwise. The angled pier created a navigational nightmare. Once again the politicians took sides depending on whether the railroads or the steamboat companies would be most grateful in a practical sort of way. Someone sent the Rock Island bridge plans to Captain Montgomery C. Meigs in Washington for his comments. Meigs, a respected army engineer, wrote back:

> *It is one of the rules of bridge building to place the piers in the line of the current. This rule is seldom violated; and in a structure such as this, exposed to the shocks of ice, drift timber, rafts, and other floating bodies in a rapid current—one under which so large a commerce must pass—it should have been carefully observed. If the maps shown me represent correctly the location of the bridge, then the effect upon the currents would be, in my opinion, to make the passage of the draw difficult, and even dangerous.*[5]

For pilots accustomed to understanding the movements of the river, the danger was clear. As the current struck the head of the long, oblique pier, the water formed a two-foot-high swell that tapered back on the right side of the draw and rolled into a huge eddy. No steamboat dared enter there. On the left side—the supposedly improved side—the compression wave traveled down the entire length of the long pier. The current shot through at a fearful clip and spawned an undertow that angled out from the long pier and made straight for the nearest short pier, 120 feet to the left.

Comments from crewmen and passengers alike all testified to the hazards of passing the Rock Island draw span. From pilot James W. Connor:

> *In high water it is impossible for an ordinary boat to go through without having all the steam that can be got, and more than the law allows them to carry. The effect upon a boat going up is to throw her upon one pier or the other; the draw is full of cross currents and whirls, which makes the boat unmanageable. In coming downstream the tendency is to throw boats upon the long pier; boats coming down are compelled to carry as much steam as in going up.*[6]

Captain Robert Herdman, of the steamer *Arizonia*, stated:

In coming down, the manner in which the water strikes the long pier has a tendency to force a boat upon it; [I] noticed this effort upon the Arizonia, *which was sunk there by striking this pier. Passing this draw is like shooting at a mark; if you hit, all is right; but if not, there is no trying it over again; no pilot can always keep his boat straight—even in an ordinary point of the river—but at the bridge the entrance must be so exact that the most skillful only make it by chance.*[7]

Captain William F. Fuller took his boat, the *General Pike*, through the bridge twice. On the second run the *Pike* slammed against the pier and sustained heavy damage. Fuller swore he never would take a boat through there again, no matter how much money the trip paid. George McClintock, captain of the *Henry Graff*, told of waiting several hours for daylight on April 21, 1856, before attempting a run through the flawed structure. His pilot took every reasonable precaution, but the *Graff* lost steerageway due to the crosscurrents and careened into the long pier. The boat did not sink but was heavily damaged. James Mellen, a clerk on the *Clara Dean*, reported that passengers on the up bound trips often asked to be put ashore below the span. They preferred to walk along the shore rather than risk the passage by boat. A businessman named D. B. Machouse, who traveled "frequently" through the bridge draw, always rode on the hurricane deck during the transit. He thought he was safer up there since the lower decks bore the brunt of the impacts with the pier. Steamboat clerk David D. More took a precaution of his own. "When we go through the draw," he stated, "I always get out my valuables to be ready in case of accident." Pilot John Kyle attempted an upward passage in 1856, but lost his nerve in the tricky swirls and backed down. The next day he paid a towboat $100 to help his boat through. And Captain Jesse T. Hurd, of the steamer *Granite State*, reported that his pilot "was a careful man," but the *Granite State* "struck the short pier and tore off about thirty-two feet of her guards. If the guards had not been so strong we should have sunk."[8]

William White, a pilot for nearly twenty-five years, gave this summation of the pilots' dilemma:

> *"When we go through the draw," he stated, "I always get out my valuables to be ready in case of accident."*

In coming down the trouble is that you cannot come into the draw straight, you have to come in at an angle; in passing the head of the turntable pier, the current carries the boat against the short pier, and thence back to the long one, so it is nearly impossible for a long boat to avoid hitting the long pier. It is worse against the short pier in coming up, and the long pier in going down. My rule in going down is to come down to the pier until I can see through the draw, then I get steady and give her all the steam I can to keep her from flanking. The velocity of the boat prevents the handling of the [tiller] wheel— have to manage her pretty much by the [paddle] wheels.

I came up through the draw this season with three long new boats for the Minnesota Packet Company: the War Eagle *and* Itasca, *each 225 feet long, and the* Milwaukee, *250 feet. The* War Eagle *wanted to run into the long pier but I got her safely through; the* Itasca *struck a pile of stones thrown in by the bridge company just above the head of the short pier, but sustained no material damage; the* Milwaukee *struck her right hand wheelhouse against the short pier.*

I think there is considerable difference in the current in the draw when a boat is there and when there is not: it is swifter, and the action of the wheels renders the boat somewhat unmanageable. If the engine should give out, or any little thing should happen to a boat while in the draw, she would be gone.[9]

Through April, 1856, twenty-three steamboats had smacked, scraped, or smashed against the Rock Island bridge piers. Most packet boat owners and officers roundly denounced the bridge. Affected steamboaters and businessmen met at the Merchants' Exchange in St. Louis and sent a committee to investigate the bridge. Then, on May 6, 1856, an accident occurred at the bridge that delighted many ardent rivermen despite its tragic overtones. The new steamer *Effie Afton*, 235 feet long, 56 feet wide—a splendid boat worth $60,000—had ascended the Upper Mississippi for the first time. "Fleet and easily handled," she arrived at Rock Island on May 5. The wind was strong—too strong to attempt a passage of the bridge. The *Afton* would tie up and wait.

At dawn no less than ten steamers were moored below the bridge, their pilots waiting for a break in the wind. As the hours wore on and the costs of standing still increased, the captains and pilots of the several boats debated the merits of making a run at the bridge. At length two boats cast off and signaled to the bridge tender. The span swung open until it rested lengthwise upon its long pier. Had the wind alone menaced the boats they may have made it through, but this was high water season. The angled pier acted like a funnel. It forced more water through one side—the channel side. In so doing it increased the current speed to eight miles an hour. The first boat came spewing and foaming toward the open gap, but her headway diminished proportionately the closer she got to the bridge. Abreast the pier she made no forward progress at all while the wind buffeted her superstructure and threatened to blow her around to some crazy, unmanageable heading; she was as helpless as a fawn on ice. She dropped back to her moorings, while the second boat made an equally futile attempt and an inglorious retreat. Both pilots felt they had earned a month's pay in one hour.

Later that afternoon the wind slackened, marginally. Two small boats successfully ran the bridge. The officers of the *Effie Afton* decided to take their turn. While the draw span swung open, the *Afton's* engineers built up a full head of steam. The gleaming white boat slid away from her moorings and cut a path into the channel. Her pilot, N. W. Parker, lined the boat up, then rang the engine bells to come ahead full. As the *Afton* moved forward a sizeable swell lifted back from her prow, then dipped into a trough amidships and rose again under her paddlewheel boxes. Like the boats before her, the *Effie Afton* lost considerable headway as she came abreast the long pier, but she kept inching ahead. Slowly she passed the centerline of the bridge. Approaching the upriver side of the long pier the pilot noticed a change in the helm—it felt slippery, as though the *Afton* were going to bolt. Every pilot knew that feel, and feared it, for it meant that an undercurrent was pushing against the side of the hull.

Suddenly the *Afton* sheered! The bow swung to starboard and nothing that Parker tried would check her. Turning perpendicular to the stream, she slid down with the fast current directly toward the nearest short pier. Parker rang for the engines to reverse. It was too late. The starboard side of the boat slammed hard against the pier and lodged squarely across it. The river now tried to pull the *Afton* down by exerting considerable pressure all along her exposed larboard beam. The entire left side sank deeper into the water while the crushed starboard side rose higher against the pier.

As the boat assumed a dangerous list to larboard, the two engineers—still at their posts—opened steam cocks to vent the high-pressure steam through exhaust escape pipes. First mate John A. Baker climbed his way from the forecastle to the boiler deck. He found that both smokestacks had been knocked off their bases. Fire burned through the deck where the stacks normally connected to the furnace breechings below. While he beat the fire down the list increased. Heating and cooking stoves throughout the boat fell over and scattered hot embers. Chief steward James Hill threw water on a fire in the main cabin only to find another one flaring up around the overturned stove in the ladies' cabin. Then another fire broke out in the barbershop. The second mate went after that one, but nobody spotted the flames licking up the bulkhead in the pantry where a cooking stove had tumbled over. It got out of hand in a hurry and the mates and stewards could do nothing except shout a warning to any passengers who might still be in their staterooms. Smoke and flames soon engulfed the upper decks while passengers and crew slid into the water and thrashed about for anything that would float. The steamers that had been waiting below the bridge sent their skiffs and yawls out to pick up the human flotsam.

Overhead, the 250-foot fixed span, well seared from the burning boat, alternately burned, hissed, steamed, and popped until its once-sturdy beams snapped like kindling and plunged into the river amidst a hailstorm of red-glowing embers.

Fueled by the rich composition of the *Afton*, fire billowed upward and wrapped itself around the timbers of the overhanging bridge span. It, too, burned quite readily, much to the astonishment of the crowds that had gathered on the Iowa and Illinois shores. The *Afton* collapsed upon itself in a terrific, roaring mass of debris; even its wetted hull succumbed and disappeared in smoke and steam. Overhead, the 250-foot fixed span, well seared from the burning boat, alternately burned, hissed, steamed, and popped until its once-sturdy beams snapped like kindling and plunged into the river amidst a hailstorm of red-glowing embers. The next morning there was no flame or smoke, or even visible debris—just a stained white bridge with a conspicuous gap in it.

Now came the litigation phase. The railroad had been deprived of its conveyance across the river, but the owners of the *Effie Afton* brought about the suit. The case was tried at Chicago in September, 1857. One of the bridge company's three-member defense team was forty-eight-year-old Abraham Lincoln. In his preparation for the case the future president had visited the bridge, had walked upon the long pier, and had posed a great many questions to the bridge engineer and the bridge master. Lincoln delivered the closing argument for the defense. He stated that steamboatmen had shouted in glee and rang their boats' bells and whistles as the burning bridge span fell into the river—a statement rhetorically, if not literally, correct. The real issues, according to Lincoln and his co-counselors, were not the technical matters of crosscurrents and undertows, but rather general principles of fact: the bridge had been legally built; bridges posed certain hazards to navigation; those hazards demanded the exercise of prudence; and the *Afton's* pilot had made no effort to examine the bridge before running it.

The jury could not reach a unanimous decision, and by their deadlock they upheld for the defendant—the bridge company. In the end, the Rock Island bridge was repaired, only to be damaged later by high winds. With the help of government subsidies a replacement bridge was built downstream and completed in 1873. This newer bridge duplicated none of the navigational hazards of the original span.[10]

Similar problems with other bridges on other rivers continued to surface in the courts. Usually the bridge in question involved a railroad. This did not bode well for boatmen, for the nation soon grew dependent upon the railroads—as once it had on the rivers. The entire country seemed to be of one accord on the matter of steamboats versus railroads. In 1886 Supreme Court Justice David Davis summarized the new national mood:

> *The officers of steamboats plying the Western Rivers must be held to the full measure of responsibility in navigating streams where bridges are built across them. These bridges, supported by piers, of necessity increase the dangers of navigation, and rivermen, instead of recognizing them as lawful structures built in the interests of commerce, seem to regard them as obstructions to it, and apparently act on the belief that frequent accidents will cause their removal. There is no foundation for this belief. Instead of the present bridges being*

abandoned, more will be constructed. The changed condition of the country, produced by the building of railroads, has caused the great inland waters to be spanned by bridges. These bridges are, to a certain extent, impediments in the way of navigation, but railways are highways of commerce as well as rivers. . . . It is the interest as well as the duty of all persons engaged in business on the water routes of transportation to conform to this necessity of commerce. If they do this and recognize railroad bridges as an accomplished fact in the history of the country, there will be less loss of life and property, and fewer complaints of the difficulties of navigation at the places where these bridges are built. [11]

Sam Clemens summed it up from the rivermen's point of view. Referring to the steel-arched Eads Bridge at St. Louis, completed in 1874 as a toll bridge, Clemens wrote:

The mighty bridge, stretching along over our heads, had done its share in the slaughter and spoliation. Remains of former steamboatmen told me, with wan satisfaction, that the bridge doesn't pay. Still,

High bridge at Louisville, Kentucky, 1872. Depending on the river stage, piers could present a real hazard to navigation. But the greater hazard to packet steamboating were the railroads that utilized those bridges. (Photo courtesy of Murphy Library, University of Wisconsin-La Crosse.)

it can be no sufficient compensation to a corpse to know that the
dynamite that laid him out was not of as good quality as it had been
supposed to be.[12]

1   U.S., Congress, House, Committee on the Post Office and Post Roads, *Minority Report,* H. Rept. 158, 32d Cong., 1st sess., 1852, p. 18.
2   *Ibid.,* p. 20.
3   U.S., Congress, House, Committee on the Post Office and Post Roads, *Wheeling Bridge,* H. Rept. 158, 32d Cong., 1st sess., 1852, pp. 1, 8-10, 13.
4   Mary Costello, *Climbing the Mississippi River, Bridge by Bridge* (Davenport, Iowa: by the author, 1995), p. 116; U.S., Congress, House, Committee on Commerce, *Railroad Bridge Across the Mississippi River at Rock Island,* H. Rept. 250, 35th Cong., 1st sess., 1858, pp. 2, 25.
5   *Ibid.,* p. 23.
6   *Ibid.,* p. 6.
7   *Ibid.,* p. 7.
8   *Ibid.,* pp. 7-9, 14-15.
9   *Ibid.,* p. 14.
10   *Ibid.,* pp. 15, 17; Albert J. Beveridge, *Abraham Lincoln, 1809-1858* (Boston: Houghton Mifflin, 1928), pp. 2:598-605; "A Rock Island Historian Spans History to Find the Truth About Local Bridges," [Davenport, Iowa] *Quad City Times,* 17 October 1989.
11   88 United States Reports 230, quoted in Hunter, *Steamboats on the Western Rivers,* pp. 595-96.
12   Twain, *Life on the Mississippi,* p. 185.

Piloting

To the typical passenger—a mere landsman—the act of piloting seemed simple enough: steer down the middle of the river. Ignorant in his bliss, the passenger knew nothing of snags, bars, reefs, or shoals. Nor could he grasp the notion that an upstream trip presented different steering problems than a downstream journey, or that navigation at night required attributes that bordered on a sixth sense. The landsman could not comprehend these things any more than an ant might comprehend a continent, for there was nothing in the normal realm of life that came close to preparing a person for the deep mysteries and hidden complexities of piloting a steamboat.

The Navigator

Considering all the difficulties of navigating the rivers, it was a wonder that anyone could have piloted a boat from one place to another. It took time to learn the rivers, and even then the channels never stayed the same long enough to accurately chart them. Of course, some tried to make piloting a textbook science. One was a Pittsburgh bookbinder named Zadok Cramer, who published an annual how-to book called *The Navigator*. Cramer based early editions of *The Navigator* entirely on hearsay reports from raftsmen. Eventually he made the trip himself and added his personal observations. Here, excerpted from the 1814 edition—the dawn of the steamboat era—are the best available steering instructions for the Mississippi between the mouth of the Ohio and New Madrid, Missouri:

> *[5 **miles down**] Island No. 1 below the Ohio, lies close to the left shore; opposite it on the same side of the river, and just above Mayfield Creek, stands Fort Jefferson, now abandoned. No. 1 is about one mile long, and the channel cannot be mistaken, being at all times on the right side of the island.*
>
> *[20 **miles down**] Iron Banks, left side. Here is a bluff mixed with an iron colored earth of a very fine sand and clay, constantly falling in, of the height of 250 feet perpendicular, and extending a mile on the river, and back from it in a ridge for five or six miles, when it breaks into small hills, and declines gradually to the common level of the country, which is there oak land. There was a post here in 1773, near the south boundary of, then, Virginia.*
>
> *Must not go too near the Iron Banks, there being an eddy near the shore under them. After passing them, hug the left shore to clear a large sandbar putting out from the head of Wolf Island, which you must keep on your right hand.*
>
> *[24 **miles down**] Wolf Island, No. 5. This is a large island lying to the right, though when opposite its head, it seems to divide the current equally, the right hand pass turning off suddenly to the right around the island.*
>
> *Wolf Island sandbar begins at the head of the island, and spreads out so far as to occupy ¾ of the breadth of the river, confining the channel to the left bank, where at its narrowest point it is not more than a quarter of a mile broad; the bar then declines towards the island, extending in length three miles, and about one mile at its broadest part, the river being a mile and a quarter wide opposite the settlement, and nearly two miles across at the head of the island. When this bar is covered, there is no danger, it is observed by boatmen, from any of the bars lower down. There are several clusters of willows on this bar, particularly near the island, where there appears to be a high water pass forming immediately under Mr. Hunter's settlement.*
>
> *This island is six miles long on its left side, while the right is ten, and 5 miles broad, containing 15,000 acres of the first rate land, well tim-*

bered, having near its middle a beautiful prairie, high and dry, pro-
ducing the finest grass for cattle. Grapes grow on the island in great
abundance. A Mr. James Hunter, the only man I ever knew who seemed
to take a pride in letting it be known that he was a professed gambler,
is the only occupant of Wolf Island at present. He says he has on it
1,000 head of hogs, a large stock of cattle, with whose
beef and pork he supplies boats, barges, keels, &c., passing up and down the river, together with butter, milk,
&c. I saw at his house a pair of wild geese tamed, running with the common geese, without any wish to leave
them.

> ∞
>
> *Cramer based
> early editions of*
> The Navigator
> *entirely on
> hearsay reports
> from raftsmen.*
>
> ∞

   A good landing can be made at the foot of the bar
near the island.

   [**45 miles down**] Island No. 10, three miles below
No. 9, lies nearest the left shore, river turns to the
right. At the head of No. 10 is an ugly sandbar covered with willows.
Best channel is to the right of both. In passing No. 10, especially in
high water, keep pretty close to the right hand point just above the
head of the island. No. 10 is about a mile in length.

   This island and the right bank opposite it, show the first evident
marks of the effects of the earthquake which commenced December
16, 1811. The right bank for several miles above and below the island,
appears to be several feet, about three or four, as near as I could judge
from the adjoining land, lower than it formerly was. Many of the
trees standing in all directions on the island, and particularly the
willows on the willow point opposite it, clearly evince the concussions
of the earth. This island is said to had cracked to that degree, that several large trees standing on the cracks, were split from the roots up to
their tops.

   [**70 miles down**] New Madrid, right side. There is a creek called
Chepousa River*, which heads in a lake 25 miles back of New
Madrid, and puts in just above the town; it affords a good landing for
boats at its mouth. To make it you must keep pretty near the right
bank for some distance above the creek, and pull in so as to clear the

---

*   Present-day St. John's Bayou.

*counter current, and make the land just below the mouth of the creek.
The nearer you land to the creek the better, for the bank opposite the
town is almost constantly falling in.* [1]

Cramer's revisions notwithstanding, frequent changes in the channel
rendered *The Navigator* inaccurate almost before the ink dried. Titian Peale,
riding aboard the *Western Engineer* on May 28, 1819, mentioned that his
boat ran aground by following the directions of *The Navigator*. [2] Yet for all
its errors and omissions, *The Navigator* remained—at least for a few years
more—the only authoritative word on Western River piloting. In 1824,
Congress began authorizing spot improvements on the Ohio and
Mississippi Rivers through annual river and harbor appropriation bills,
but not until the 1880s did massive channel stabilization projects get under
way. And only then would maps or charts come close to delineating a safe
channel line.

Reading the River

Piloting proved to be more art than science. It was taught by word of
mouth and reinforced with hands-on training. A pilot would tell his
apprentice, or "cub," that the only book to read was the river itself.
"Reading the river" meant the ability to discern the water's depth and the
bottom's characteristics by careful observation of the motion and appearance of the river's surface. The clues were subtle and easily misread by an
inexperienced pilot. For example, it was an accepted fact that higher waves
formed over the deepest water, *provided* the wind came from upstream; if
the wind blew from the opposite direction then high waves meant shallow water.

Pilots also located deep water by searching the river's surface for signs of
a reef. A reef was an underwater ledge created and sustained by a deflection
of water and sand moving along the bottom. Usually a reef presented a
shallow incline on its upstream side and rose to within a few feet of the surface, then dropped off in an almost perpendicular wall. The deep water
was immediately downstream of the reef. The problem was in getting over
the reef itself. A down bound boat might pass over with no trouble save for
a little grinding on the hull; but an up bound boat risked the real chance
of crushing its hull if it hit the bluff side of the same reef. Fortunately,

most reefs extended outward only a short distance from a point on the bank or the head of an island. A pilot could run his boat around the end of some reefs—but not all of them. So-called rainbow reefs formed a long arc that extended all the way across the channel. Rainbow reefs did have "breaks," or passes. The difficulty lay in finding the break; sometimes it could be located only by sounding with a pole or weighted line.

Then there were crossings. Some were deeper than others, some more easily read, but there were few that a pilot took for granted. Crossings made in a falling river were an adventure. In the midst of it the channel might suddenly disappear, its tenuous line obstructed by a malevolent sandbar. The wary pilot knew what to look for: a slick, flat-looking lesion—a trouble sign as sure as if the river had waved a red flag.[3]

The more observant passengers grew to appreciate, if not understand, the art of piloting.

The more observant passengers grew to appreciate, if not understand, the art of piloting. The following passage, written in 1892 by a novice river traveler, reflects a layman's admiration for the piloting craft:

> I spent much time every day in the pilothouse. I heard very much about the skill and knowledge the river pilot's calling required, but I saw even more than I heard. This giant river does not impress those who study it with its greatness so much as with its eccentricities. It runs between banks that are called earth, but act like brown sugar; that cave in and hollow out, and turn into bars and islands in a way that is almost indescribable. Islands which were on one side one year are on the other side another year. Channels which the steamboats followed last month and for years past are now closed. Bars no one ever saw before suddenly lift above the surface. Piloting on the Mississippi is a business no one ever learns. It is a continual subject of study. It is the work of years to understand the general course of the channel, and then the knowledge must be altered with each trip. The best pilot on the river, if he stops ashore a few months, becomes greener than a new hand. The pilots not only report their new experiences for publication in the newspapers, but they make notes of remarkable changes, and drop them into boxes on the route for the guidance of others in the business.[4]

Steering

Good piloting required more than mere knowledge of the river, it implied a steady hand at the wheel, as well. A pilot had to anticipate the "swing" of his boat and stay ahead of her, or else she would "run away" from him. Sometimes the simple act of heading a boat downstream could cure a body of ever wishing to become a pilot. A further lesson in this maritime art form comes to us from the reminiscences of George Byron Merrick, whom we already have met as a boy at Prescott, Wisconsin. He writes now of his days as a "cub" on the Upper Mississippi:

> The skilled steersman, combining his art with exact knowledge of the bottom of the river, will give his boat only enough wheel to lay her into her "marks," closely shaving the points of the reefs and bars, and will "meet her" so gradually and so soon as to check the swing of the jackstaff at the exact moment when the marks are reached. There is then no putting the wheel over to bring the boat back, after having overreached her marks, and the rudders have at no time been more than a quarter out of line with the hull of the boat. It is this delicate handling of the wheel, which differentiates between the artist and the athlete.
>
> Steamboats have their individuality, the same as pilots and steersmen. There are boats (or have been), that would almost steer themselves, while there are others so perverse and tricky that no one could feel sure of keeping them in the river for any consecutive two miles. A sternwheel boat going downstream when the wind was blowing up the river, was about as helpless a craft to handle as could well be imagined. After she was once "straightened down" she was all right; but in attempting to get her nose pointed down river, after having made a landing, there were more profane possibilities than the uninitiated ever dreamed of. The current, acting on the stern of the boat and the partially submerged wheel, was all the time pulling that end of the boat downstream; while the wind, acting upon the tall chimneys and the pilothouse and "texas," was at the same time pushing the bow of the boat upstream; and the pilot was all the while endeavoring to reverse this position, and get the bow of his boat pointed in the direction in which he wished to go. It sometimes took

hours to accomplish this, particularly if caught in places where the river was narrow and correspondingly swift, and the wind strong and contrary. The only way to swing a sternwheel boat was to put the steering wheel hard over, throwing the four rudders as far to one side as possible, and then back strongly against them. Under this leverage, if there was no wind, the boat would swing easily and promptly until her head was pointed downstream; and then by coming ahead and gaining steerageway, the boat was under perfect control. But when the wind was blowing upstream, it was often found impracticable to back fast and far enough to gain the necessary momentum to swing her in a narrow place; the engines would have to be stopped before the boat was swung to more than a right angle with the river, and then, before steerageway was gained after coming ahead, the bow of the boat would again be pointing upstream, and the same performance would have to be [repeated]—sometimes a dozen or twenty times, before the boat would get underway in the proper direction.

In 1881 I saw Henry Link, after having made a landing at Newport [Minnesota], back the Mary Morton, *of the Diamond Jo Line, more than five miles down the river, she having swung stern-down at that place. He seesawed back and forth across the stream, first in one direction and then in another, and failed at last to swing his boat against the strong south wind which was blowing. He finally gave it up and ran ashore, and getting out a line to a big tree, backed his craft around until her bow was pointed downstream, and then made a start from a broadside position against the bank. I happened to be a passenger on the boat at the time. His remarks on that occasion were unprintable.*[5]

Sam Clemens knew a few bad moments in steering. Though the world would eventually honor him as the gifted writer and humorist Mark Twain, Clemens was merely another relief pilot in the years just before the War Between the States. Only once in his career as a pilot did he run aground; that was in heavy smoke and fog in the sugar cane region of Louisiana. One other time, though, he came near getting himself in trouble while trying to steer a sluggish boat on a bad night. This story, told many years later by Clemens, did not make it into *Life on the Mississippi;* perhaps it should have, for it well illustrates the skill required to steer a steamboat:

> There was a pilot in those days [1861] by the name of Jack Leonard who was a perfectly wonderful creature. I do not know that Jack knew any more about the river than most of us and perhaps could not read the water any better, but he had a knack of steering away ahead of our ability, and I think he must have had an eye that could see farther into the darkness.
>
> I had never seen Leonard steer, but I had heard a good deal about it. I had heard it said that the crankiest old tub afloat—one that would kill any other man to handle—would obey and be as docile as a child when Jack Leonard took the wheel. I had a chance one night to verify that for myself. We were going up the river and it was one of the nastiest nights I ever saw. Besides that, the boat was loaded in such a way that she steered very hard, and I was half blind and crazy trying to locate the safe channel, and was pulling my arms out to keep her in it. It was one of those nights when everything looks the same whichever way you look: just two long lines where the sky comes down to the trees and where the trees meet the water with all the trees precisely the same height—all planted on the same day, as one of the boys used to put it—and not a thing to steer by except the knowledge in your head of the real shape of the river. Some of the boats had what they call a "night hawk" on the jackstaff, a thing which you could see when it was in the right position against the sky or the water, though it seldom was in the right position and was generally pretty useless.
>
> I was in a bad way that night and wondering how I could ever get through it, when the pilothouse door opened, and Jack Leonard walked in. He was a passenger that trip, and I had forgotten he was aboard. I was just about in the worst place and was pulling the boat first one way, then another, running the wheel backward and forward, and climbing it like a squirrel.

I do not know that Jack knew any more about the river than most of us and perhaps could not read the water any better, but he had a knack of steering away ahead of our ability, and I think he must have had an eye that could see farther into the darkness.

"Sam," he said, "let me take the wheel. Maybe I have been over this place since you have."

I didn't argue the question. Jack took the wheel, gave it a little turn one way, then a little turn the other; that old boat settled down as quietly as a lamb—went right along as if it had been broad daylight in a river without snags, bars, bottom, or banks, or anything that one could possibly hit. I never saw anything so beautiful. He stayed my watch out for me, and I hope I was decently grateful. I have never forgotten it.[6]

The pitch-blackness of night navigation eventually would yield to brighter times in the post-war years. In 1869 a pilot association began erecting marker lights on the Ohio. By 1880 the federal government had taken over the responsibility and navigation lights were widespread on the Ohio and Mississippi Rivers. These "government lights" were simply lanterns perched on white-painted tripods, which suggested "an immaculate chicken coop" to at least one observer. Typically they were placed at the head and foot of islands and other prominent shore features, and at the opposite ends of crossings—so that a pilot could line up his boat between them. The task of keeping them lit fell to local residents. It could be a dangerous and onerous task, but there was no shortage of applicants. The job paid ten to fifteen dollars a month—a princely sum to sharecroppers and tenant farmers along the river, most of whom were former slaves. As one grateful light tender said, "I's fixed for life, boss, if de gover'ment done hold out."[7]

Searchlights were installed on steamboats beginning in 1875, but only served to confirm what the pilot already *knew*.[8] The following account illustrates the point—

We left the dancing lights of [Memphis], and moved out into a pall of smoke suspended in fog, and then I saw how well and thoroughly the men in the pilothouse knew the mighty river. After a run of a few miles the captain declared it unsafe to go farther. The electric searchlight was thrown in all directions, but only illuminated a small circle closed in by a fog bank. In absolute, black darkness the pilot and the captain discussed the character of the shores, to hit upon a hard bank with heavy timber to which it would be safe to tie up. They agreed that some unseen island would serve best.

"Look out for the bar just above there," said the captain.

"Yes," said the pilot. "I know where she is."

The wheel was spun around, the boat turned into a new course, and presently the searchlight was thrown upon the very timber-studded reef they sought—as fine an exhibition of knowledge, experience, and skill as I ever witnessed.[9]

At times piloting could be quite a physical activity, even at the hands of the smoothest pilot. This was never more so than at dead low stage when the river came to resemble an obstacle course of reefs, bars, and snags. In 1880, the Baron de Wartegg saw this sort of river and learned firsthand why steamboats wore out so quickly and why pilots were paid so well:

We are speaking of January and therefore the very low river of winter. Anxiously the pilots sought their guideposts—tree trunks, hills, bends, other physical features. Often the engines must be shut off and the boat left to the current. But that precaution will not always do. A skiff, let down by chain and manned by two deckhands and the two pilots, precedes the heavy-laden boat and sounds with the lead for safe passage. Suddenly the news comes back: the pilot-boat has found shallows, a sandbar. The obstruction intersects the width of the river and could have taken shape in the last few days. Pilots file reports at the end of the run so that other pilots may benefit from what they have observed. But this sandbar has not yet been mentioned.

> *Jump with a steamboat? This 3,000-ton vessel plus cargo, across that barrier of sand?*

Nothing remained to us but, as they say in river vernacular, "to jump the bar." Jump with a steamboat? This 3,000-ton vessel plus cargo, across that barrier of sand? Yes, it poses a delicate situation, a thorny problem. The danger did not escape the passengers. It left its mark on them. But it could not be dodged; it had to be faced. The boat, maneuvering slowly, positioned itself at the shoals of danger, then laid on all steam and struck the bar full speed ahead.

A jolt. A scraping. A grinding on the sand. They send a shiver through the boat and—we find ourselves on the other side in deep water! Danger remains, looms large. From the pilotboat suddenly the cry, "Larboard snag!" At that moment our boat swerves to the right in a lunge, the great wheel in the pilothouse whirling like the smaller one that spins thread, and we drive perpendicular to the current— straight for the west bank. There the journey resumes. We have cleared the peril! The steersman has executed a masterpiece![10]

1   Zadoc Cramer, *The Navigator* (Pittsburgh: Cramer, Spear & Eichbaum, 1814), pp. 174-78.

2   Peale Journals.

3   William L. Heckmann, *Steamboating: Sixty-Five Years on Missouri's Rivers* (Kansas City: Burton Publishing, 1950), pp. 68-70.

4   Ralph, p. 178.

5   Merrick, pp. 100-02.

6   Albert B. Paine, *Mark Twain: A Biography,* 3 vols. (New York: Harper & Brothers, 1912), pp. 1:152-54.

7   Ralph, p. 173.

8   Wayman, p. 167; Way, p. 182.

9   Ralph, p. 183.

10 *Travels on the Lower Mississippi,* p. 41.

PART 2

Crew & Passengers

The Boatmen

In his classic work, *Life on the Mississippi*, Samuel Clemens relates that there was "but one permanent ambition" among the boys growing up in antebellum Hannibal, Missouri—and that ambition was "to be a steamboatman."[1] Although other interests might intrude, the river and the steamboats were the only real connections to the outside world for thousands of boys just like Clemens. Somewhere, beyond distant river bends, was a world different from anything they had seen. To work on a steamer—to share its pleasures, dangers, and hardships—was to know all the world's secrets. And to return home someday—tanned and worldly—as part of a steamboat crew, betokened unsurpassed glory.

Crew Complement

In the river cities of St. Louis, Pittsburgh, Cincinnati, and New Orleans, steamboats were a major employer. The number of persons working on a single packet boat* usually ranged from 40 to 80 souls, according to the size of the vessel, the level of passenger service, and the amount of freight handled. At times the crew outnumbered the passengers.

---

* A packet boat was one that carried both passengers and cargo. A packet company, or packet line, consisted of mutually owned or affiliated steamboats that operated on a regular schedule.

On a typical steamboat of the middle period, plying the waters between St. Louis, Cincinnati, and New Orleans, the officers consisted of a captain, two pilots, a chief clerk, a steward, two engineers, and two mates. There were, in addition, the junior officers, or apprentices, known by various titles. The pilot's apprentice was called a "cub" or steersman. Chief clerks enjoyed the services of two or more assistants, known as second clerks, or "mud clerks." Engineers in training were listed as strikers.

Boat crews also included deckhands, firemen, roustabouts, porters, cooks, chambermaids, a carpenter, a watchman, and a barber. In postbellum days, with all crew members drawing salaries, the captain of a large packet could expect to pay some $3,000 per month in wages.[2]

Though not normally associated with the crew of a steamboat, virtually every St. Louis, Cincinnati, and New Orleans packet contracted for the services of a barkeeper. The bar was located in the main cabin, forward, opposite the clerk's office, in what generally was referred to as the gentlemen's cabin. It was also conveniently close to the tables where the poker players congregated. On the big packets the barkeeper did not mix the drinks himself, but rather employed someone else to do it. More often the barkeeper mingled amongst the passengers and assisted the professional gamblers in fleecing unwary victims. For this he received a commission from the gamblers.[3]

Mates

First and second mates directed the work of the deckhands and rousters. Many mates had a reputation—probably well deserved—as coarse, profane fellows who regarded passengers as a nuisance. When young Sam Clemens, a disenchanted printer's apprentice at the time, took steamboat passage from Louisville to New Orleans in search of a new career, he attempted to make himself useful to the boat's mate. Writing many years later as Mark Twain, Clemens recalled that awkward moment:

> I particularly longed to acquire the least trifle of notice from the big stormy mate, and I was on the alert for an opportunity to do him a service to that end. It came at last. The riotous pow-wow of setting a spar was going on down on the forecastle, and I went down there and stood around in the way—or mostly skipping out of it—till the

mate suddenly roared a general order for somebody to bring him a capstan bar. I sprang to his side and said: "Tell me where it is—I'll fetch it!"

If a rag-picker had offered to do a diplomatic service for the Emperor of Russia, the monarch could not have been more astounded than the mate was. He even stopped swearing. He stood and stared down at me. It took him ten seconds to scrape his disjointed remains together again. Then he said impressively: "Well, if this don't beat h--l!" and turned to his work with the air of a man who had been confronted with a problem too abstruse for solution.

If a rag-picker had offered to do a diplomatic service for the Emperor of Russia, the monarch could not have been more astounded than the mate was.

I crept away, and courted solitude for the rest of the day. I did not go to dinner; I stayed away from supper until everybody else had finished. I did not feel so much like a member of the boat's family now as before. However, my spirits returned, in installments, as we pursued our way down the river. I was sorry I hated the mate so, because it was not in (young) human nature not to admire him. He was huge and muscular, his face was bearded and whiskered all over; he had a red woman and a blue woman tattooed on his right arm—one on each side of a blue anchor with a red rope to it; and in the matter of profanity he was sublime. When he was getting out cargo at a landing, I was always where I could see and hear. He felt all the majesty of his great position, and made the world feel it, too. When he gave even the simplest order, he discharged it like a blast of lightning, and sent a long, reverberating peal of profanity thundering after it. I could not help contrasting the way in which the average landsman would give an order with the mate's way of doing it. If the landsman should wish the gang-plank moved a foot farther forward, he would probably say: "James, or William, one of you push that plank forward, please"; but put the mate in his place, and he would roar out: "Here, now, start that gang-plank for'ard! Lively, now! What're you about! Snatch it! snatch it! There! there! Aft again! aft again! Don't you hear me? Dash it to dash! are you going to sleep over it! 'Vast heaving. 'Vast heaving, I tell you! Going to

heave it clear astern? WHERE 're you going with that barrel! for'ard
with it 'fore I make you swallow it, you dash-dash-dash-dashed split
between a tired mud-turtle and a crippled hearse-horse!"
I wished I could talk like that.[4]

Rousters

At the busier ports captains hired local labor to work freight; most masters, though, found it preferable to retain an ample crew of rousters on
the boat. These onboard stevedores performed exhausting work at all hours
and in any weather. They were fed as part of their compensation, but they
received no permanent quarters—they berthed on the main deck wherever space permitted. Writing in 1855, Thomas Thorpe noted: "It is astonishing what an amount of hard work they will perform, and yet retain their
vivacity and spirits. If they have the good fortune to be employed on a
'bully boat,' they take a lively personal interest in its success, and become
as much a part of the propelling machinery as the engines."[5]

That was the antebellum view, when most rousters on the lower rivers
were chattels of the captain or the boat owner. Emancipation after 1865 did
not materially improve their lot. In 1870, writer George W. Nichols thought
that "perhaps there are worse occupations in life than theirs; but if I had a
choice in the way of manual labor it would not be in the line of a rouster."[6]

Even in the 1890s the hard work and meager existence of the
roustabout had not changed. Nor had they ceased to attract the wonder-
ment of travel writers who found the rousters life an intriguing subject for
Northern readers:

> *Now they would jog along rolling barrels aboard with little spiked*
> *sticks, next they appeared each with a bundle of brooms on his shoul-*
> *der, and in another two minutes the long, zigzagging, shambling*
> *line was metamorphosed into a wriggling sinuosity formed of soap-*
> *boxes, or an unsteady line of flour bags, each with ragged legs beneath*
> *it, or a procession of baskets or of bundles of laths. As each one picked*
> *up an article of freight, an overseer told him its destination. The*
> *Negro repeated this, and kept on repeating it, in a singsong tone, as*
> *he shambled along, until one of the mates on the boat heard him*
> *and told him where to put it down.*

Two views of roustabouts unloading Mississippi steamboats. The sidewheeler (top photo) is so heavily laden that her main deck is nearly awash, while the sternwheeler (bottom) carries eight tiers of cotton bales—weighing some 500 pounds each. Most freight was loaded and unloaded by hand. (Top photo U.S. Army Corps of Engineers; bottom photo Murphy Library, University of Wisconsin-La Crosse.)

Some wear coats and vests and no shirts; some wear overcoats and shirts and no vests; some have only shirts and trousers—shirts that have lost their buttons, perhaps, and flare wide open to the trousers band, showing a black trunk like oiled ebony. They earn a dollar a day, but have not learned to save it. They are very dissipated, and are given to carrying knives, which the mates take away from the most unruly ones. The scars on many of their bodies show to what use these knives are too often put.

The work is hard, and they are kept at it, urged constantly by the mates on shore and aboard, as the Southern folks say that Negroes and mules always need to be. But the roustabouts' faults are excessively human, after all, and the consequence of a sturdy belief that they need sharper treatment than the rest of us leads to their being urged to do more work than a white man. There were nights . . . when the landings ran close together, and the poor wretches got little or no sleep. They "tote" all the freight aboard and back to land again on their heads or shoulders, and it is crushing work. Whenever the old barbaric instinct to loaf, or to move by threes at one man's work, would prompt them, one of the mates was sure to spy the weakness and roar at the culprits.

I mentioned the fact that the roustabouts were worked very hard.

"Dat dey is," said the barber. "We call 'em 'roosters' on de ribber, but rous'about is more correc'. Dey wuk hard night an' day, an' dey git mo' kicks dan dollars. Ef I got rejuced so's I had to do manual labor, I'd go to stealin' 'fo' I'd be a rooster."[7]

Firemen

The kindred spirits to the rousters were the firemen. In round-the-clock watches they fed the massive furnaces with wood, and in latter years with coal, until the boilers fairly swelled from the heat and pressure.[*] The fire-doors faced forward in order to increase the draft, and the rush of air tugged fearfully at the meager vestments of the stokers. With long iron prods they arranged the burning fuel evenly over the grates, then stood

---

[*] This is not an exaggeration. Over the years observers on different boats reported seeing boilers expand and contract with every stroke of the pistons.

back to wipe the sweat from their tinted goggles. A man could go blind peering into the glare of the furnaces. And yet no cry of anguish gushed from their throats, but rather the cadence of a song from which they timed their efforts and took their consolation. We hear of it in this glimpse from the 1830s:

> Among the beings attached to a Western steamer, there is one class too remarkable to be passed by, and this is composed of the firemen, the sphere of whose labor is directly on the bow of the boat, upon which the long row of gaping furnaces open. They are almost invariably athletic Negroes, or mulattos. The labor, which would be considered pretty severe by all but themselves, is generally performed amid bursts of boisterous merriment, jests, and songs; and the peculiar character of the latter has often made me hang over the boiler deck railing to listen; particularly after dark, when the scene was very striking from the bright ruddy glare thrown upon and around them, while with a thousand grimaces they grasped the logs and

Though often depicted as a carefree way of life, the roustabouts' lot was brutally hard and unremitting. Periods of rest were infrequent—the roustabout took his sleep wherever and whenever he could. (From *Harper's New Monthly Magazine.*)

whirled them into the blazing throat of the furnaces. Their ordinary song might strictly be said to be divided into a rapid alternation of recitative and chorus—the solo singer uttering his part with great volubility and alertness, while the mass instantly fell in with the burden, which consisted merely of a few words and notes in strictly harmonious unison.[8]

Clerks

Many successful businessmen got their start as mud clerks on a river steamer. The steady work, fair pay, and ample travel appealed to young lads who hoped to obtain a foothold in the realm of free enterprise. Indeed, clerks often became shareholders in their boats and would someday own a vessel outright, either as captain or shore-bound entrepreneur. First, though, they had to endure an initial trial as an apprentice clerk—a time when all was new and the world lay before them. Days in port were spent receiving and discharging freight, and reconciling those exchanges with bills of lading and dray tickets. Once underway mud clerks usually found time to socialize with passengers, especially the young ladies. Since many of the upper river boats went into dry dock during the winter, some mud clerks used the time off to attend business or professional schools.

Mud clerk Henry M. Blossom kept a journal of his day-to-day routine on the steamer *Polar Star*. His boat normally ran in the Missouri River trade, but the following entries record one of the *Star's* occasional runs on the Mississippi:

> *[St. Louis] Monday, Oct. 17th [1853]—I was awakened at 2 o'clock this morning by calls from passengers who had just arrived on the* Arabia *and wished to secure berths. Before night we had our rooms full; but it was determined by the "master spirits" of the* Star *that we should go South and our trip* was accordingly transferred to the* Aubrey.
>
> *Tuesday, Oct. 18th, 1853—During the day have been extremely hurried with the rush of freight. [This evening] tried to sleep, but mosquitoes wouldn't let me.*

---

* By "trip," he is referring to freight and passengers bound up the Missouri River.

October 19th—Left St. Louis at 4 o'clock p.m. with a fair freight and scarcely any passengers.

October 20th—At 8 o'clock arrived at Hat Island where we found six or eight boats detained by the bar. We lost about three hours at the bar. At Tower Island we took aboard 56 head of hogs, 25 head of cattle, 9 head of horses, and 1 mule. We had a big chase for the hogs, several going in the river repeatedly. Hogs bring $2 freight; horses and cattle $9.

October 21st—Took on board about 700 barrels and boxes of apples and 20 coops of chickens at Hickman [Kentucky]. Wooded about 30 miles below—16 cords at $2 [per cord], fine dry ash.

October 23rd—Landed at Napoleon [Arkansas] and put off mail. Yellow fever yet raging with considerable virulence.

October 25th—We were detained all of last night in a fog. Met Bunker Hill No. 3 below Natchez [Mississippi] after discharging freight at that place consisting of 70 barrels flour, 10 barrels ale, and 5 barrels whiskey.

October 27th—Arrived at New Orleans early in the morning. We could discharge no freight, owing to heavy rain, until afternoon.

October 28th—We got out most of our cargo early in the day.

October 29th—Early in the morning commenced receiving freight [for the up bound trip]; of which New Orleans was not prolific, as [ocean] vessels had been unable to discharge owing to rains. Left New Orleans . . . with light freight and drawing 4½ feet. No passengers, scarcely.

November 3rd—[Near Helena, Arkansas.] Left the bank at 5:30 a.m. The Crescent tried to pass us at the foot of Horseshoe Cut-off and we had a jolly race.

*Arrived at St. Louis at 6 o'clock a.m. of **Sunday, 6th November**.*

Owing to the Sabbath, *Polar Star* held her freight until Monday, when it was discharged in a cold, drizzling rain. Henry Blossom and the other clerks counted the bundles, barrels, and boxes of freight as they came out of the hold and matched them against the bills of lading. On this day all were correct except for one box of glass and one bundle of gunny material. With the freight off, the clerks enjoyed three days shore leave. As was his habit, Blossom attended theatrical performances and visited friends. Each night he would return to the boat and write letters home. Then it was back to work receiving freight for the next run to New Orleans.[9]

Stewards

Every packet boat had a chief steward and yet the job seldom was mentioned in travel literature. Passengers rarely paid attention to the steward; they regarded him as little more than the *maître d'* of a floating restaurant. The best description of the steward and his realm comes to us from George Merrick who, besides cubbing on a steamer, spent summers as a striker, mud clerk, and cabin boy. What he knew about the steward's job came from long hours of observation at the working end of a mop and broom:

> It was a saying on the river that if you wished to save the meals a passenger was entitled to on his trip, you took him through the kitchen the first thing when he came aboard. The inference was, that after seeing the food in course of preparation he would give it a wide berth when it came on the table. It would be unfair to the memory of the average river steward to aver that this assertion was grounded upon facts; but it would be stretching the truth to assert that it was without foundation. Things must be done in a hurry when three meals a day are to be prepared and served to three or four hundred people; and all the work had to be accomplished in two kitchens, each ten by twenty-feet in area—one for meats and vegetables, and the other for pastry and desserts.
>
> The responsibility of providing for meals at stated times, with a good variety, cooked and served in a satisfactory manner, devolved upon the steward. Under him were two assistants, with meat cooks, vegetable cooks, pastry cooks, and bread makers, and a force of waiters and pantrymen conditioned upon the boat's capacity for passengers. While the steward was, in the thought of outsiders, rated as an officer of the second class, he was as a matter of fact in the first class. When the pay of the captain was three hundred dollars per month, and that of the mate two hundred, the average steward of any reputation also commanded three hundred, the same as the captain, and his services were sought by the owners of a dozen boats. Likewise, he earned every cent of his salary, whatever it might be.

Unlike the other officers he had no regular watch to stand, after which he might lay aside his responsibility and let the members of the other watch carry the load while he laid off and watched them sweat. He was on duty all the time, and when and how he slept is to this day a mystery to me. He might have slept in the morning, when the cooks were preparing breakfast, had he felt quite confident that the cooks were not likewise sleeping, instead of broiling beefsteaks and making waffles. This being a matter of some doubt, and of great concern, he was usually up as soon as the cooks, and quietly poking about to see that breakfast reached the table promptly at seven o'clock. If the floor of the cabin was covered with sleepers, it was the steward who must awaken them, and, without giving offense, induce them to vacate the premises that the tables might be set. This was a delicate piece of business. The steward also saw that the assistant in charge of the waiters was on hand with all his crew, to put the cabin to rights, set the tables, and prepare to serve breakfast, while the cabin steward and the stewardess, with their crews, were making up the berths, sweeping, dusting, and tidying up.

As soon as breakfast was out of the way, the menu for dinner was prepared and handed to the chief cook. Shortages in provisions were remedied at the first landing reached, and stocks of fish, game, fresh eggs, and fresh vegetables were bought as offered at the various towns. While there was a cold-storage room on all first-class packets, its capacity was limited, and with a passenger list of two hundred and fifty or three hundred in the cabin, it was often found necessary to lay in additional stocks of fresh meats. Often, a dozen lambs could be picked up, or a dozen "roaster" pigs, and these were killed and dressed on the boat by one of the assistant cooks. Live poultry was always carried in coops, and killed as wanted.

Of course the darkies are not the cleanest-appearing people aboard the boat, but if the steward is up in his business he sees to it that a reasonable degree of cleanliness is maintained, even in the starboard galley. On the opposite side of the steamer is the pastry cook's domain, and that is usually the showplace of the boat. Most stewards are shrewd enough to employ pastry cooks who are masters of their profession, men who take a pride not only in the excellence of their bread, biscuit, and pie crust, but also in the spotlessness of their workshops.

They are proud to receive visits from the lady passengers, who can appreciate not only the output but the appearance of the galley. It is a good advertisement for a boat, and the steward himself encourages such visits, while discouraging like calls at the opposite side.

In old, flush times in the steamboat business, pastry cooks generally planned to give a surprise to the passengers on each up trip of the steamer. I remember one such, when no less than thirteen different desserts were placed in front of each passenger as he finished the hearty preliminary meal. Six of these were served in tall and slender glass goblets—vases, would more nearly describe them—and consisted of custards, jellies, and creams of various shades and flavors; while the other seven were pies, puddings, and ice creams. The passenger was not given a menu card and asked to pick out those that he thought he would like, but the whole were brought on and arranged in a circle about his plate, leaving him to dip into each as he fancied, and leave such as did not meet his approval. It was necessary to carry an extra outfit of glass and china in order to serve this bewildering exhibition of the pastry cook's art, and it was seldom used more than once on each trip.

Serving such a variety of delicacies, of which but a small portion was eaten by any person at the table, would seem like an inexcusable waste; but the waste on river steamers was really not as great in those days as it is in any great hotel of our day. Each steamer carried forty or more deckhands and rousters. For them, the broken meat was piled into pans, all sorts in each pan, the broken bread and cake into other pans, and jellies and custards into still others—just three assortments, and this, with plenty of boiled potatoes, constituted the fare of the crew below decks. One minute after the cry of "Grub-pile!" one might witness the spectacle of forty men sitting on the bare deck, clawing into the various pans to get hold of the fragments of meat or cake which each man's taste particularly fancied. It certainly wasn't an appetizing spectacle. Only familiarity with it enabled an onlooker full to appreciate its grotesqueness without allowing the equilibrium of his stomach to be disturbed. It usually had but one effect upon such lady *passengers as had the hardihood to follow the cry of "Grub-pile!" and ascertain what the thing really was.*

Altogether the duties of the steward were arduous and tormenting. The passengers expected much; and after getting the best, if any slip occurred they were sure to enter complaint—a complaint so worded as to convey the impression that they never had anything fit to eat while on the boat, nor any service that white men were justified in tolerating. [10]

Another account of work in the steward's department comes from the reminiscences of George H. Devol, of Marietta, Ohio. There is a something of a dark side to Devol's story, for although he was only ten years old at the time, Devol soon would learn the rudiments of a less honorable profession on the river:

In the year 1839, while at the river one day, I saw a steamer lying at the wharf-boat by the name of Wacousta. *The first steward said I could ship as a cabin boy at $4 per month. I thought this a great opportunity, so when the boat backed out I was on board without saying anything to my parents or anyone else. My first duty was to scour knives. I knew they would stand no foolishness, so at it I went, and worked like a little trooper, and by doing so I gained the good will of the steward. At night I was told to get a mattress and sleep on the floor of the cabin; this I was glad to do, as I was tired.*

About four o'clock in the morning the second steward came up to me and gave me a pretty hard kick in the side that hurt me, and called out: "Get up here, and put your mattress away." I did get up and put away my bed, and then I went to the steward who kicked me and said: "Look here! Don't kick me that way again, for you hurt me." He let go and hit me a slap in the face that made my ears ring; so into him I pitched. I was a big boy for only ten years old; but I struck the wrong man that time, for he hit me another lick in the nose that came very near sending me to grass, but I rallied and came again. This time I had a piece of stone coal that I grabbed out of a bucket; I let it fly, and it caught him on the side of the head and brought him to his knees. By this time the passengers were getting up to see what was the matter; the pilot and first steward soon put a stop to the fight. I told my story to the boss, and he took sides with me. He told the officers of the boat that I was the best boy to work that he had; so they discharged the second steward at Cincinnati, and you can bet I was glad. I remained on the Wacousta *for some time, and thought myself a good steamboat man. I knew it all, for I had been there.*

The next boat I shipped on was the Walnut Hills, *at $7 per month. I would get up early in the morning and make some "five-cent pieces" (there were no nickels in those days) by blacking boots. I quit the* Walnut Hills *after three months, and shipped with Captain Peterson on the* Cicero, *bound for Nashville. The first trip up the Cumberland River the boat was full of passengers, and I had a fight with the pantryman. The captain said I should go ashore. They brought me up to the office, and the clerk was told to pay me my wages, which amounted to the large sum of one dollar and fifty cents. I was told to get my baggage; but as two blue cotton shirts and what I had on my back was all I possessed, it did not take long to pack. My trunk was a piece of brown paper with a pin lock. They landed me at a point where the bank was about one hundred feet high, and so steep that a goat could not climb it. They commenced to pull in the plank, when the steward yelled out to the captain that he "could not get along without that boy," and asked him to let me go as far as Nashville. I was told to come aboard, which I did, and I remained on that boat for one year, during which time I learned to play "seven-up," and to "steal card," so that I could cheat the boys, and I felt as if I was fixed for life.* [11]

Captain

The captain was the chief administrative officer, and often an owner of the vessel—sometimes the sole owner. He held a master's license (after 1871), which made him legally responsible for the overall safe operation of the boat, but it did not entitle him to pilot the craft or to operate the engines. Captains worked closely with their chief clerks in obtaining freight contracts and passenger business, and in balancing the ledgers. Captains decided when to put their boats in for repairs, and when to enter into the trade of a certain city or river. Most of them worked for several years as clerks, pilots, mates, and even engineers before obtaining their master's license.

William B. Miller was master of the *Thompson Dean* (the second vessel of that name) in 1875. In a remarkably vivid letter to his family, he details the trips of the *Dean* and touches upon the many aspects of his job as captain:

> *Upward bound, December 6, 1875*
>
> *My Dear Children,*
>
> *I am a bad correspondent these days, as I suppose you already know. This is the busiest winter I have ever had. I seem to find no time to write letters except occasionally on my upward trips, and then my boat shakes so that it is almost impossible to use a pen. I am reduced to the necessity of a pencil and even then it is difficult business. I wish for your company a great deal this winter. There is much that would interest you in the course of a trip, the chief of which is the change from winter to summer and again from summer to winter which I undergo every trip.*
>
> *I wear winter underclothing and overcoats in Memphis one week and next in New Orleans I put on my lightest underwear and go in my shirt sleeves for comfort. Down there the leaves are green on the trees and the gardens full of roses as they are with you in summer. On my table as I write you tonight are three large bouquets given me at Baton Rouge and Bayou Sara [Louisiana] as I came up. They contain the choicest roses and camellias and although they have been four days in my room they are almost as fresh as when cut, and new buds open every day. One of the bouquets contains 26 roses and camellias besides smaller flowers that I don't know the names of.*
>
> *We leave Memphis always on Wednesday night, every alternate week, and the weather there is usually chilly, although not so cold as with you. We generally start with one or two thousand bales of cotton and fifty or sixty passengers. The first night out we land at Bennet's, and Mhoon's, and O.K., and Trotter's landings, where we usually add three or four hundred bales to our cargo and arrive at Helena [Arkansas] (90 miles) at daylight. Here we generally spend three or four hours, and sometimes longer. Last trip I was there all day and took on board there 1,700 bales. Leaving Helena we stop during*

The *Thompson Dean*. She is loaded heavy by the bows with her lower deck guards covered by five tiers of cotton bales. The 306-foot-long *Dean* was built in 1872 and dismantled in 1882. Her namesake was a prominent Cincinnati businessman and boat owner. (Photo courtesy Murphy Library, University of Wisconsin-La Crosse.)

Thursday and Thursday night at Delta, Friar's Point, Sunflower, Australia, Laconia, Carson's, Waxhaw, White River, Terrene, Floryville, Riverton, Napoleon, Prentiss, Niblett's, Storm's, Bolivar, Kentucky, and Chicora, adding 30, 50, or 100 bales of cotton and hundreds of sacks of cottonseed at each place, and passengers are getting on and off at every landing.

The cotton bales, as you know, are about five feet long, two feet thick, and three feet wide, and weigh about 500 pounds each. The seed is in sacks nearly the size of a wheat sack and weighs about 120 pounds per sack.

Friday morning we usually reach Chicot City [Arkansas], and by that time business has commenced in earnest with us. Leaving there we make the crossing of Choctaw bar, where the Indiana *lies sunk, and rounding to at the head of Choctaw Bend we land at Eutaw, Stop's, Mound Place, Delome, and Wilkinson's; the landings being so near together that we back down from one to the other the whole* length of the bend—about six miles. This is a wealthy bend and the plantations are yet white with unpicked cotton although the pickers have been three months at work.*

The darkies come running from the fields in droves to see "de big Dean" and our brass band has an appreciative audience. In this bend we add several hundred bales and sacks and then go on down the river stopping at Arkansas City, Port Anderson, Greenwood, Utopia, Gaines' Landing, Point Comfort, Shady Side, Lewellyn, Linwood, Luna, Point Chicot, Argyle, and Greenville adding freight and passengers everywhere. By this time it is Saturday night and we begin to notice that we are entering a different country and climate.

From Memphis to White River is almost an unbroken wilderness except at the little landings I have mentioned, but the past 24 hours we have been in a better country and the weather is growing warmer. Leaving Greenville [Mississippi] Saturday night we are nearly loaded but we still take on board a few hundred bales and sacks from those who ship by us regularly at Leland, Sunnyside, Refuge, Eggs Point, Auburn, Longwood, Bernard's, Leota, Maryland, Carolina, Pilcher's Point, Duncan's, Skipwith's, Wilson's Point, Homochitta, Ben Lomond, and Lake Providence.

By this time it is Sunday morning and we are looked for by every darky and colored child along the shore for the next 100 miles. Sunday is their holiday, the day of their best clothes, and our band plays for them as we take on a few thousand sacks at Tallula, Wilton, Melbourne, Goodrich's, Bell's, Duvall's, Chotard, Henderson's, Villa Vista, Ditchley, Omega, and Millikin's Bend. The antics these colored folks—old, middle aged, and young—can cut up of a Sunday, under the influence of a brass band, are more than I can hope to convey a faint idea of. . . .

We are now loaded, 5,000 bales and 10,000 sacks, and the cotton is twelve tiers high on our guards; if our passengers get a peep of daylight they have to go on the hurricane deck or in the pilothouse. Our guards are dragging the water and our mates and our 100 men

---

* Choctaw Bend, as well as Eutaw and Mound's Landings, still appear on navigation charts of the Lower Mississippi.

on deck are worn out with four days constant work night and day. We are now at Vicksburg, 400 miles from Memphis and halfway to New Orleans. We take on 2,000 bushels of coal here and swing out into the stream at 10 p.m. and stretch off to Natchez (107 miles) without a landing. We are there at daylight Monday morning, and the flowers begin to come on board, sent by the friendly hand of those who have traveled with us perhaps, or those who are connected with us in a business way.

After this we are in a different country and probably stop only at Bayou Sara and Baton Rouge. The cotton plantations have disappeared and far as we can see is the sugar cane, looking very much as the cornfields do in summer with you. The steam of the sugar mills is seen in all directions. Liveoak and orange and china trees dot the landscape. Elegant mansions along the "coast" are so near each other as to make an almost continuous village, and over all the fleecy clouds and the bright sunshine make it a continual summer.

Sometime during Tuesday afternoon the church steeples of New Orleans come in view and we are over an hour making the circuit of the crescent on which the city is built. . . . About 4 p.m. we move into our dock at the foot of Canal Street . . . and I leave the deck with a feeling of relief that "another trip is ended."

Here we put out our cargo and receive on board hundreds of hogsheads and barrels of sugar and molasses, boxes and barrels of oranges and coconuts, bunches of bananas, etc., etc., and on Thursday evening we drop out into the stream and commence our upward journey.

We make the same landings that we did going down but our stops are shorter, merely putting off the small lots of plantation supplies that were ordered as we went down. Our brass band plays at the principal points during the day and in the evenings our very excellent string band amuses the passengers in the cabin and our old French darky quartet sings "Silver Threads Among the Gold" in a way that always brings down the house. So we go, and amid it all I have little time for play, or letter writing, or anything else but attending to all the thousand demands upon my time that are necessary to keep the machine moving.

> *Tuesday morning we reach Memphis and then begins precisely the same program over again. I write you tonight about 100 miles below Memphis and the weather is growing rapidly cold and flurries of snow are in the air. I suppose it is winter with you tonight. Write me oftener, can't you? I don't get many letters from you, and the few I do get indicate that you are both in need of a little practice in that line, and, do you know, I find misspelled words in them. So you must brush up a little, both of you, and write to me oftener. My best love to you all.*
>
> *Affectionately,*
> *Papa*[12]

Pilots

The riverboat pilot was an American classic. He ranked with cowboys and railroad engineers as an enduring symbol of the romance of the Western frontier. But the pilot had the better of it, for he was at least as independent as the cowboy and far better paid than the engineer. The pilot was a professional contractor, not an employee of a boat or packet line. In busy times he could stipulate his own terms. Pilots signed on for a trip or for a season and captains frequently paid extra to retain a competent pilot through the off-season. Pilots enjoyed the greatest prosperity in the late 1850s, when their wages reached $300 per month—an exquisite salary matched by few other professions. This prosperity owed to the fact that the pilots had formed a professional union at that time, the Pilots' Benevolent Association. The Association's use of river channel reports, which were shared and continually updated by member pilots from New Orleans to St. Louis, won favor with insurance underwriters, shippers, and the traveling public, and ensured that the pilots could very nearly dictate their own terms to owners and captains.[13]

If compelled to list from memory all the famous pilots of the era, most Americans could name only one: Samuel Clemens—Mark Twain. Such is the misplaced emphasis of history. In point of fact, Clemens was not very well known at the time. He worked on the river only five years—two of those as a cub—and never held more than a second-class pilot's license, which he received on September 9, 1858. Still, he was the man who made them all famous, and his entertaining book, *Life on the Mississippi*, remains

Samuel L. Clemens, steamboat pilot, circa 1859. The world did not yet know him as the humorist, Mark Twain. Indeed, had it not been for the disruption of the Civil War, Clemens might have spent his life as a pilot—a profession he dearly loved. (Photo courtesy of Vassar College Library.)

the best single source on the making of a pilot. Avid readers of Mark Twain realize, however, that as an author Clemens never let facts get in the way of a good story. His official biographer, Albert Bigelow Paine, found that Clemens' account of securing a steersman's berth under the tutelage of Horace Bixby was reworked for the benefit of the readers. Paine interviewed Bixby in 1910 and came away with a more detailed, if not different, story of Clemens' bid to become a pilot:

> In the Mississippi book the author conveys the impression of being then a boy of perhaps seventeen. Writing from that standpoint he records incidents that were more or less invention or that happened to others. He was, in reality, considerably more than twenty-one years old, for it was in April, 1857, that he went aboard the Paul Jones; and he was fairly familiar with steamboats and the general requirements of piloting. He had been brought up in a town that turned out pilots; he had heard the talk of their trade. One at least of the Bowen boys was already on the river while Sam Clemens was still a boy in Hannibal, and had often been home to air his grandeur and dilate on the marvel of his work. That learning the river was no light task Sam Clemens very well knew. Nevertheless, as the little boat made its drowsy way down the river into lands that grew ever pleasanter with advancing spring, the old "permanent ambition" of boy-

hood stirred again, and the call of the faraway Amazon, with its coca and its variegated zoology, grew faint.

Horace Bixby, pilot of the Paul Jones, *then a man of thirty-two, still living (1910) and at the wheel, was looking out over the bow at the head of Island No. 35 when he heard a slow, pleasant voice say:*

"Good morning."

Bixby was a clean-cut, direct, courteous man.

"Good morning, sir," he said, briskly, without looking around.

As a rule, Mr. Bixby did not care for visitors in the pilothouse. This one presently came up and stood a little behind him.

"How would you like a young man to learn the river?" he said.

The pilot glanced over his shoulder and saw a rather slender, loose-limbed young fellow with a fair, girlish complexion and a great tangle of auburn hair.

"I wouldn't like it. Cub pilots are more trouble than they're worth. A great deal more trouble than profit."

The applicant was not discouraged.

"I am a printer by trade," he went on, in his easy, deliberate way. "It doesn't agree with me. I thought I'd like to go to South America."

Bixby kept his eye on the river; but a note of interest crept into his voice.

"What makes you pull your words that way?" ("pulling" being the river term for drawling), he asked.

The young man had taken a seat on the visitor's bench.

"You'll have to ask my mother," he said, more slowly than ever. "She pulls hers, too."

Pilot Bixby woke up and laughed; he had a keen sense of humor, and the manner of the reply amused him. His guest made another advance.

"Do you know the Bowen boys?" he asked—"pilots in the St. Louis and New Orleans trade?"

"I know them well—all three of them. William Bowen did his first steering for me; a mighty good boy, too. Had a Testament in his pocket when he came aboard; in a week's time he had swapped it for a pack of cards. I know Sam, too, and Bart."

"Old schoolmates of mine in Hannibal. Sam and Will especially were my chums."

"Come over and stand by the side of me," said Bixby. "What is your name?"

The applicant told him, and the two stood looking at the sunlit water.

"Do you drink?"

"No."

"Do you gamble?"

"No, sir."

"Do you swear?"

"Not for amusement; only under pressure."

"Do you chew?"

"No, sir, never; but I must smoke."

"Did you ever do any steering?" was Bixby's next question.

"I have steered everything on the river but a steamboat, I guess."

"Very well; take the wheel and see what you can do with a steamboat. Keep her as she is—toward that lower cottonwood snag."

Bixby had a sore foot and was glad of a little relief. He sat down on the bench and kept a careful eye on the course. By and by he said:

"There is just one way that I would take a young man to learn the river: that is, for money."

"What do you charge?"

"Five hundred dollars, and I to be at no expense whatever."

In those days pilots were allowed to carry a learner, or "cub," board free. Mr. Bixby meant that he was to be at no expense in port or for incidentals. His terms looked rather discouraging.

"I haven't got five hundred dollars in money," Sam said; "I've got a lot of Tennessee land worth twenty-five cents an acre; I'll give you two thousand acres of that."

Bixby dissented.

"No; I don't want any unimproved real estate. I have too much already."

Sam reflected upon the amount he could probably borrow from (his sister) Pamela's husband without straining his credit.

"Well, then, I'll give you one hundred dollars cash and the rest when I earn it."

Something about this young man had won Horace Bixby's heart. His slow, pleasant speech; his unhurried, quiet manner with the wheel; his evident sincerity of purpose—these were externals, but beneath them the pilot felt something of the quality of mind or heart which later made the world love Mark Twain. The terms proposed were agreed upon. The deferred payments were to begin when the pupil had learned the river and was receiving pilot's wages. During Mr. Bixby's daylight watches his pupil was often at the wheel, that trip, while the pilot sat directing him and nursing his sore foot. Any literary ambitions that Samuel Clemens may have had grew dim; by the time they had reached New Orleans he had almost forgotten he had been a printer; and when he learned that no ship would be sailing to the Amazon for an indefinite period the feeling grew that a directing hand had taken charge of his affairs.

From New Orleans his chief did not return to Cincinnati, but went to St. Louis, taking with him his new cub, who thought it fine, indeed, to come steaming up to that great city with its thronging waterfront; its levee fairly packed with trucks, drays, and piles of freight, the whole flanked with a solid mile of steamboats lying side by side, bow a little upstream, their belching stacks reared high against the blue—a towering front of trade. It was glorious to nose one's way to a place in that stately line, to become a unit, however small, of that imposing fleet.

At St. Louis Sam borrowed from Mr. Moffett the funds necessary to make up his first payment, and so concluded his contract. Then, when he suddenly found himself on a fine big boat, in a pilothouse so far above the water that he seemed perched on a mountain—a "sumptuous temple"—his happiness seemed complete.[14]

> *... Albert Bigelow Paine found that Clemens' account of securing a steersman's berth under the tutelage of Horace Bixby was reworked for the benefit of the readers.*

Clemens had chosen his master well. Bixby was one of the best pilots on the Mississippi. Horace Ezra Bixby was born in rural New York state in 1826 and ran away to Cincinnati at the age of fourteen. After four years as a tailor's apprentice, he took a job as mud clerk on a packet boat. Two years later he earned his pilot's license. Over the next decade his keen eye, prodigious memory, and unshakable self-confidence gained him the reputation as a "lightning" pilot—a master of his craft. When he met twenty-two-year-old Sam Clemens in 1857 and agreed to take him on as a cub, he unwittingly ensured himself a place in history. During the War Between the States Bixby piloted the Union's most formidable gunboat, the *Benton*. In post-war years Bixby invested in the Anchor Line of St. Louis and captained two of its finest boats, the *City of Alton* and the *City of Baton Rouge*.

Clemens' departure from the river in 1861 placed him out of contact with Bixby for some two decades. When their paths crossed again in 1882, Clemens found his mentor just as he had left him:

> *[Bixby has] the same slender figure, the same tight curls, the same spring step, the same alertness, the same decision of eye and answering decision of hand, the same erect military bearing; not an inch gained or lost in girth, not an ounce gained or lost in weight, not a hair turned. It is a curious thing, to leave a man thirty-five years old and come back at the end of twenty-one years and find him still only thirty-five.* [15]

Bixby lived to see the decline of the packet steamboat era, but he was not finished with the river. Instead he took a berth with the Mississippi River Commission—a government entity tasked with improving navigation and flood control on the river. Bixby was the oldest active captain and pilot when he died in 1912. He was eighty-six. [16]

There came a time in the education of every apprentice pilot when he would have to take the wheel alone and unassisted and guide his boat safely to its destination. No pilot could ever forget the experience; it became part of his initiation to the guild, and a permanent grade card by which all other rivermen judged him. George Merrick's first test of nerve and self-reliance came on the St. Croix River, between the states of Minnesota and Wisconsin, in 1860:

> *I had been running with Charley Jewell on the* H.S. Allen, *from Prescott to St. Croix Falls. Mr. Jewell fell sick and was laid off at Prescott. On the levee, the day he went home, was a steamboat load of rope, rigging, boats, and camp equipage, together with a couple of*

*hundred raftsmen landed from a downriver packet that did not care
to make the run up the lake. The disembarked men were anxious to
reach Stillwater with their cargo, that night. Our regular starting
time, as a United States mail boat, was at 7 o'clock in the morning.
They offered extra compensation if we would take them up that night,
and the proposition was accepted by Captain Gray. All hands were set
to work loading the stuff. I felt quite elated at the prospect, as it was
a bright evening, and I felt sure of finding my way, for there were only
three or four close places to run in the thirty miles of lake navigation
between Prescott and Stillwater.*

*We got everything aboard, and I backed her out and started up the
lake. There had been some lightning in the north, where there was a
bank of low-lying clouds. So far away were they, apparently, that no
one thought of a storm, certainly not a serious one. We were running
toward it, however, and as we soon discovered, it was coming to meet
us at a rattling pace. We met when about six miles above Prescott.
First a terrific wind out of the north, followed by torrents of rain,
and incessant lightning, which took on the appearance of chain-mail
as it shimmered and glittered on the falling rain drops. I put up the
breast-board, and let down the head-board as far as I could and still
leave room between to look out ahead; but the fierce wind drove the
rain in sheets into the pilothouse, and in a minute's time I was completely soaked.* The lightning and thunder were terrifying in bril-
liancy and in sharpness of sound, the flash and the report coming in
so closely together as to leave no doubt that the bolts were getting
seriously close to the smokestacks. The pilothouse was not the place I
would have chosen from which to enjoy these effects, had I my choice.
The place I really longed for was somewhere down below, where I
would have felt less conspicuous as a target.*

*I managed to work my way around the Kinnickinnic bar, and
made the run up to the Afton (or "Catfish") bar, around which the
channel was quite narrow and woefully crooked. Thus far, the high*

---

* The pilothouse of a river steamboat was glassed in on three sides. In order to afford
the pilot an unimpeded and distortion-free view, the forward-facing window contained no glass. The breast-board, which hinged downward, and the head-board,
which propped upward like a sunshade, could be closed to fill the void.

banks had sheltered us somewhat from the wind. Here, however, the low-lying prairie came down to the water's edge. The sweep of the wind was terrific, while the downpour of rain was such that at times it was impossible to see any landmarks a hundred feet away. Captain Gray, wrapped in his storm clothes, who had, since the tempest broke, stayed on the roof, one eye on the banks, when he could see them, and the other on the young man at the wheel, finally called up and wanted to know if I did not think we had better feel our way ashore and tie up until the storm abated, even at the risk of being late in getting back to Prescott to take up our regular trip in the morning. I was shivering so that my teeth clattered, and the captain would have been fully justified in assuming that I was shaking as much from fear as from cold. I had a deal of pride in those days, however, and a fair allowance of inherited courage, with perhaps a dash of pig-headedness. I did not wish to have it bulletined from one end of the river to the other that the first time I was left in charge of a steamboat, I had hunted a tree to tie up to because it happened to thunder and rain a little. That would have been the popular version of the incident, in any case. I replied, therefore, that if Captain Gray would send his waiter up with a glass of brandy, I would take the steamer to Hudson levee before taking out a line, and from there to Stillwater and back to Prescott in time for our morning run. The captain said nothing, then or thereafter, but sent his "boy" up with the brandy. This was applied inwardly, and served to take the chill off.

> *I did not wish to have it bulletined from one end of the river to the other that the first time I was left in charge of a steamboat, I had hunted a tree to tie up to because it happened to thunder and rain a little.*

Thus fortified—temperance people will please not be horrified at this depravity of a nineteen-year-old novice, under such extraordinary provocation—I worked around "Catfish" and followed along the west shore as far as Lakeland. From Lakeland across the lake to the Hudson levee, is about three-quarters of a mile. It was still blowing a gale, and the rain came down in torrents, so that the opposite shore could not be seen—in fact one could not distinguish an object ten rods *ahead. I had felt my way along, sometimes under the "slow bell," until the present. I must now cut loose from the west shore, and make the crossing to Hudson. There was plenty of water everywhere; but I could not see any landmarks on the opposite side of the lake. I got a stern bearing, however, and headed across. In a minute's time I could see nothing, either ahead or astern, and having no compass I had to rely on the "feel" of the rudders to tell me which way she was swinging. As it turned out, this was of little value, owing to the strength of the wind. For five minutes I ran under full head, and then slowed, trying to get a glimpse of the east bank, and "find myself." When I did, the H.S. Allen was headed squarely down the lake, and fully a mile below the Hudson landing. The force of the wind on the chimneys had turned her bow downwind and downstream. As the rain began to slacken and I could see my marks, it took but a few minutes to straighten her up and make the run to the landing.*

On leaving Hudson there were two ways of running the big bar opposite and below the mouth of Willow River. One, the longest, was to cross back to Lakeland and then run up the west shore—all of it straight work. The other was to run half a mile, then quartering west-northwest across the lake to the opposite shore. This crossing saved a mile or more of steaming over the other course; but it was crooked and narrow, and the possibility of hanging up was much greater. Captain Gray asked me, when backing out, which crossing I would make. I replied that I was going to take the upper to save time. He said nothing, but again took his place by the bell. He made no suggestion, nor offered any opinion as to my decision. That was a part of the river etiquette, which he adhered to even in the case of a boy; for which I sincerely thanked him in my inner being, while accepting it outwardly quite as a matter of course—which it would have been, with an older and more experienced man at the wheel.

I made the crossing without calling for leads, or touching bottom, and the rest of the way was easy. When we made Stillwater the stars were out, and the storm clouds hung low on the southern horizon. I went below and got into dry clothes, and [grabbed] a few hours' sleep while the freight was being put ashore. Along about two o'clock in the morning I started back, with the mate on the roof. In confidence he [told] me the gratifying news that the "old man says you're all right. He says that you've got nerve enough to last you through." As "nerve" was one of the things needed in the business, I was certainly proud that my night's work, alone on a heavily-loaded boat, in one of the worst storms, had given me a standing with the "old man"; and I felt reasonably certain that his report would carry weight among the rivermen who might chance to discuss the merits of the young "cub," and his equipment for serious work.[17]

To hear pilots tell their stories, one would come to believe that the piloting fraternity was unhampered by laws and regulations. Such was not the case; piloting was one of the first professions to come under federal scrutiny. After the passage of the landmark Steamboat Inspection Act of 1852, the printing on the back of every pilot's license reminded the holder of his responsibilities, and the penalties for ignoring them. For example, any steersman working alone who was not fully licensed to operate a passenger steamboat was subject to a (then) stiff one hundred dollar fine for each occurrence. Any pilot who was deemed incompetent, or who placed his boat and passengers in peril through misconduct or neglect, could lose his license permanently; and anyone who was injured through the misconduct or neglect of a pilot could sue that pilot for damages. It was the duty of all pilots to point out any defects in the hull or steam apparatus of their vessel to government inspectors. Failure to do so could result in the revocation of the pilot's license (though compliance might result in the pilot being fired by the boat's owner). Pilots also were required to report all serious accidents to the inspectors, regardless of culpability. Finally, as the wording on their licenses pointed out, pilots were divided into three categories. First-class pilots were qualified to act as chief pilots on any boat by virtue of their "long experience in the navigation and management of all classes of steam vessels." Second-class pilots, whose experiences were more limited, could work as chief pilots on medium or small vessels, but only could serve as relief, or second, pilots on the largest steamboats. (Large steamers were defined as any vessels that registered over 750 tons displacement.) The lowest category was that of assistant pilot. These were the cubs. They were "not considered to have sufficient knowledge of the route" for which their license was to be granted. They were never to be left "in charge of the deck."[18]

True fans of river lore cannot help but feel envy over the stories of green kids and gray-haired veterans who took their places at the wheel of a steamboat. What measure of pride and confidence they must have felt to "steady her up" and "set her on her marks!" Their work was the culmination of practice, knowledge, and sheer determination. And there was no other way—no easy way of learning the river, no shortcut to the pilothouse. Well, . . . unless your name happened to be Solomon Smith.

Sol Smith was a genuine character of his times. Sol came to the river in the 1830s as an actor and theatrical manager. He purchased a floating theater on the Ohio River with the idea of staging plays from Louisville to New Orleans. It was not to be; the theater sank, literally. Discouraged, but not defeated, Sol went on to sample a multitude of careers while at the same time supporting a large family at St. Louis. During thirty years in the Mississippi Valley, he dabbled in medicine, law, journalism, business, politics, theology, and theatrics. He succeeded tolerably well at all of them. We will cross Sol's path again, farther down the river; but for now we meet him as a scribbler of tales; in this case the tale is an autobiographical account of how he became a steamboat pilot on a trip to New Orleans:

> *The incidents I am about to relate occurred in the summer of '40. The river was low, and it was not thought advisable to run nights, at any rate until we got below Memphis.*
>
> *There was considerable sickness among the deck passengers, and as I was the only physician on board, my time was much occupied in weighing out grains and scruples of calomel, jalap, and ipecacuanha from the medicine chest. This I got along with very well, having a faithful assistant in the clerk, Thompson, who went the rounds with me, and took particular care that my prescriptions were attended to.*
>
> *One evening a steward came to my stateroom and said Captain D—— desired to speak with me.*
>
> *"What!" I exclaimed, more than half asleep—for truth to say I was snatching an afternoon's nap to make up for the loss of rest caused by my professional attendance on the lower deck. "Is the captain taken sick? Well, bring me the medicine chest. How was he taken—fever? Tell Thompson to give him the usual dose of ipecac to clear out his stomach, and I'll be with him before it operates."*

"You are mistaken, Doctor. The captain is not sick; he wants to see you on particular business."

"Oh, that's a different matter—ask the captain to come to my stateroom."

Away went the steward, and soon after the captain made his appearance. After the usual inquiries from me of "how do we get on?" and "how far have we run today?" and an apology from him for disturbing me, the worthy captain opened the business of the evening.

"I fear our first pilot's in a bad way—nothing will stay on his stomach," remarked Captain D——, taking a chair, and stretching out his legs in the easy way that captains of steamboats will. "Can't you do anything for him?" he asked.

"I fear not," was my answer. "I have tried everything in the medicine chest—there is no hope whatever of his being able to take his post at the wheel during this voyage; soon as we arrive at New Orleans he had better go to Stone's hospital—a month's care in that excellent institution will probably restore him."

"This is devilish unlucky," grumbled the captain. "I wanted to run nights after tonight, and the second pilot cannot stand double watches. What's to be done?"

I quietly told him I didn't know what was to be done, and supposed the business was over; but Captain D—— lingered, gave two or three "h-hems," spat violently through the stateroom door and over the guards, changed his position several times, and at length continued the conversation.

"Mr. Smith, I understand that during your life you've turned your hand to most everything."

"Well, I have—"

"I have heard of your merchandising, your preaching, your acting, and your doctoring—did you ever try your hand at PILOTING?"

"Piloting? Never—unless occasionally lending a hand at steering a flatboat may be considered piloting."

The captain looked somewhat disappointed when he received my answer, and rose to depart.

"What is it you want?" I asked.

Looking up in my face, he said, "I want a pilot; we can't run nights with one—Jim being down with the fever, and there being no *hope of getting him up, I thought if you—"*

"Am I to understand you that failing to get Jim on his legs, you wish me to stand watch as a pilot?"

"Why, if you would—Thompson says you can, if you will."

"But what would the insurance companies say in case of accident?" I inquired.

"That's the point," answered the captain. "I want you to take Jim's place at the wheel, and assume his character at the same time! If you will do this, we shall save at least 48 hours between this and Orleans."

I pondered a moment, and then asked when he wished me to assume my new duties.

"At 6 p.m., tomorrow," he answered.

"Enough said—I'LL DO IT! Consider me engaged, and be so good as to send Thompson to me."

The captain departed, rejoiced at my ready acquiescence, and that same evening a report went through the boat that Jim was much better, and would be able to resume his post at the wheel very shortly. Thompson came to me, and I arranged with him to give our patients a farewell dose all around, and pronounce them cured.

Next evening, I visited the pilot's stateroom, and just before 6 o'clock the tall figure of Jim was seen (or was supposed to be seen) enveloped in his greatcoat, a large hat pulled over his eyes, and a bandanna tied around his neck, coat collar and all, stalking up to the wheel house. A supposed sore throat, the effects of salivation, was a sufficient reason for the pilot's taciturnity during the remainder of the voyage.

In my character of doctor, I had had some difficult duties to perform; as an actor and manager, my path had not always been strewn with roses; as a preacher, I had perspired a few; and as a lawyer, some hard cases had come under my superintendence; but this PILOTING was by far the most difficult job I had ever undertaken! It was observable that while passing over bad places, Captain D——
was always in the pilothouse, which was somewhat strange, as Jim was known to be one of the most careful and competent pilots on the Mississippi; but this was accounted for in the fact that the captain was young at the business, and wanted to learn the river.

We arrived without accident at New Orleans—and I do assure you I felt much relieved, myself—though as a faithful physician, I felt it to be my duty to recommend that poor Jim, being much worse from his constant duties at the wheel, should be sent to Dr. Stone's hospital for a month.

I am happy to say that Jim recovered, and was ready to resume his post in the wheelhouse on the very next trip of the Vandalia. *He never met me without calling out, "Sol, WHO'S AT THE WHEEL?"*[19]

1 Twain, *Life on the Mississippi*, p. 32.
2 Salaries varied, of course, over the ninety years of packet steamboat operations. Most crew wages remained flat when compared to the cost of living of the day, with the notable exception of pilot salaries. From a high of $300 per month in the years immediately prior to the Civil War, pilot pay plummeted to $75 per month in the 1890s. See, for example, the crew account book of the steamer *Helena*, in the E. B. Trail Collection, 1858-1965, Joint Collection—Western Historical Manuscript Collection and State Historical Society of Missouri Manuscripts, Kansas City, volume 42; see also Hunter, *Steamboats on the Western Rivers*, pp. 465-66.
3 Hanson, pp. 22, 23.
4 Twain, *Life on the Mississippi*, pp. 40-41.
5 Thorpe, "Remembrances of the Mississippi," p. 37.
6 Nichols, p. 844.
7 Ralph, pp. 166, 175, 176.
8 Latrobe, p. 304.
9 Henry Martyn Blossom Journal, 1851-1853, Missouri Historical Society Collections, St. Louis.
10 Merrick, pp. 126-29.
11 George H. Devol, *Forty Years a Gambler on the Mississippi*, 2nd ed. (New York: George H. Devol, 1892), pp. 10-11.
12 Letter, Captain William B. Miller to "My Dear Children," December 6, 1875, in the Inland Rivers Library, Rare Books and Special Collections, Public Library of Cincinnati and Hamilton County.
13 Nichols, pp. 836-38; for details of the Pilots' Benevolent Association, see Twain, *Life on the Mississippi*, chapter 15, and Hunter, *Steamboats on the Western Rivers*, pp. 468-72.
14 Paine, pp. 1:116-20.
15 Twain, *Life on the Mississippi*, p. 382.
16 "Mark Twain Hero Dies," [St. Louis] *Globe-Democrat*, 2 August 1912, p. 8.
17 Merrick, pp. 106-09.
18 "Duties and Liabilities of Pilots under the Steamboat Law of August 30, 1852," in the E. B. Trail Collection, folder 88.
19 Solomon F. Smith, "Who's at the Wheel?" *Weekly Reveille* 2, no. 44, (11 May 1846): 852.

The Traveling Public

The novelty of maritime travel in the midst of a continent made for a marvelous contradiction, and those who traveled by packet steamboat nearly always found something of interest on the trip. They expressed a wide range of emotions in their travel accounts—from surprise and delight, to boredom, confusion, and even fear. It is not so farfetched from what today's travelers experience. The recollections presented here are many and varied, for this is a rich and bountiful topic.

Fares and Schedules

Although passenger revenue on the river amounted to only a small portion of total earnings, the traveling public primarily thought of steamboats as people movers. Owners and captains fostered this belief with elaborate cabin motifs and generous meal offerings. Steamboat travel was less expensive than other forms of transportation—given the generous amenities provided. Fares fluctuated with the season and stage of the river; but at one time in mid-century cabin passage from St. Louis to New Orleans fell to twelve dollars, one-way. Fares also varied according to locality. Below Memphis, the minimum fare on many boats was five dollars, even if the passenger were traveling only a few miles. And on Red River in Louisiana, steamboat clerks set their prices according to the wealth of the region: cotton planters paid more than tobacco farmers, and sugar plantation owners paid more than the cotton growers.[1] Usually, passengers were entitled to room and board on the steamer from the moment they paid their fare, even if departure were several days off; in some cases, captains allowed passengers to keep their berths while the vessel lay over at the port of destination. There were other considerations, too. One boat's master might grant free transit to a plantation owner as payback for a cotton shipment; another would reduce the price to repeat customers; and on *rare* instances some captains allowed stranded or impoverished travelers to ride without paying. All things were negotiable and predicated upon the reputation of the captain and the general flow of business.

> ∞
>
> *By the 1850s, reservations could even be made by telegraph from a distant city.*
>
> ∞

A traveler wishing to book passage could make arrangements either by applying directly at the boat, or through the office of the boat's agent. By the 1850s, reservations could even be made by telegraph from a distant city. Steamboat owners regularly advertised coming departures in the newspapers of all the major river port cities. The following is a typical listing in a St. Louis daily of 1842:

> *REGULAR PACKETS FOUR TIMES A WEEK from St. Louis to Hannibal, Marion City, Quincy, Warsaw, and Keokuk.*
>
> *The splendid, fast-running passenger steamers* ROSALIE *and* ANNAWAN *will run during the season to the above and all intermediate places, as Regular Packets, making four trips per week.*
>
> *The well-known, fast running passenger steamer* ROSALIE, *N. Camron, master, will leave St. Louis every Tuesday and Saturday, at 4 o'clock p.m. Returning will leave Keokuk at 8, Warsaw and Churchville at 9 o'clock p.m., every Sunday and Wednesday; Quincy at 8, Marion City at 9, and Hannibal at 10 o'clock a.m., every Monday and Thursday.*
>
> *The new and splendid, fast-running steamer* ANNAWAN, *W. S. Randolph, master, will leave St. Louis every Monday and Thursday at 4 o'clock p.m. Returning will leave Keokuk at 8, Warsaw and Churchville at 9 o'clock p.m.; Quincy at 8, Marion City at 9, and*

Hannibal at 10 o'clock a.m. every Wednesday and Saturday.

Passengers will please be on board in season, and in no case will the boat be detained beyond her hour of departure. For freight or passage apply on board or to:

STETTINIUS & JANUARY
VON PHUL & McGILL, or
FINNEY, LEE & CO.
St. Louis, Mo.[2]

These new, splendid, fast-running, well-known steamers making their regular calls at Hannibal would have been familiar to young Sam Clemens. He was, at that time, a seven-year-old lad, and probably just coming under the spell of the river. The same issue of the newspaper ran 28 similar ads, in addition to three "Steamboat for Sale" listings—asking prices not given.

With delays caused by late-arriving freight, difficult navigation, and mechanical breakdowns, published departure times were presumptions, at best. Packet-line boats tried to get out on schedule, but transient steamers more often would tarry until they had gotten enough freight and passengers to make a profitable run; this meant attracting riders and finding ways to retain them beyond the advertised departure time. From 1889—

It must be borne in mind that in the early days of steamboating there were few or no regular packets running in regular trades, and leaving on regular days, and queer tricks were often resorted to, to get a trip of freight and passengers when other boats were up for the same destination.

I have often and often known Ohio River boats [to] lie at St. Louis with steam up and all the appearances of starting in an hour—lay there five or six days, and all the time the captain and officers protesting they were going in as many hours. If some passengers were in sight, they would ring the big bell, fire up so as to throw out a column of black smoke from the chimneys, and work the wheels so as to give every indication of starting, when they had not half a cargo and had no idea of going. One noted captain, nicknamed "Ephraim Smooth," was in the habit of pulling out his watch and saying: "If you are over an hour away from the boat you will be left."

❦ 133 ❦

There was another dodge resorted to by some, and as they wanted to make all the show of starting by keeping up a fire without the expense and waste of fuel, or from keeping firemen, one captain full of inventive genius was caught by a passenger—who had been waiting three days in the delusive hope of starting—building a fire in the breeching of the chimneys, and when asked what was he doing that for, said: "They are a new kind of boiler, and have to be fired that way."[3]

When a great packet backed out from the wharf of a large city, the roustabouts gathered on the forecastle for a stirring chorus of song. Captains promoted the practice because it encouraged loyalty from the deck crew; passengers looked upon it as the sign of a well-ordered boat— "a pleasing and novel effect."[4] One passenger described the effect as his boat left St. Louis in 1870:

At the hour appointed the lines were cast loose, and we backed easily out from among the crowd of steamers which lay at the levee. There was a raw wind from the north, and the sun shone cold and cheerless through the gray and white clouds which covered the sky. At the bow of the boat were gathered the Negro deckhands, who were singing a parting song. The leader, a stalwart Negro, stood upon the capstan shouting the solo part of the song, the words of which I could not make out, although I drew very near; but they were answered by his companions in stentorian tones at first, and then, as the refrain of the song fell into the lower part of the register, the response was changed into a sad chant in mournful minor key. Very soon we were fairly out into the river, and with head downstream, with choking gasps from the steampipes, and bulging columns of smoke from the huge, lofty smokestacks, and swift revolutions of the large paddlewheels, we sped away toward our destination.[5]

Up from the Gulf

Thousands of immigrants, as well as Americans from the East Coast, caught their first glimpse of the Mississippi River from the deck of an oceangoing vessel as it entered the river from the Gulf of Mexico. It was a very different introduction than steaming onto the Mississippi from the broad mouth of the Ohio or arriving by rail opposite St. Louis. There were no wooded bluffs nor sweeping vistas to greet the traveler. The banks of the Mississippi took shape gradually—as though rising slowly out of the deep. Indeed, they were, for as the river mingled with the Gulf, the river's great load of sediment settled to the bottom and built itself upward and outward.

Most ships entering the passes of the Mississippi Delta were deep-draft sailing vessels. They had to be towed upriver. In fair weather, steam-powered towing boats, which bore a striking resemblance to sidewheel river packets, hovered about the entrance to the passes to await the arrivals of the great ships. These towing boats would steam alongside a sailing ship, lash the windjammer to its side—sometimes one on each side—and begin the slow, 100-mile trip up the channel to the magnificent confusion of New Orleans. Lulled by the monotony of a long ocean voyage, the passengers lined the railings to watch the great transformation, as in this account from 1857:

> *Presently there come to the traveler, through the fog, sounds of some living thing—that incessant "pough, pough" like a cough, or snort of the working giant; and when the fog lifts, you catch sight of the black monster bearing down toward you over the long, lazy swells, with its fiery eyes and its steam-breathing nostrils.*
>
> *It is the tug, with its deck flush and clean, only the engine and little cabin on its center, and no living person to be seen, except possibly on the top of its high ladder a single figure, till, as it closes with you the master of the machine is discovered with the magic wheel in his hand.*
>
> *A few words suffice, and the black monster seizes the white-winged ship. Her wings are closed, and she is borne away with irresistible power over the bars and through the slimy mud till she enters between long, low mud lines, which here border the "Father of Waters."*
>
> *The Delta of the Mississippi is a boundless waste of mud, water, and reedy thicket—the haunt of countless waterfowl, and the sunny retreat of hosts of alligators, whose notes of love are sometimes heard sounding like the bellowing of bulls of Bashan.*
>
> *After some fifty miles of tug between these low, marshy shores, trees begin to appear—dense thickets of cypress swamp; then the artificial mud-banks, called the levee, soon appear. These have been built*

with great labor on both sides of the river below and above New Orleans for many miles, and are intended to keep out the waters, which during the rise of the river would sweep away all crops and houses.

Then, some sixty miles from the mouth of the river, your eyes are gratified with a sight of the first sugar plantation, with its picturesque-looking mansion, and its Negro huts with black groups around them. From this point the traveler watches the shores to see the estates which succeed each other, until he reaches New Orleans; that is the longed-for end of his voyage, and he looks eagerly till he sees its forests of masts rising above the low banks, and hears the distant but deep roar of the city.

This sloping levee at New Orleans is a strange place to an unsophisticated man; it is from one or two hundred feet in width, and extends along the front of the city some four miles, following the curve of the river, which . . . gives to New Orleans its name of "the Crescent City." 'Tis a busy, driving, dreadful place, piled with bales and boxes, and hogsheads and casks, and cattle and bureaus, and bedsteads, and horsecarts, and pulpits, and all the other multitude of things which come pouring out of that wonderful cornucopia, the Valley of the Mississippi, of which New Orleans may be called the mouth.

Sailors are heaving, and hauling, and yo-hoing—mates are smoking, and puffing, and splashing about—and the river is all the while rushing swiftly down, ready to sweep everything along to the wide ocean.[6]

> *The Delta of the Mississippi is a boundless waste of mud, water, and reedy thicket—the haunt of countless waterfowl, and the sunny retreat of hosts of alligators, whose notes of love are sometimes heard sounding like the bellowing of bulls of Bashan.*

Melting Pots

One characteristic in common among every boatload of passengers, regardless of the river they traveled or the direction from which they came, was the commingling of nationality, occupation, and political persuasion. It was a wonder that steamboat passengers got along at all. Thefts, quarrels, fights, and even serious crimes of passion did occur on board, but most passengers felt secure and they tolerated each other rather well. Indeed, river travelers usually found fascination and pleasant diversion in the mix. The multiformity of life and culture on a steamboat is addressed in this essay from 1855:

The crowd of passengers ordinarily witnessed on our Mississippi steamers present more than is anywhere else observable in a small space, the cosmopolitanism of our extraordinary population. Upon their decks are to be seen immigrants from every nationality in Europe; in the cabin are strangely mingled every phase of social life—the aristocratic English lord is intruded upon by the ultra-socialist; the conservative bishop accepts a favor from the graceless gambler; the wealthy planter is heartily amused at the simplicities of a "Northern fanatic"; the farmer from about the arctic regions of Lake Superior exchanges ideas, and discovers consanguinity, with a heretofore unknown person from the everglades of Florida; the frank, open-handed men of the West are charmed with the business-thrift of a party from "Down East"; politicians of every stripe, and religionists of all creeds, for the time drop their wranglings in the admiration of lovely women, or find a neutral ground of sympathy in the attractions of a gorgeous sunset.

Upon an examination of the baggage you meet with strange incongruities—a large box of playing cards supports a very small package of Bibles; a bowie knife is tied to a life preserver; and a package of garden seeds rejoices in the same address as a neighboring keg of powder. There is an old black trunk, soiled with the mud of the Lower Nile, and a new carpetbag direct from Upper California; a collapsed valise of new shirts and antique sermons is jostled by another plethoric with bilious pills and cholera medicines; an elaborate dress, direct from Paris, is in contact with a trapper's Rocky Mountain costume; a gun case reposes upon a bandbox; and a well-preserved rifle is half concealed by the folds of an umbrella. The volume of a strange, eventful, and ever changing life is before you, on the pages of which are impressed phases of original character such as nowhere else exhibited, nowhere seen, but on the Mississippi.

The passengers being usually together from five to seven days, there is, from necessity, encouraged a desire to be pleased, and many of the happiest reminiscences of well-spent lives are connected with the enjoyments, novelties, and intellectual pleasures of such prolonged trips.

After the "first day out" genial minds naturally gather into sympathetic circles; conversation is relieved by continued change of scene; every "landing place" suggests a reminiscence of "early times," and varies, without interrupting, the flow of conversation. Groups of persons snugly dispose of themselves under the shady side of the "guards"; among which are often found ladies and gentlemen but recently from the worn out fields and ruined cities of Central Europe, and they find something particularly inspiring in the surrounding evidences of vitality as exhibited in the rich soil and hopeful "settlements." There are also present persons who have for many years been in some way connected with the river, who have learned its traditions, and love to repeat over the thousand reminiscences that are constantly revived by the moving panorama.[7]

Daily Routine

Steamboat travel was noisy. First, there was the incessant puffing of the engine that exhausted high-pressure steam directly into the atmosphere. It bothered some more than others. One passenger commented: "The steam goes out with a roar like the sound of a distant cannon, about every five seconds, and it is very oppressive."[8] Then, there was the noise of the cargo—not only the sound of loading it, which justly could be described as a late night irritant, but the noise of the cargo itself. "Last night the boat stopped to take in some hogs," wrote one Nathanial Hobart in 1837, "and you never heard such squealing as they did make."[9] In many cases upper decks were crowded with cages of cackling and gobbling domestic fowl while horses, mules, and cattle neighed, brayed, and lowed from pens on the main deck.

After a night of racket and disturbances, the novice steamboat passenger, thus deprived of a good rest, might expect to sleep late in the morning. Forlorn hope! On most boats built before 1835, the men slept in the large, open cabin with drawn curtains as their only means of privacy. As British tourist Charles J. Latrobe discovered in those early days, the curtains came open at breakfast, like it or not:

Staterooms are not always to be had by gentlemen, as they are commonly found to be attached to the ladies' cabin alone—but in case they are unoccupied they may be secured, and your position is so far more than ordinarily a favored one, as you have private access to them by the outward gallery. Otherwise it must be conceded that nothing is omitted that the known ingenuity of this people can contrive, to render the berths in the main cabin as tidy and ornamental in appearance by day, and as secluded and convenient by night as circumstances permit of. They are also arranged, that when you retire to rest, the thick curtains with their valance can slide forward upon brass rods, two or three feet from the berth itself, and this form a kind of draped dormitory for you and your companion.

About an hour before the time appointed for breakfast, after the broom has been heard performing its duty for some time, a noisy bell rung vociferously at the very porches of your ear, as the domestic marches from one end of the cabin to the other, gives notice that the hour of rising has arrived, and it is expected that every one will obey it and be attired in such time as to allow the berths to be arranged, and the whole cabin put in its day-dress, before the breakfast, which like all other meals is set out in the gentlemen's cabin, is laid upon the table. In vain you wish to indulge in a morning doze and thus to cut short the day; every moment your position becomes more untenable. Noises of all kinds proceed from without. You persevere—shut your eyes from the bright light which glares upon you through the little square window which illumines your berth, and your ears to all manner of sounds. Suddenly your curtains are drawn unceremoniously back, the rings rattle along the rods, and you see your place of concealment annihilated and become a part of the common apartment, while the glistening face and bright teeth of the black steward are revealed, with eyes dilated with well-acted surprise, as he says, "Beg pardon, Colonel! Thought him whar up; breakfast almost incessantly on de table." He retrogrades with a bow, half-closing the curtains; but you have no choice, rise you must. Happy he, whose foresight has secured to him all the enjoyment of the luxury of his own clean towels, as none but the disagreeable alternative of drying his person by the heat of the stove, can be the fate of him who has not done this. As to making use of the common articles, hung up for the accommodation of some thirty citizens in rotation, no one need blush at being termed fantastically delicate in avoiding that.

The table is spread with substantials, both in profusion and variety; and considerable impatience is generally observable to secure places, as it frequently happens that the number of cabin passengers is greater than can be seated with comfort at the table, however spacious. The steward, or his assistant, after many a considerate glance at his preparations, to see that all is right, goes to the ladies' cabin, and announces breakfast —an announcement which is generally followed by their appearance. They take their places at the upper end of the table, and then, and not till then, the bell gives notice that individuals of the rougher sex may seat themselves. There is little or no conversation, excepting of the monosyllabic and ejaculatory kind which is absolutely necessary. Many of the males will leave the table the moment they are satisfied—the ladies leave it as soon as they well can; and then come in the barkeepers, engineers, carpenter, pilot, and inferior officers of the boat: the table again groans with its load of plenty, and is again stripped and forsaken, to be a third time the scene of feasting for the black steward and colored servants of both sexes. During these latter scenes of the same act of the same play, I need hardly press you to quit the cabin for the seats on the boiler deck, or, still better, for the hurricane deck above.

> ❧
>
> *Suddenly your curtains are drawn unceremoniously back, the rings rattle along the rods, and you see your place of concealment annihilated and become a part of the common apartment . . .*
>
> ❧

The time occupied [at mid-day] by the supple-limbed black boys, Proteus and William, in drawing out the long table, laying the cloth, and other preliminary preparations, will not be far short of an hour; while a quarter of that suffices for the demolition of the various courses, whole meal, as already described, consisting of a shove to the table, a scramble, and a shove from the table. Things are cleared away, and the sliding table pushed together again; William and Proteus placing themselves at either end, twenty feet apart, and straining with might *main till the ends meet. You take a dozen turns across the floor—you read a little, write a little, yawn a little—when before you could have believed it possible, the steward's myrmidons, with looks of infinite importance, enter again, seize on the two ends of the table, strain them once more asunder, and the work of preparation recommences.* [10]

The Anchor Line ran one of the last great packet operations on the river. Their several boats, all named after river cities, were large, well-appointed, and dependable. Thomas J. Hand rode the Anchor Line's *City of Greenville* to New Orleans in December, 1882. Hand was a seventeen-year-old lad from Ossining, New York. He traveled alone across the South as an agent for his father's cattle breeding business, and he kept his parents well informed with letters written every other day. Hand came away favorably impressed with Western River steamers, though he considered the daily routine on them rather dull:

The men sit around one end of the saloon, the ladies the other, both near their respective stoves. Occasionally one of the passengers walks out on the deck, to gaze at the monotonous scenery, or watch the boatmen, as they heave the lead and cry, "quarter-less-four," or "mark twain," and then, having become thoroughly chilled, comes in again, toasts himself for a few minutes before the stove, and then settles down to snooze, or reread his thrice read paper. Breakfast is at seven, dinner at twelve, and supper at six. Half an hour before the [meals] the waiters set the tables, which are in the middle of the saloon. This operation is watched with intense interest by the passengers, as meal time is almost the only break in the day's monotony. At length a waiter appears bearing a gong. At sight of him every passenger starts for the tables; they have all been watching for his appearance for some time, but he goes through the form of beating the gong nevertheless, through the saloon and around the deck, finishing with a vicious bang twang, in a louder note than the rest. Everybody orders as many dishes as it is possible to manage, and delays as long as possible over the meal, and at length returns to the stove again. After supper a few play casino and euchre (gambling is done, if at all, in private) and finally everybody turns in early, more tired than by the hardest day's work. [11]

The generous meals and enforced idleness of a steamboat trip might have brought relaxation to some travelers, but not to everyone. Henry B. Miller rode a steamer in 1838 on a relatively short trip of 300 miles from Galena, Illinois, to St. Louis. For his tastes, he found it too much of a good thing:

> *This is one of the effects that traveling on steamboats will have on a person used to active exercise: the table is filled with the luxuries of life, and all things fitted up in an inviting manner; you sit down with a great variety before you; you are paying well for it and have every encouragement to eat (with the exception of a keen appetite sharpened by active exercise); breakfast over, you sit and lounge about or walk the deck if you see fit; about 11 o'clock comes a lunch; here again is eating for you—cakes, raisins, almonds, &c., &c.; dinner about 2; still very little exercise; dull and drowsy, you may retire to your berth and sleep an hour or two to drive away a heavy hour or more; supper comes, and after drinking a good portion of tea or coffee, you are ready to go to sleep quite tired with dullness and eating; thus time is too frequently spent on board the steamers.*[12]

A sort of stupor eventually set in with many travelers—a nineteenth century version of jet lag in which time slowed down and the emotions hit bottom. "Conversation became odious," reported Briton Thomas Hamilton, "and I passed my time in a sort of dreamy contemplation." On a long passage down to New Orleans, Hamilton admitted that he "could scarcely have smiled at the best joke in the world; and as for raising a laugh—it would have been quite as easy to quadrate the circle."[13] American John H. Gilman took a two-day river trip in 1846 and summed up his feelings about it in one terse comment: "I am heartily tired of steamboating."[14] Many travelers, unaffected by the lure of the river, would have agreed with him.

In many ways, travel by steamer on the Mississippi and Ohio Rivers differed little from a hotel stay except, of course, that the hotel in this case moved about. People of all backgrounds came and went, including certain petty individuals who seemed to delight in making a boorish nuisance of themselves. Pity the cabin crew who had to cater day after day to the ridiculous whims of difficult passengers. It was all part of dealing with the public, and it has not changed much over the years. A tongue-in-cheek satire from 1844 will serve to illustrate the point:

> *Two ladies in an adjoining stateroom . . . kept incessantly calling upon that indispensable Figaro, the steward.*
>
> *"Steward!" called one, in a smothered voice, as if of intense suffering. "Do come and open this window, or I shall die!"*
>
> *The window was accordingly opened; but directly the other lady exclaimed, "Steward! Do come and shut this window, or I shall die!"*
>
> *This, too, was obeyed, when the first order was repeated, followed by the other in the same terms—and this continued until things began to grow serious, and the poor steward commenced turning very red and perspiring with vexation.*
>
> *At this moment a gentleman, who had been a quiet observer of the scene, cried out in a loud voice, "Steward, why don't you wait upon the ladies there? Shut the window till one of them is dead, and then open it and finish the other!"*[15]

Amazing Graces

Europeans traveling in the United States always found fault with American social graces. This was especially true on steamboats, where the combination of close quarters and assorted rustic types led to a certain familiarity and ease to which Europeans were unaccustomed. An astounded French visitor of high upbringing, Madame Marie Fortenay de Grandfort, took pains to record some incidents of this order in her 1855 book, *The New World:*

> *There were about three hundred passengers on board. Some passed the day asleep in their staterooms; others conversing, that is, talking very loudly, in the cabin; the majority seated in a circle on the front guard of the boat, smoked in silence, or cut up pieces of wood assuming the while the most singular attitudes. It is a mania with Americans, when they talk or walk or are waiting for some one or some thing, to "whittle." Provided with a large or small knife, they lay hands on the first bit of stray wood that falls in their way, or the branch of a tree, or a cane, or an umbrella left in a corner. If they are deprived of these, they attack the furniture; they pitilessly cut into*

counters, window sills, doors, chairs, sofas, billiard tables, church pews; in fact, nothing is sacred against their knife blades. The railings of the guards on certain boats on the Mississippi have been transformed into gigantic saws by this Yankee process. I have often seen, on steamboats on the Ohio, gentlemen vigorously whittling away the arms of the chairs they were seated on, beneath the eyes of the captain himself.

But it is the attitudes of the Americans that merit special study. I have rarely seen one whose position, when he was seated, was not a miracle of equilibrium and imagination. Generally they place their feet on a mantle piece, or against a stovepipe, or a wall, or a post, but always so that the feet are more elevated than the head. On the steamboat I was traveling on, I one day heard the sounds of a piano. They came from the ladies' cabin. Some of the passengers walked thither; I followed their example. They took seats in the cabin, and with loud discordant voices, joined in the national air that an adorable young lady of thirty-two years was playing. Four of these gentlemen seated themselves around a slender pillar, in the middle of the cabin, supporting the ceiling. Their feet were gathered in a bunch around this pillar at so great a height that the only portions of their bodies resting in the chairs were their heads and their backs. A fifth, seated in front of the musician, majestically displayed his legs on the piano itself, appearing thus to make the lady an offer of his boots; a sixth had taken possession of a sofa, whilst several ladies, not finding seats, were standing, grouped around the player; a seventh had climbed upon his chair, and was seated on the back of it, tilted against the partition; and to conclude, an eighth, having sought in vain for a place for his feet, ended by putting them on the shoulders of the gentleman seated near the piano. That person received the compliment gracefully and smilingly. When the song was over, these amateurs applauded, by whistling and giving *utterance to loud cries. The one perched on the chair, carried away by enthusiasm, and forgetting that his position did not allow him much freedom of movement, applauded by clapping his hands. He lost his equilibrium, and falling on the corner of another chair, came near putting out an eye. Notwithstanding, ten minutes after, I saw him seated in a position more dangerous and incredible than before.*[16]

In 1893, writer Julian Ralph set off from New York bound for New Orleans in order to write an article about the Mardi Gras. He took the train to St. Louis and had intended to continue by rail to New Orleans. But then he heard that packet steamboats still plied the Lower Mississippi, and the thought of riding a relic of bygone times intrigued him. When he asked an acquaintance in St. Louis if many folks still rode the packets, he was told that not as many rode the best boat in one season as used to ride in a single trip. "The boats are not advertised," said the friend. "The world has forgotten that they are still running." Here, thought Ralph, was rich material for the readers back East. No more rail travel for him, he would go by steamboat and try to capture the essence of a bygone day. He did:

I packed up at the Southern Hotel, and was on board the City of Providence, *Captain George Carvell, master, an hour before five o'clock, the advertised sailing hour. The strange, the absolutely charming disregard for nineteenth century bustle was apparent in the answer to the very first question I asked.*

"Does she start sharp at five o'clock?"

"No, not sharp; a little dull, I expect."

The City of Providence *lay with her landing planks hoisted up ahead of her like the claws of a giant lobster. She was warped to a wharfboat that was heaped with barrels, boxes, and bags, and alive with Negroes. It was after six o'clock when the long-shore hands were drawn up in line on the wharfboat and our own crew of forty roustabouts came aboard. In a few moments the great island of joiner work and freight crawled away from the levee and out upon the yellow, rain-pelted river, with long drawn gasps, as if she were a monster that had been asleep and was slowly and regretfully waking up.*

After supper I was asked to go up into the pilothouse then in charge of Louis Moan and James Parker, both veterans on the river, both good storytellers, and as kindly and pleasant a pair as ever lightened a journey at a wheel or in a cabin. That night, when a dark pall hung all around the boat, with only here and there a yellow glimmer showing the presence of a house or government light ashore, these were spectral men at a shadowy wheel. In time it was possible to see that the house was half as big as a railroad car, that Captain Carvell was in a chair smoking a pipe, that the gray sheet far below was the river, and that there was an indefinable something near by on one side which the pilots had agreed to regard as the left-hand shore.

Back in the blaze of light in the cabin I saw that the women had left their tables, and were gathered around a stove at their end of the room, precisely as the men had done at theirs. The groups were 200 feet apart, and showed no more interest in one another than if they had been on separate boats. I observed that at the right hand of the circle of smoking men was the neatly kept bar in a sort of alcove bridged across by a counter. Matching it, on the other side of the boat, was the office of Mr. O. W. Moore, the clerk. To Mr. Moore I offered to pay my fare, but he said there was no hurry, he guessed my money would keep.

To the bartender I said that if he had made the effervescent draught which I drank before supper I desired to compliment him. "Thank you, sir," said he. "You are very kind."

How pleasant was the discovery that I made on my first visit to the South, that in that part of our Union no matter how humble a white man is he is instinctively polite!

I slept like a child all night, and mentioned the fact at the break-fast table, where the men all spoke to one another and the clerk addressed each of us by name as if we were in a boarding house. Everyone smiled when I said that the boat's noise did not disturb me.

"Why, we tied up to a tree all night," said the clerk, "and did not move a yard until an hour ago."

I had not been long enough in the atmosphere of Mississippi travel to avoid worrying about the loss of a whole night while we were tied up to the shore. There had been a fog, I was told, and to proceed would have been dangerous. Yet I was bound for New Orleans for

Mardi Gras, and had only time to make it, according to the boat's schedule. But I had not fathomed a tithe of the mysteries of this river travel.

"It's too bad we're so late," I said to Mr. Todd, the steward.

"We ain't late," said he.

"I thought we laid up overnight," I said.

"So we did," said he. "But that ain't goin' to make any difference; we don't run so close to time as all that."

"Don't get excited," said Captain Carvell. "You are going to have the best trip you ever made in your life."

"Come on up to the pilothouse," said Mr. Moan. "Bring your pipe and tobacco and your slippers, and leave 'em up there, so's to make yourself at home. You're going to live with us nigh on to a week, you know, and you ought to be friendly."

It was this tone, caught from each officer to whom I spoke, that I, all too slowly, imbibed the calm and restful spirit of the voyage. Nothing made any difference, or gave cause to borrow trouble—not even hitching up to the river bank, now and then, for a night or two. I alone was impatient—the only curse on the happy condition. In the middle of a lifetime of catching trains and riding watch in hand I found that I did not know how to behave or how to school myself for a natural, restful situation such as this. I felt I belonged in the world, and that this was not it. This was dreamland—an Occidental Arabia. True, we were moved by steam, and swung red farm wagons to the hurricane deck and blew whistles, all by steam; but it was steam hypnotized and put to sleep. Could I not hear it snore through the smokestacks whenever the engineer disturbed it?

As we swung away from Chester [Illinois], Mr. Moan pointed across the river and said: "That's Claraville over there. It's a tidy place. Been that way since I was a boy. It don't grow, but it holds its own."

I harbored the hope that I would appreciate that remark, and the

In the middle of a lifetime of catching trains and riding watch in hand I found that I did not know how to behave or how to school myself for a natural, restful situation such as this.

spirit which engendered it, in five days or so of life on the lazy boat. Even then I could see that it was something to "hold one's own." It was an effort and perhaps a strain. It is more than we men and women are able to do for any length of time.

We stopped at Cairo on the second morning out, and were pulling away from there while I ate my breakfast. I told Captain Carvell that I was sorry to have missed seeing that important town, but I found that, as before, my regrets were groundless. Nothing is missed and nothing makes any difference on that phenomenal line.

"You ain't missed Cairo," said the captain. "We are going up a mile to get some pork, and down half a mile to get some flour. We shall be here some hours yet."

I ate a leisurely breakfast, saw the town to my heart's content, and was back on the boat an hour before it got away for good. A railroad train whizzed along above the levee like a messenger from the world of worry and unrest, and I looked at it as I have often looked at a leopard caged in a menagerie. It could not get at me, I knew.

Down and down we went with the current, and no longer noticed the deep snoring of the engine, or thought of the rushing world to the north and east. The table fare remained remarkably good, the nights' rests were unbroken; never did I stop marveling that the boat was not crowded with the tired men of business, to whom it offered the most prefect relief and rest.

There was mild excitement and much blowing of whistles when we passed our sister boat, the City of Monroe—*the prize Anchor liner from Natchez.*

"Hark!" said the first mate in his society voice. "Stop talking. Listen to her wheels on the water. It's music. It's for all the world like walnuts dropping off a tree."

As the days went by it was apparent that the woods extended along both sides of the turbid river, with only here and there a clearing for a town or farm or house. The population does not cling to the shore; it is too often overflowed. At Pecan Point (pecan is pronounced "pecarn" along the river) we saw the first green grass on February 23rd, and the first great plantation. It was, as we have all read, a great clearing, a scattering of Negro cabins, and then the big mansion of the planter, surrounded by tidy white houses in numbers sufficient to form a village. Here a darky put a history of his life into a sentence. Being asked how he got along, he said: "Oh, fairly, fairly, suh. Some days dere's chicken all de day, but mo' days dey's only feathers."

To tell in detail what we saw and did during two more days; how we saw green willows and then dogwood and jasmine in bloom, or even how Captain Carvell got out his straw hat at Elmwood, Mississippi, would require a second article. . . . They are mere incidents in the laziest, most alluring and refreshing journey that one tired man ever enjoyed.[17]

Deck Passage

Most foreigners traveling by steamboat were neither writers, noblemen, nor tourists. They were immigrants who, together with impoverished Americans, rode on the main deck alongside the freight, livestock, and machinery. On ocean vessels they called it steerage class, on the river it was deck passage; in either instance it could be a rough experience, especially for a family with small children. Deck passage averaged about half the cost of cabin fare; it entitled the rider to basic transportation between two points, and little else. Deck passengers were not allowed access to the staterooms or the cabin; they had to provide their own bedding; they paid extra for meals or brought their own; and they were required to make space for the cargo. They huddled amid filth and noise, with no privacy and only minimal shelter from the elements. Epidemic disease, especially cholera, frequently decimated the deck passengers as a result of their unsanitary living conditions.[18] Some boats required deck passengers to assist in wooding and firing. The deck crews frequently abused them for getting in the way, stole from them, and even left them stranded at woodyards or freight landings. A boat that carried eighty cabin passengers might carry 300 deck passengers, and the deck passengers were several times more likely than their more fortunate brethren above to be killed in an explosion or sinking.

Captains seldom did anything to alleviate the hardships of deck passage. To the contrary, they frequently overloaded their boats with "deckers" to offset losses in cabin passage revenue. Immigrants, who made up the largest population of deck passengers, usually did not complain to authorities about their treatment even though the law favored them in many instances.

According to the federal statutes, a minimum of fifteen square feet of deck space was allotted to each deck passenger. The space had to be "clear of obstruction, and easy of access." Furthermore, the area was to be in a "suitably enclosed deck-room, which shall be properly warmed in cool weather, and properly vented at all times."[19] Such was the intention. A passenger aboard the *Helen McGregor,* in the cold December of 1832, described the deck-room of that boat as a "man-pen" with nothing more than tattered canvas curtains to keep the weather out. Berthing spaces consisted of plank "shelves."[20]

A Journal from Marietta to St. Louis

In 1833 a group of Swiss immigrants entered the United States in the hope of establishing a Swiss colony near St. Louis. They were more fortunate than most immigrants in that they possessed trades and skills that would serve them well in the new country—and they brought enough money to insure a successful journey. After arriving at New York, they traveled by canal boat and steamer via the Hudson River, Erie Canal, and Lake Erie to the state of Ohio. By coach and by keelboat they ventured southward to Marietta, where the Muskingum River flowed into the Ohio. Among the group was one Joseph Suppiger, who kept a diary of the trip. We join Suppiger as the colonists prepare to depart Marietta on the aptly named low-pressure boat, the *Emigrant:*

> *Friday, August 19 [1833]. The steamboat we were expecting did not come until 10:00 a.m. The fare for the 325 miles from here to Cincinnati is $8 per person cabin class; without meals on the deck $2.50. The deck passengers can prepare their own meals on a stove which is provided or buy them from the captain at 25¢ a meal. Every traveler has sixty pounds free, but this is not strictly adhered to. Excess weight costs 20¢ per hundred pounds.*
>
> *The fare for a large group is very advantageous here. For all of our baggage and eleven persons cabin class we had to pay only $25. By 11:00 A.M. all of our things were loaded, and the journey began. Now in the middle of the Ohio we saw that we had been much mistaken the day before concerning the size of the two rivers. The Ohio here is almost twice as wide as the Rhine below Zurzach, but flows very gently. The surface is smooth as a mirror. At high water it may*

be different. At a few places there is a slight fall, and there are frequently large islands. In many places the river is more than twenty to forty feet deep, while in others it is hardly four, but the channel used by the boats is seven to eight feet deep. If high water did not rip trees and stumps from the wooded banks, creating a hazard, travel on the river could be most pleasant. Boats have been wrecked here and there on the river, but in no instance with loss of life.

Saturday, August 20. Our steamboat makes good progress. Yesterday at 10:30 P.M. we already had reached Point Pleasant opposite Gallipolis [at the mouth of the Kanawha River]. I had expected the settlements on the Ohio to be better developed. With the exception of important communities there were small, recently established general stores. Nearly everywhere the shores and the low hills still are covered with virgin forest, with space enough for centuries to come for thousands of settlers.

> *Nearly everywhere the shores and the low hills still are covered with virgin forest, with space enough for centuries to come for thousands of settlers*

The construction of the steamboats here is entirely different from those on Lake Erie and the Atlantic coast, but it is perfectly adapted to the depth of the waters on which they operate. Here on the Upper Ohio, where at low water stages there are often places that have only a depth of five or six feet, the vessels that can keep running the longest are built for a depth of only four feet. And since the engines as well as the passenger salons must be kept above the water line, it requires two decks in order to have space for all. The hold, or what is below water line, is now generally used for freight. On the lower deck just above the water line is the boiler, toward the bow, and just behind it is the engine with cylinder, pistons, condenser, and pump. The working beam extends to the cranks of the paddlewheels, which are approximately in the center of the boat. In all of these vessels the flywheel is on the axle of the paddlewheels.

On both sides, next to the engine, the space is used for the galley, toilets, sailors' bunks, etc., and the stern for the deck passengers, with an iron stove. The upper deck has a place forward for the pilot as well as the office and sleeping quarters of the captain, and, inside, the cabins for the men and women. On many steamboats the captain is situated below, behind the engine, and the deck passengers occupy the upper deck. Our boat, the Emigrant, commanded by Captain Thomas Baylett, runs between Pittsburgh and Louisville and has sleeping accommodations for twenty males and eight females. The occupants of the men's cabin eat at one table.

Most of the steamboats are neatly painted and the interiors most beautifully decorated and carpeted. Each berth has its own small window that can be opened or closed according to the weather, and this is fitted with jalousies. The berths can be curtained off for privacy.

At 6:00 P.M. today we passed Maysville in the state of Kentucky. This place must have developed recently, for it already has a good deal of masonry along the river, partly to facilitate the landing of boats at every level and partly to prevent the washing away of the earthen banks. Our boat had a substantial load of freight for this place from the factories of Pittsburgh. We did not proceed again until midnight, and at 6:00 P.M. we arrived at Cincinnati.

Cincinnati could well become the second largest city in the United States after New York. It already has won the advantage of becoming the largest in the interior. Many steamboats are being built here, and there are numerous other industries. A good number of steamboats arrived today and many departed, all to different places. Each seeks advantage through commendations from its patrons.

Tuesday, August 23. At 5:00 A.M. we were in Louisville. As for steamboats to St. Louis, it was just as we had been told, for we had not been here long before a captain asked us if we would not like to travel with him. He told us then that his boat definitely would have to stop at Shippingport. On arriving there we found several steamboats larger than any we had seen before.

There was another steamboat scheduled to leave for St. Louis in addition to the Cumberland, about which the captain had told us earlier in the day in Louisville. The Cumberland was just being reconditioned, which would require at least three days. Since the other steamboat, the Talisman, was due to leave this very afternoon, we made arrangements for passage on it, and the competition unquestionably helped us to get a better rate.

Steamboat under construction at Cincinnati, 1848. She rides high in the water, for she has yet to receive her texas and pilothouse—nor does she carry any freight. The boilers can be seen mounted horizontally on the main deck, immediately aft of the chimneys. The commercial buildings that line the riverfront cater almost exclusively to the steamboat trade. (From the Collection of The Public Library of Cincinnati and Hamilton County.)

At Louisville we were still six hundred miles from St. Louis. For this distance the cabin fare is usually $12 per person plus 50 cents for freight charges. The captain of the Cumberland *had wanted to take us with all of our freight for $120. On the far superior* Talisman, *however, we had to pay only $100, with the captain standing the cost of carting our things over to Shippingport, two miles below Louisville. These two captains were so competitive the captain of the* Cumberland, *who spoke German, now offered to take us for $20 less.*

They formerly had operated a ship in a joint venture but had taken separate paths a few weeks before, hence their enmity. Especially in the spring the steamboats earn a tremendous amount of money. A company that procured a new ship this year for nine thousand dollars is said to have earned thirty-six thousand dollars in the past eight months. This is the absolute truth! However, it is said to be one of the largest and most beautiful of vessels. On its maiden voyage from New Orleans it had more than 300 deck passengers and 150 in cabins, not all at one time, but on its entire trip to Louisville.

A canal has been built from Louisville to Shippingport on which steamboats will be able to operate at all times, with no worry about water level. It has been blasted entirely through rock, the cause of the rapids here, and the work is still going on. The cost is said to run into many millions of dollars, and its success is being questioned because of the possibility that at low water level there still will not be enough at its beginning at Louisville. However, the canal is not yet finished at that very important point, and I cannot believe that such a gigantic and costly work would have been undertaken without the sponsors having considered all contingencies. It is laid out in a straight line, and at Shippingport four locks lead back down into the Ohio.

Wednesday, August 24. Although we brought our things aboard hurriedly at 5 P.M. yesterday and the boilers were already being fired, we are still here today. Apparently our captain was expecting more freight or passengers, for this afternoon quite a few more passengers came aboard.

We left at 3:00 P.M. As soon as one has arranged for passage on a ship, one is eligible for board and lodging on it. For some miles below the falls the current of the Ohio was somewhat brisker, but then it gradually resumed its gentle flow, moving along a rocky channel that must be considered potentially dangerous for vessels, for the depth was being measured constantly. Naked rock was visible in only one place near the falls.

Thursday, August 25. A clattering noise of the left paddlewheel gave us a cause for disturbance last night. It had torn something loose in the paddlewheel box which broke several paddles and crossbars. Today it was quickly repaired. It appears that such accidents are not rare, for a good supply of crossbars is kept in readiness. These are shaped to fit in the cast iron sockets of the paddlewheel frame and merely need to be screwed on.

Friday, August 26. Toward 5:00 P.M. we reached the Mississippi.

Before this the Ohio had spread out in some places like a large lake, but here at the confluence of these two great rivers the width was even more impressive. Quietly and gently they merged, much as if the arms of the Ohio—separated by islands—had united again. Our progress now changed in that we were traveling upstream and through far murkier water. Just as beautiful to my mind had been the mingling of waters at the junction of the Cumberland and Tennessee Rivers with the Ohio, where the clear waters of the tributaries delayed mingling with the murky waters of the main stream. For almost six miles the muddy water of the Ohio had been visible suspended in the clearer waters of the tributaries.

Sunday, August 28. Last night we strayed from the channel twice. On the Mississippi, as on other rivers, it is always necessary to know exactly where the channel is in order to be sure of deep water. It flows just as gently and smoothly as the Ohio and the Hudson. At one place this morning where our boat had to back up for some distance in order to find another channel, the river formed a lake-like basin more than two leagues wide.

At 3:00 P.M. we finally glimpsed the long-awaited St. Louis. I cannot describe the impression this place first made on me. We expected a small town something like Sursee, but it exceeded Lucerne in every respect. "Here," my heart spoke, "must I remain. Here it is good to live; let us build here."[21]

Joseph Suppiger's heartfelt desire came prematurely. After examining the country west and south of St. Louis, the group decided to look elsewhere. They had grown discouraged by the thick woods of the Ozark foothills (it would have to be cleared in order to farm), and they disliked the institution of slavery in Missouri. They eventually established their colony in Illinois.

Steamboat Melodrama

The following story explains itself well enough without a lengthy introduction. The author, Mrs. Eliza Steele, published it as part of her book of travel in 1841. While there is a good deal of steamboating in this episode, it is also a fine example of nineteenth century melodrama:

[July 16, 1840.] A stateroom was observed to be constantly closed, and a young man about twenty, who occasionally came from it, squeezed himself in, as if afraid his companion would be seen from without. The curiosity of the young ladies was soon excited, and by means of the chambermaid they ascertained it was the young man's wife, a young girl, apparently about fourteen, who was thus carefully secluded. A runaway match was immediately whispered about; the young people became quite in a fever to obtain a glimpse of the fair heroine. It was a long time ere their wish was gratified, as she never left her room, taking even her meals there.

Our mornings on board are generally very social, the ladies sitting with the gentlemen of their party upon the guards, or gathering in groups with their work, while the male passengers are smoking, talking politics, or gambling. The Negro banjo, and merry laugh or joke of some son of Erin, echoes up from the lower deck; but in the afternoon the siesta is the fashion, and every one turns in his berth to take a nap. I did not follow this custom, as I was unwilling to lose any of the scenery, so that I usually stole out of my stateroom, like a mouse from its hole, and after a long look up and down the river, stole in again, the heat being too great to allow of a long stay.

Yesterday afternoon, oppressed with thirst and with heat, for the thermometer on board stood at ninety-six, I went into the ladies' cabin in search of water, a jar of which filled with lumps of ice, was placed upon a marble table in one corner of the cabin. The ladies were all in their berths except two, who were using every "means and appliance," to keep themselves cool. They were each in a rocking chair kept in motion, their feet upon an ottoman, [which] made a table for their books, while a large feather fan in one hand, and a lump of ice in another, were tolerable arms against the fire king.

As thirsty as I was, I hesitated to drink the thick muddy water, for while standing in our tumblers, a sediment is precipitated of half an inch. Oh how I longed for a draught of cool spring water, or a lump of Rockland lake ice! While drinking, one of the ladies advanced for the same purpose.

"Dear me! What insipid water!" she said. "It has been standing too long. I like it right thick."

A water cooler in the main cabin. Most boats were equipped with an ice locker to cool the drinking water of the cabin passengers—an absolute must on the lower rivers in summer. Note that the cups are chained to the cooler. (From *Harper's New Monthly Magazine.*)

I looked at her in surprise. *"Do you prefer it muddy to clear?"* I asked.

"Certainly I do," she replied. *"I like the sweet clayey taste, and when it settles it is insipid. Here Juno!"* calling to the black chambermaid who was busy ironing, *"Get me some water fresh out of the river, with the true Mississippi relish."*

Everyone's back is indeed fitted to his burden. This person had lived upon the banks of the Mississippi, had drank its waters all her days, and now it required to be muddy ere it was palatable. The chambermaid descended to the lower deck, where a gallant black beau drew a bucket from the river, and after satisfying the lady, she resumed her ironing.

Against this practice of ironing in the ladies' cabin I must uplift my voice. I suffered from this annoyance upon the Illinois, Mississippi, and Ohio. Constantly there was a woman washing upon the lower deck, where the water thrown from the wheel falls upon the deck in a pretty cascade, and another is ironing above. All the ironing of the boat, and crew, and often of the passengers, is done in the ladies' small sitting room, the steam and perfume of the wet clothes, charcoal furnace, and of the ironer is extremely disagreeable. In one instance I knew this to be the case all night, the girls taking it by turns; and I never traveled one day without this addition to the heat and other discomforts of a steamboat. In such long voyages it may be necessary to wash for the captain and crew, but surely bed and table linen enough might be provided to reach Cincinnati, where they stop long enough to have them washed. If not, why may there not be a room in some other part of the deck? The captain in some instances reaps the profits, as the chambermaids are his by hire or purchase, and if they charge all as they did us, one dollar and fifty cents a dozen, the profit must be considerable. It is sometimes, as in our case, a great convenience to travelers, but another place should be provided.

But to go on with my afternoon adventures. I left the cabin and walked out upon the shady side of the guards. All was still except the booming steampipe; every one was asleep or reading. I leaned over the railing and found the banjo player and his audience all in slumbering attitudes, or swinging in their hammocks, and everything denoted silence and repose. Suddenly a terrific and astounding bang, clang, and clatter, as if the boat had been cracked to atoms; the wheelhouse was broken in pieces, the boards flew over me, and a torrent of water flowing from it nearly washed me from the deck. In a moment every one tumbled out and rushed upon the deck exclaiming, "What's the matter?"; "Are we snagged?"; "Had the boiler burst?"; "Is it a sawyer?"

The old Kentucky lady who had stepped out first, took her pipe from her mouth and said quietly, "It's only a log."

"Oh, only a log"; "Nothing but a log," echoed from every mouth, and returning to their cabins they all stepped into their berths again.

I looked around me in amazement. "Only a log!" said I to myself. And what is a log? The steamboat is broken and stops, all is confusion, and crash, and I am told it is nothing but a log. "Madam," said I, turning to the Kentucky woman, "will you have the goodness to tell me what a log is?"

"There they are," she said, pointing with her pipe to the river. Floating along like so many alligators, were long branchless trunks, which had been wafted along thousands of miles from the Rocky Mountains perhaps.

"But, pardon me, madam, how are these logs able to create such a disturbance?"

"You seem a stranger, child," she replied. "As these are floating along, and we are riding among them, what more natural than that they should get in the water wheel, break it, and stop the boat. But see, the carpenters are already at work, and I dare say they will have it repaired in the course of two or three hours." So saying, she knocked the ashes out of her pipe, took off her cap, and passed into her stateroom, to sleep away the hours we were doomed to pass under a July southern sun inactive.

The most remarkable event connected with this accident was the discovery of the fair unknown of the closed stateroom. When the noise was first heard, the young man rushed out bearing a plump rosy girl in his arms who, as soon as he put her down, began to tell the beads of a long rosary which hung from her neck. One glance sufficed to tell him the nature of the accident, and he left her to walk towards the wheelhouse just as the Kentucky lady disappeared. Seeing the poor thing's agitation, I turned towards her and endeavored to soothe her.

"I thank the Virgin Mary it is no worse," she said kissing her cross, "but something dreadful will come to punish my wickedness. Oh, how could I leave my dear mother abbess and the sisters!" Stopping suddenly she gazed around her in affright, for she had unconsciously said more than she intended. "Oh dear, what am I saying!" she exclaimed. "Where is Edward? Why did he leave me?"

I soon succeeded in soothing her, and when I related my conversation with the old woman, she laughed merrily at my ignorance. Her young husband returned, and was so delighted to see her cheerful, that he immediately drew chairs, we all sat down and were soon as social as old friends. I was much amused with the surprise of my companion who had come in search of me, when he saw me upon such familiar terms with this mysterious couple.

At sundown we stopped to take in wood and to procure milk. As it was rather damp I did not land, but was much amused with the antics of men and boys who, delighted to have space, frolicked and jumped about the woods. The southerners in their thin pink and purple or blue-striped coats, added to the gaiety of the scene. Our steward with his tin kettle entered a small cottage, or rather log cabin, near, and procured a supply of fresh milk, which we saw a young country lass draw from their cow she had just driven home.

While our husbands strolled together, my little Catholic confided to me her history, after the fashion of traveling heroines you know. She was the daughter of a wealthy planter in Kentucky who, although of the Presbyterian faith, had sent his child to a Catholic nunnery to be educated. She had, as is very common in such cases, become a convert to the Catholic faith, and when her parents came to carry her home, declared it her intention to take the veil and never leave her convent. Her parents' entreaties and despair were of no use; stay she would, and did. A convent, however, was not to be her destiny, for she fell in love with a young gentleman, brother of a friend of hers at the same convent, who often came there to see his sister. The attachment being mutual, they had, with the assistance of the sister, contrived to elope. They were now on their way to New York, and she was so fearful of being recognized and brought back that she would not at first leave her stateroom.

"Were you not sorry to leave your mother?" I asked her.

"Oh dear yes, she and the sisters were always so kind to me."

"I mean your mother and your father, not the mother abbess."

"Alas! My parents are such sad heretics that I ought not to love them. I shall never see them in the next world, and it is better to be separated here."

The heat drove me into the ladies' cabin, which being empty, I sat down to put down a few notes. I had scarcely seated myself, when the young Catholic runaway rushed in, and throwing herself beside me, hid her head in my lap exclaiming, "Oh, they are here, my mother, my father! They will separate me from Edward forever!"

I looked towards the door with much anxiety, for I had heard the southern planters were a gouging, raw head and bloody bones sort of people, who whipped a slave to death once a week, and I feared for the fate of the poor young wife. My information, however, had been taken from foreign tourists, and I found this idea, like so many others I had imbibed from them, was far from truth. Imagine my surprise, when a pleasant, good-humored looking man entered the room and, seating himself in a chair, gave way to a hearty fit of laughter. His wife, a tall, slender, lady-like looking personage, walked directly up to her daughter, and folded her in her arms, while gentle tears flowed over her cheeks. I looked at the father in perplexity, wondering at this extraordinary merriment, and at Edward, who stood beside him, having, I thought, a most unbecoming smirk upon his countenance. The lady looked up to her husband reproachfully, but said nothing.

> ... I had heard the southern planters were a gouging, raw head and bloody bones sort of people, who whipped a slave to death once a week ...

"My dear madam," he said at last to me, "I understand you have taken a kind interest in my little girl's concerns, and I owe it to you to explain the circumstances of the case. Anxious to give my daughter the best of education, I sent her to a convent not far from my estate, where there were some very accomplished ladies from Europe, who could teach her all I wished her to know. But when I went to take her home, my lady fancied herself a Catholic, and renounced her home and friends forever. I returned home in despair, and while revolving my future proceedings in this disagreeable affair, Edward, the son of a dear friend, who several years since had removed to New York, came to make us a visit. In telling him my difficulties, I added how glad I should have been, had this not occurred, to give her and my plantation to him. 'I will scale the convent and carry her off,' he said in a jest. The idea struck me as a good one; I pressed it upon him, and you see here they are, and have my hearty blessing."

The bride, as her father spoke, had gradually dried her tears, and raised her head a little. When she began to understand the denouement, she first blushed deeply with mortification, then pouted, and at last burst suddenly into a merry laugh, and ran like a fawn into her father's outspread arms, exclaiming, "Oh, you naughty papa! You good for nothing papa!" The party soon after departed, and I received kind expressions and adieus from all, and a few tears from the bride.[22]

Solomon Smith, Midwife

No one could outdo Solomon Smith when it came to offbeat adventures on the river. In an earlier tale, Sol Smith told of administering medicine to the sick passengers and crew of a steamboat, and subsequently filling in for the pilot. Now we will discover, through the published letter of a chum, exactly how he came to be an itinerant physician. His swift education in medicine took place aboard a steamboat, naturally. The unidentified writer of this letter, a soldier apparently from Jefferson Barracks, Missouri, was heading south as the United States prepared for war with Mexico:

Steamer Missouri, *Sept. 3, 1845*

Dear Drummers:

Being now fast speeding on my journey to join my comrades in arms, at the theater of "Rumors of War," and having, just now, nothing else to do, the idea occurs to me of scribbling a word, to unfold to you the further awakened genius of one of your old friends.

We have on board two bank agents; one trader in Negroes; one bishop; one lawyer; one Frenchman, wife, dogs, and all—no children; three blacklegs,* busy at their profession; eleven ladies, three of whom are beautiful and unmarried—which you will wonder that I, a young United States officer, did not mention first; seven aristocratic "gen'lmen ob color" of the South; 129 head of horned animals, besides ducks, pigs, sheep, guinea hens, geese, chickens, turkeys, etc., etc.; all which are truly amusing to one just let out, as his mother knows.

The French gentleman is, today, in a world of trouble because, in all this crowd, he cannot find a doctor. He says his "wife is vare seek," he must have somebody "do some ting to his wife—she seek, by gar! She will get seeker vare soon; some lady, some gentleman—must go help my wife!"

"Halloo! Halloo there, captain! Stop the boat! Captain! I want to get aboard!" shouts a genius from one of the darkest, deepest bends in the turbid Mississippi, just below the earthquake city—New Madrid. He is a lank fellow, full seven feet high, and looks as if he

---

* Professional gamblers, especially those known to cheat or swindle their opponents.

Solomon Smith, 1801-1869, was best known as a comic actor and showman. Ever restless and plagued by debt, he often turned to itinerant careers—with results not far removed from the stage roles he played. (From *Theatrical Management in the West and South.*)

had waded through the swamp from all the West.

"Where do you want to go?" roars the captain.

"To New Orleans!" he replies, and draws himself up to his full height on the verge of the river bank, where the descent to the water's edge seems almost perpendicular, and about fifty feet. "Will you take in a stranger?"

"Certainly," replies the captain. "We're charged with that anyhow. Down with the wheel, hard a-starboard! Stop that larboard engine! Stop both engines! Back her," cried the captain, "on the larboard wheel!"

Round swings the huge mass into the bend, and the noble Missouri chafes and snorts like a war horse under effect of these orders and rides majestically up to the shore.

"Launch out a plank!"

"Aye, aye, sir!"

"High up on the bank there!"

"Aye, aye!" And up goes the plank, about halfway to the feet of the stranger.

"Now get aboard—jump down!"

"I can't jump that, Captain!"

"Well, slide then, or you won't get aboard!"

And sure enough the backwoodsman, as we took him to be, places his saddlebags half over the verge of the precipice, and seats himself—like the urchins between school hours on their sleds in winter—and down he comes with a rush!

"Who, and what, is this?" is in the mouth of each and all as the passengers gather on the boiler deck to see what is going on.

"I guess it's a half-breed," says a Yankee who had never seen an Indian, and was traveling to gratify his verdant curiosity.

"It's a land speculator," says another.

But the clerk knew him. Now, for fun, says he, "It's a doctor. Don't you see his saddlebags?"

This was enough! The Frenchman was the first to greet him.

"How do you do, sir," replies Saddlebags, as some called him.

"Me be vare much glad you come, sair—me want you—dat is, my wife want you bad—you practice your pro-fessione—eh?"

"Oh, yes—anything to help an individual," says the stranger. "But, pray, let me get to a room and put on t'other shirt—'twas clean two weeks ago—but since I have walked across from above Cape Girardeau, where that damned boat sunk and left us to wait for another to sink on, or to wade our path through by land—I am not certain whether 'tis much lighter in color than the one I have on— and that is not much for white as you can see."

"Well," says the Frenchman, "please be vare soon—I wait."

The stranger goes to a room thinking, "Well, somebody knows I am a lawyer, and I have picked up a case already." Not long after he appears and the Frenchman is in ecstasies.

"Now, sair, for my wife, sair—I much make rejoice dat you come in time, sair! She vare seek."

"Sick, ah! Oh, this is a different case, sir, from those in which I practice—I am not a doctor!"

"Ah, mon dieu—no vat you call—back out, sair—I know you for one doctaire—I see your saddlebags with the med'cines, sair, what you call 'em—you must see my wife, sair, or fight me, sair!"

"Oh! Well I may as well go and look at her then—it is easier, anyhow, than to fight."

"Thank you, sair, thank you—I know you understands about de lady and de childs, eh?"

"Why, yes, I ought to know something of 'em; seven call me father!"

"C'est heureux! *Well, sair, walk in."* And in went Solomon Smith to see the Frenchman's sick wife. Monsieur went in too, and locked the door and took out the key!

The clerk, Thompson, my old crony, takes me aside and says he: "We'll I've got Sol Smith into a scrape at last unless he can play the midwife as well as everything else!"

Sol must tell the rest of the story; that evening, however, a neatly painted shingle was put up over the door of his stateroom, as indicating the office of THE REVEREND SOLOMON SMITH, ATTORNEY AT LAW, M.D. AND MIDWIFE![23]

Games of Chance

The "Father of Waters" bears upon his bosom a crowd of men (often gentlemenly, jovial fellows) who have erected gambling into a profession; they are a "breed" peculiar to the river, and are wanted; they dress well, smoke well, drink well, and with a dash of swagger and a spice of blackleg, they flatter young, tender pigeons, and then pluck them. Among the scrambling speculators who congregate at New Orleans, they have their place, and except for an occasional fight and slaughter, are not thought so ill of.[24]

The preceding quote, from a magazine article of 1857, aptly sums up the life and times of professional riverboat gamblers. Games of chance were strictly forbidden on a few boats, and the captains promptly tossed off anyone caught violating the rule. But on most steamboats gamblers were tolerated—even encouraged. It gave the passengers something to do. The gamblers themselves were a tough lot who survived by chicanery and quick wits. Their greatest danger came from the suckers they fleeced, suckers that carried guns and demanded the return of their money. George Devol was the best known of the professional riverboat gamblers. He not only survived forty years of his dangerous occupation, but he also wrote a book about it—with no apologies to the "pigeons." We've met Devol before, as a belliger-

George Devol, professional gambler. Devol rode the steamboats and railroads of mid-America, always willing to separate a fool from his money. (From *Forty Years a Gambler on the Mississippi*.)

ent cabin boy learning the rudiments of his dangerous trade. Two stories from Devol's book suffice now to illustrate the life and times of blacklegs and the curious turn of events that often befell them:

> We were once coming down on the steamer Belle Key, of Louisville, and my partner was doing the playing that day. We had won some big money, and were about to quit, when up stepped a very tall man, who looked pale and sickly. He watched the game for some time, and then pulled out a $1,000 note and laid it on the card he wanted, and of course he lost. He did not say a word, but started back to his room. I thought he acted strangely, and I concluded to keep an eye upon him. Pretty soon out he came with an overcoat on his arm, and he walked up as near the table as he could get, and commenced to push some of the crowd away so as to get closer. Finally he got at my partner's back, with me close at his heels, when he commenced to pull from under his coat a large Colt's pistol. As he leveled it to shoot [my partner] in the back of the head, I knocked him stiff, and the gun dropped on the floor. It was cocked, but it did not go off.
>
> They carried him to his room, put cold water on him, and finally brought him to. He sent for me, and when I went back he reached out

his hand, and said: "Friend, you did me a kindly act, for I had made up my mind to kill that man. I am glad it happened so, for it was all the money I had, and it was raised by my friends who, knowing that I never would reach home again, were sending me to Florida, as all the doctors had given me up; and I thought I would kill him, as I do not expect to get off this boat alive. I have got consumption* in its last stages."

So I pulled out $1,000, counted it out to him, and he cried like a child. His pistol I gave to the mate, as I thought he had no need of such a weapon.

⌘

Another time I was coming up on the steamer Fairchild with Captain Fawcett, of Louisville. When we landed at Napoleon there were about twenty-five of the "Arkansas Killers" came on board, and I just opened out and cleaned the party of money, watches, and all their valuables. Things went along smoothly for a while, until they commenced to drink pretty freely. Finally, one of them said: "Jake, Sam, Ike, get Bill, and let us kill that damned gambler who got our money."

"Alright," said the party, and they broke for their rooms to get their guns. I stepped out of the side door, and got under the pilothouse, as it was my favorite hiding place. I could hear every word downstairs, and could whisper to the pilot.

Well, they hunted the boat from stem to stern—even took lights and went down into the hold—and finally gave up the chase, as one man said I had jumped overboard. I slipped the pilot $100 in gold, as I had both pockets filled with gold and watches, and told him at the first point that stood out a good ways to run her as close as he could and I would jump. He whispered, "Get ready," and I slipped out and walked back, and stood on the top of the wheelhouse until she came, as I thought, near enough to make the jump, and away I went . . . and struck into the soft mud clear up to my waist. Some parties who were standing on the stern of the boat saw me and gave the alarm, when the "killers" all rushed back and commenced firing at me, and the bullets went splattering all around me. The pilot threw

* Tuberculosis.

her into the bend as quick as he could, and then let on she took a
sheer on him, and nearly went to the other side.

The shooting brought the Negroes from the fields to the bank of the
river. I hallooed to them to get a long pole and pull me out, for I was
stuck in the mud. They did so, and I got up on the bank and waited
for another boat.[25]

In an 1868 autobiography, Sol Smith relates his own encounter with ship-board gamblers. The episode took place on the steamer *Dr. Franklin*, bound up from New Orleans in December, 1844. If anyone else had told the story, it would have been termed fiction; but in the case of Smith, the consummate actor who never could turn down a role, it may be considered factual:

I don't know how or why it is, but by strangers I am almost always
taken for a preacher. It was so on this voyage. There were two
Methodist circuit riders on board, and it happened that we got
acquainted and were a good deal together, from which circumstances
I was supposed to be one of them, which supposition was the means
of bringing me into an acquaintance with the female passengers,
who for the most part were very pious, religiously-inclined souls. We
had preaching every day, and sometimes at night; and I must say, in
justice to [the preachers], that their sermons were highly edifying
and instructive.

In the meantime a portion of the passengers "at the other end of
the hall" continued to play sundry games with cards, notwithstand-
ing the remonstrances of the worthy followers of Wesley, who fre-
quently requested the captain to interfere and break up such unholy
doings. The captain had but one answer—it was something like this:
"Gentlemen, amuse yourselves as you like; preach and pray to your
hearts' content—none shall interfere with your pious purposes; some
like that sort of thing—I have no objection to it. These men prefer to
amuse themselves with cards. Let them. They pay their passages as
well as you, gentlemen, and have as much right to their amusements
as you have to yours, and they shall not be disturbed. Preach, play
cards, dance cotillions, do what you like; I am agreeable. Only under-
stand that all games (preaching among the rest) must cease at 10
o'clock." So we preachers got very little comfort from [the captain].

Up, up, up, up we went. Christmas day arrived. All the other *preachers had holden forth on diverse occasions, and it being ascertained that it was my intention to leave the boat on her arrival at Cairo, a formal request was preferred that I should* preach the Christmas sermon! *The women (God bless them all!) were very urgent in their applications to me. "Oh do, Brother Smith; we want to hear you preach. All the others have contributed their share to our spiritual comfort—you* must *oblige us—indeed you* must."

I endeavored to excuse myself the best way I could, alleging the necessity of my leaving the boat in less than an hour—my baggage was not ready—I had a terrible cold, and many other good and substantial reasons were given, but all in vain; preach I must. "Well," thinks I, "if I must, I must."

> *"The poor miserable sinners have filled the measure of their iniquity by opening a faro bank!"*

At this crisis, casting my eye down toward the social hall, and seeing an unusual crowd assembled around a table, I asked one of the brethren what might be going on down there. The fattest of the preaching gentlemen replied, "The poor miserable sinners have filled the measure of their iniquity by opening a faro bank!"

"Horrible!" *exclaimed I, holding up my hands, and "Horrible," echoed the women and missionaries in full chorus.*

"Cannot such doings be put a stop to?" asked an elderly female, addressing the pious travelers.

"I fear not," groaned my Methodist colleague (the fat one). "We have been trying to convince the captain that some dreadful accident will inevitably befall the boat if such proceedings are permitted, and what do you think he answered?"

"What?" we all asked, of course.

"Why, he just said that, inasmuch as he permitted us to preach and pray, he should let other passengers dance and play, if they chose to do so; and that, if I didn't like the proceedings complained of, I might *leave the boat!"*

This announcement of the captain's stubbornness and impiety was met with a general groan of pity and sorrow, and we resumed the con-

versation respecting the unhallowed faro bank. "It is much to be regretted," remarked the gentlewoman who had spoken before, "that something *can't be done. Brother Smith*," she continued, appealing directly to me, and laying her forefinger impressively upon my arm, "cannot you break up that bank?"

"Dear madam," I answered, "you know not the difficulty of the task you impose upon me; faro banks are not so easily broken up as you may imagine; however, as you all appear so anxious about it, if you'll excuse me from preaching the sermon, I'll see what can be done."

"Ah! That's a dear soul!"

"I knew he would try!"

"He'll be sure to succeed!"

"Our prayers shall not be wanting!"

Such were the exclamations that greeted me as I moved off toward the faro bank. Elbowing my way into the crowd, I got near the table in front of the dealer, and was for a time completely concealed from the view of my pious friends near the door of the ladies' cabin. I found the bank was a small affair. The betters were risking trifling sums, ranging from six to twenty-five cents.

"Mr. Dealer," I remarked, "I have come to break up this bank."

"The deuce you have!" replied the banker. "Let's see you do it."

"What amount have you in the bank?" I inquired.

"Eleven dollars," was his answer.

"What is your limit?" asked I.

"A dollar," he replied.

"Very well," said I, placing a ragged Indiana dollar behind the queen—"turn on."

He turned, and the king won for me. I took the two dollars up and let him make another turn, when I replaced the bet, and the queen came up in my favor. I had now four dollars, which I placed in the square, taking in the 5, 6, 7, and 8, and it won again! Here were seven dollars of the banker's money. I pocketed three of them, and bet four dollars behind the queen again; the jack won, and the bank was broken! The crowd dispersed in all directions, laughing at the breaking up of the petty bank, and I made my way toward the ladies' cabin, where my new friends were anxiously awaiting the result of my bold attempt.

"Well? Well? Well?" they all exclaimed. "What success? Have you done it? Do let us hear about it!"

I wiped the perspiration from my brow, and putting on a very serious face, I said solemnly, "I HAVE BROKEN THAT BANK!"

"You have?" they all exclaimed.

"Yes, I'll be damned if he hasn't!" muttered the disappointed gamester, the keeper of the late bank, who was just going into his stateroom. In the midst of the congratulations which were showered upon me, I received a summons from the captain to come forward with my baggage—we were at Cairo.[26]

Showboats

As evidenced by the improbable adventures of Sol Smith, folks along the river were starved for entertainment. Out of that glaring need came the era of showboats. River showboats were nothing more than enclosed, ornate barges or rafts, with plenty of seating. The *Floating Palace*, built in 1852 to accommodate a traveling circus, could seat a thousand spectators. *Floating Palace* also began a notable river tradition about 1855 when the owners installed a steam calliope on board. The *Palace* toured up and down the river for seven years. Another showboat, *Romance Wonderland*, plied the Western Rivers for thirty years.[27] Showboats were towed—or sometimes drifted—from town to village, from one end of the river to the other. They were purely an American institution, and the showmen entrepreneurs who operated them made quite a reputation in the Valley. We are about to meet one of them and learn of his business in this encounter written by the wandering German, Ernst von Hesse-Wartegg:

In Memphis I bought newspapers to help pass the time on this long, boring steamboat journey downriver. You can get little reading there but the daily press. In it, as a rule, Americans find everything that could interest them, every subject from the Orient to theater to art. In the four-page, five-foot-square Memphis Avalanche, *theater and art are relegated to a microscopically small space of notices about opera troupes performing locally. In that category this notice interested me most: "Dan Rice's opera boat sails slowly south. Like all Rice's enterprises, this boat is 'the world's greatest.'"*

I did not understand it. Had American opera impresarios' enterprise gone astray on the Mississippi? Thespians on tour in land conveyances, yes, but Thespians afloat, Thespian steamboats? Who had ever heard of such a thing?

"It's nothing new, sir—not at all unusual for us," said a fellow passenger. "We are a wonderful race, sir."

"But why opera on a boat? Why doesn't the troupe go from place to place by train, like all the rest?"

"Well, sir," my Yankee friend answered, "I'll explain it to you. People in this country must always have something cute and different. Dan Rice is a smart fellow. He always has what's wanted and makes money hand over fist. On this river, these thousand miles to New Orleans, you'll see hundreds of plantations, settlements, and towns; but damn few theaters. People here don't even know what 'opera' means. Dan Rice built himself an opera house and sails it downstream from place to place. Look, stranger, the best thing for you to do is look at it for yourself. Dan Rice's boat is anchored off Helena."

That night we arrived in Helena, Arkansas. Our boat to stay until morning to take on cotton. I wasn't sure I should believe that Yankee; his tales of a "floating opera house" sounded too tall. So I got up early and went to see for myself. There was the proof in big letters! Six giant posters, side by side on the wharf, featured the flashy portrait of Dan Rice, the famous impresario. A slight importunity, true, but effective. The advertisement framed the portrait. Above and below the smooth-shaven, roguish face, I read: "Dan Rice's Floating Opera House and Museum"; and on the sides: "Playing here three days, the 25th, 26th, and 27th."

> *Admission to the floating opera house . . . . 50 cents.*
> *Reserved seats . . . . 75 cents.*
> *Children . . . . 25 cents.*
> *Admission to the museum . . . . 25 cents.*

No doubt about it now! It was over there, that wonder rivaling the Hanging Gardens of Babylon, Dan Rice's floating opera house. Its outward appearance would best be compared to Noah's ark as depicted in children's illustrated Bibles. The keel of this operatic ark was a large flatboat or better, a raft of long logs bound together; and the weather deck, a small wooden playhouse of the kind we meet so often (but, of course, only on dry land) at European fairs. Pictures of all kinds of monsters covered the four walls, probably the cast of the museum rather than the opera. Big portraits of Dan Rice, placards, slogans, etc., gave this strange opera house the look of an American street corner. Above it flew the Stars and Stripes and below them a large white flag that asserted: Grand Opera House.

The craft was anchored at the riverbank but the gangplank was up. I shouted: "Hello! Opera!" Dan Rice himself appeared, Yankee hat pushed back on his head, quid in cheek, hands in pockets.

He roared at me: "What the hell do you want here at seven in the morning?"

"Sir, my boat sails in a quarter of an hour. Before it does, I want to visit your famous opera house.

"Come aboard, sir," he answered obligingly and pushed the gang-plank to shore.

I paid my fifty cents.

"I'm afraid you're early for the opera. My troupe is still asleep inside."

"At least show me where they perform!"

"Can't do that, either. Occupied."

"And just how big is your troupe?"

"Well, you see, the women sleep on the stage, the men in the audi-torium, with the curtain down between. But you can look at my museum, the greatest, most beautiful, most inter—."

I interrupted him. The museum contained the usual curiosities to be found in roving European shows, plus an Indian, also asleep. My time short, I couldn't wait for the first performance. (There were two a day.) But Dan Rice did tell me why and how he runs this enterprise.

"Well, sir, you see, people along the Mississippi and near bayous and on adjoining rivers in Arkansas and Louisiana could never watch such a show if I didn't bring it to them. I've tried to tour the region with only my troupe, but it costs a lot of money and these towns have no theater or hall for my performances. Here I had to make do in a cotton shed, there in an old warehouse. The show didn't pay until I used a flatboat. I live on it with my people, have my opera house always with me, and sail downriver from place to place. In two months I'll be in New Orleans and the trip won't have cost me a cent."

"But then what? How do you get the boat back upriver?"

"I don't. In New Orleans, you see, I pack my museum, costumes, and sets, sell the boat for wood, and my troupe 'busts' and scatters to other theaters. I buy a ticket on the first steamboat for St. Louis and there have another flatboat and opera house built. Then I announce new artists in 'star engagements' and head downriver with a fresh troupe."

"And your repertory? What do you perform, Colonel?"

"Well, stranger, whatever the people down there want. We try everything. They like singing best. I have a prima donna now, sir, the greatest in the world. Too bad you can't hear her. Voices crack a little when we approach New Orleans. You know how it is, two months or more on the river—think of it! It's hard work, sir!"

"I can imagine, Colonel. God be with you. You are great man, Colonel. Until we meet again, downriver!"

"Thanks, stranger! So long!"

Dan Rice's picture stayed with us the whole trip. At every wharf, in every newspaper, there was the smooth-shaven face of the impresario. He had sent a "drummer" ahead, an advance man who pasted it on each post and on every wall. Dan Rice is surely the Mississippi's Barnum.[28]

1   Knox, pp. 468-69.
2   *Daily Missouri Republican*, 2 July 1842.
3   Gould, pp. 677-78.
4   Thorpe, "Remembrances of the Mississippi," p. 37.
5   Nichols, p. 835.
6   "Up the Mississippi," pp. 433-35.
7   Thorpe, "Remembrances of the Mississippi," p. 34.
8   Letter, Thomas J. Hand to "Darling Mama," 9 December 1882, in the Hand Papers, Columbiana and Special Collections, Columbia University, New York.
9   Manuscript Letter-Journal of Nathanial Hobart, 1837-38, in the Western Americana Collection, Yale University Library, New Haven, Connecticut.
10   Latrobe, pp. 1:286-302.

11 Letter, Thomas J. Hand to "Darling Mama," 9 December 1882, in the Hand Papers.

12 Henry B. Miller, "Journal," *Missouri Historical Society Collections* 6 (1931): 242.

13 Hamilton, pp. 2:193-94.

14 Letter, William H. Gilman to John Gilman, 4 June 1846, in the William Henry Gilman Dairy, 1846-1858, Rare Books and Manuscripts Division, New York Public Library.

15 "Steam Boat Wit," *Weekly Reveille* 1 (28 October 1844): 128.

16 Marie Fontenay de Grandfort, *The New World* (New Orleans: Sherman, Wharton & Co., 1855), pp. 77-81.

17 Ralph, pp. 165-66, 168-72, 174, 177-78, 182-84.

18 *Daily Missouri Republican*, 5 & 8 May 1849.

19 Passenger Steamer Inspector's Certificate, in the E.B. Trail Collection, folder 38a.

20 Cowell, pp. 92-93.

21 *Journey to New Switzerland: Travel Account of the Koepfli and Suppiger Family to St. Louis on the Mississippi and the Founding of New Switzerland in the State of Illinois*, ed. John C. Abbott, trans. Raymond J. Spahn (Carbondale: Southern Illinois University Press, 1987), pp. 119-28.

22 Eliza R. Steele, *A Summer Journey in the West* (New York: Taylor & Co., 1841), pp. 199-229.

23 "A New Branch of Business," *Weekly Reveille* 2, no. 11 (22 September 1845): 497.

24 "Up the Mississippi," p. 441.

25 Devol, pp. 28-30.

26 Solomon F. Smith, *Theatrical Management in the West and South for Thirty Years* (New York: Harper's, 1868), pp. 189-91.

27 Dorsey, *Master of the Mississippi*, pp. 255-56.

28 *Travels on the Lower Mississippi*, pp. 88-91.

PART 3

Fast and Furious

Taking the Horns

Americans always seemed in a hurry. The country was so large, and the obstacles so immense—to be the first or the fastest counted more than anything. Naturally, on the river, that instinct translated into racing. Whenever two boats in the same trade found themselves side by side, the competitive spirit burst forth (along with the boilers, sometimes) and the race was on. Nothing was prearranged; rules were nonexistent. It was sport, but the foundation of this sport rested on solid business practice. The fastest boat between major cities displayed deer or elk antlers on the hurricane deck or pilothouse as a symbol of her speed. A boat that carried the "horns" attracted a larger share of the trade.

For the Thrill of It

Racing was such an exhilarating experience that everyone on board looked forward to it—well, almost everyone. There were the detractors; but upon what grounds could they object to an innocent contest of speed between gentlemen of commerce? Perhaps the answer can be found in the 1855 account that follows:

> We resumed our trip up the river. Hardly had we lost sight of
> Memphis, when we saw, about two miles ahead, a steamboat that had

just finished taking in a supply of wood, and was bound, like us, for St. Louis. It was five o'clock in the afternoon; the captain had reached at least his eighth "drink" for the day. He threw out a signal and determined on having a race. The boat ahead answered by another signal, which meant that our challenge was accepted. Immediately our captain called up the engineers, and ordered them to "fire up" as much and as speedily as possible. Our steamer, like most of those on the Mississippi, was a high-pressure boat. The furnaces were crammed full of combustibles in order to raise the hottest fire; oil, turpentine, and even barrels of tar were thrown in. Far from being alarmed, the passengers were running below every moment and calling out to the crew: "Fire up! Fire up! That rascal must not show his stern any longer!"

One of the passengers however, frightened at the jerks of the boat and loud hissing of the steam, went to the captain saying: "Sir, I have on board with me five young men from different schools in New Orleans. I have undertaken to bring them back in safety to their homes; I am responsible for their lives. In the name of Heaven, give up a struggle that nothing obliged you to commence, and which may end, for us, in a terrible catastrophe!"

"You are a fool!" replied the captain. "In five minutes, we will pass that 'shoe' ahead of us, or else we'll be blown a hundred and fifty feet in the air!"

The poor mentor said nothing in reply, but his countenance spoke for him. Like a certain character in an old comedy, he looked as if he were saying to himself: "I wish I could get out of this."

Little by little it was evident we were gaining on our opponent. But our boat creaked and labored all over; she rushed through the water like a dolphin, the howling of the piston was loud and continuous; the wheels seemed to be whirled around by an invisible but tremendous hurricane. At length, after several anxious moments, we caught up with the "rascal." A frightful outburst of exclamation and cries took place on our boat. Then when we had got somewhat ahead of our rival, our captain wheeled the stern of his boat directly in front of the other's bow, and ironically called out to him that he might throw a rope to us, as we would tow him gratis. The cries and noise with us then became indescribable—captain, officers, crew, servants, passengers, firemen—all were gathered on our guards, insulting by voice and gestures the few persons who ventured to appear on the other boat.

This event was for our captain a complete triumph, and the passengers noticed it appropriately. Like all rejoicings in the United States, this ended in a series of libations that lasted all night.[1]

The bold declaration of a captain that he would pass a competitor at the risk of blowing up his own boat seems an exaggeration. Perhaps it was not. An article that appeared in 1845, if it can be taken literally, suggests that the Mississippi was the country's longest race track, and strongly implies that steamboats were the preferred vehicle of lunatics:

From New Orleans thus far on the trip up, the two boats, of nearly equal speed, have alternately passed each other during the stop to wood, showing no gain of consequence on the part of either, and the grand struggle has been as it at present is, to rush the operation so as to get a start before being overtaken. The bank is reached—the boat made fast—gangways are formed.

"Lively, men! Lively!" cries the mate, and while the upper cabins pour out their crowds upon the boiler deck, the hands, and the swarms of wild-looking passengers below (obliged by contract) dash ashore among the brush.

Now ensues a scene that tasks description! The fire, augmented by piles of the driest wood, crimsons the tangled forest! Black and white, many of them stripped to their waist, though others, more careful, protect their skins by ripping and forming cowls of empty salt sacks, attack the lengthened pile, and amid laugh, shout, curse, and the scarcely unremitting scream of the iron chimneys, (tortured by the still-making steam,) remove it to the boat.

"Lively, men! Lively!" rings the cry, and lively, lively is the impulse inspired by it! See that swarthy, gigantic Negro, his huge shoulders hidden beneath a pyramid of wood, hurl to the deck his load, cut a caper along the plank, and, leaping back, seize a flaming brand to whirl it round his head in downright enjoyment!

"Lively! Lively!"

Laugh, shout, whoop, and the pile is rapidly disappearing, when a cry is heard from the hurricane deck: "Here she comes, round the point!"

'Tis the rival steamer, sure enough; and once more she will pass during this detention. Now dash both mate and captain ashore to rush the matter. The bell is struck for starting, as if to compel impossibility; the accumulated steam is let off in brief, impatient screams, and the passengers, sharing the wild excitement, add their cries.

"Passed again, by thunder!"

"We've got enough wood!"

"Leave the rest!"

In the meantime, around the point below, sweeps the up-comer—all lights and sparks—moving over the water like a rushing fire-palace! Now her "blow" is heard, like a suppressed curse of struggle and defiance, and now, nearing the bank where lies her rival, a sort of frenzy seizes on the latter—

"Tumble it in!"

"Rush her!"

"Damn the rest!"

"You've got enough!"

> *The struggle is to leave the bank before she can be passed, and fuel, flame, and frenzy seemingly unite to secure the object; barrels of combustibles are thrust into the furnaces, while, before the doors, the firemen, naked and screaming, urge their wild efforts!*

Ra-a-a-s-h *goes the steam! The engine, "working off," thunders below. Again, the bell rings, and the hurly-burly on shore is almost savage. At length, as the coming boat is hard astern, the signal tap is given: "All hands aboard!" The lines are let go, the planks are shoved in by the Negroes who are themselves drawn from the water with them, and amid a chaos of timber, a whirl of steam, and a crash of machinery, once more she is under way. The struggle is to leave the bank before she can be passed, and fuel, flame, and frenzy seemingly unite to secure the object; barrels of combustibles are thrust into the furnaces, while, before the doors, the firemen, naked and screaming, urge their wild efforts!*

"Here she is, alongside!" *And now the struggle indeed is startling; the one endeavoring to shoot out from the bank across the bows of the*

other, and she, authorized by river custom, holding her way; the con-
sequences of collision resting alone on her imprudent competitor.
Roar for roar—scream for scream—huzza for huzza—but now, the
inner boat apparently gaining, a turn of her antagonist's wheel leaves
her no option but to be run into or turn again towards the bank! A
hundred oaths and screams reply to this maneuver, but on she
comes—on, on—a moment more and she strikes! With a shout of
rage the defeated pilot turns her head—at the same moment snatch-
ing down his rifle and discharging it into the pilothouse of his oppo-
nent! Fury has now seized the thoughts of all, and the iron throats of
the steamers are less hideous than the human ones beneath them. The
wheel for a moment neglected, the thwarted monster has now taken
a sheer in the wild current, and, beyond the possibility of prevention,
is driving on to the bank! A cry of terror rises aloft—the throng rush
aft—the steam, every valve set free—makes the whole forest shiver,
and, amid the fright, the tall chimneys [are] caught by the giant
trees, and wrenched and torn out like tusks from a recoiling
mastodon.[2]

For all the inherent danger of steamboat racing, very few people thought
seriously of pressing for laws to ban it. Most passengers and steamboatmen
viewed racing as a calculated risk that got them where they wanted to go
quicker than they expected to get there. Though at times reticent, the traveling public came to develop a sense of humor about racing and its more
ardent proponents. It was humor with a biting, satirical edge, as evident in
an 1855 issue of *Harper's New Monthly Magazine:*

> *Squire Blaze was a model woodchopper. He settled at low water at*
> *a place so infested with snags that the flatboatmen christened it the*
> *"Devil's Promenade." It lies at the mouth of "Dead Man's Bend," just*
> *at the foot of "Gouge-your-eye-out Island." Here he prospected a wood-*
> *yard, and soon after exchanged some of his dry goods for whiskey and*
> *tin cups; and then, for the accommodation of travelers, he connected*
> *a grocery to his other occupation. His early life had been "devarsi-*
> *fied," and he gave some of the principal incidents with great zest.*
>
> *Having served for a long time as first mate on a raft, he grew*
> *ambitious for higher distinction. By one of those magical elevations*

so peculiar to a new country, he got possession of a "starn-wheeler," and entered the pine-knot business, the pursuit of which took him so high up Red River, that he says he "got sometimes clean out of the way of taxes." His pride was to be called "captain"; his ambition, to run a race. Circumstances occurred that brought about the wished for consummation. We give the particulars in his own words:

"I was coming down 'Little Crooked' with a full head of steam on, when I overtuck the Squatter Belle, loaded, like myself, with pine knots, and bound for the Massissipp. The race was excitin', a parfect scrouger—the steam yelled and the hands swore; you'd a-thought all the univarse was poundin' sheet iron. 'Twas no use—I was always a misfortunate man: the Fairy Queen's ingin (that was my boat) had light weights on the safety valve, and the furnaces got choked with rosin. The Squatter Belle was getting ahead; twice I raised my rifle to shoot her pilot—for you see I didn't like to be beat—when I smelt something warm, and the next I knew [the boilers exploded and] I was lodged in the limbs of a dead cypress, thirty-two feet six inches from the ground. This was the proudest moment of my life.

"What grieves me," continued Squire Blaze, with unusual feeling, "what grieves me is, that my title of 'captain' didn't stick, and I've been called 'squire' ever since."[3]

The Race of the Century

Contests of speed on the river fell into two categories: racing against another boat, which usually consisted of short sprints, and racing against the clock, which was done most often over long distances. Several boats were revered for their speed. Legend has it that the *Princess*, of 1844, consistently ran so fast that no boat ever overtook her, although many tried. The first *J. M. White*, built also in 1844, put on such a display of swiftness on a trial run from New Orleans to St. Louis that posts later were placed on the shore to mark and commemorate her location at each twenty-four hour interval; would-be challengers measured their performance against those posts. The *A. L. Shotwell* and the *Eclipse*, both speedsters of their day, got into a race, of sorts, in 1853. The course was 1,440 miles from New Orleans to Louisville. The *Eclipse* left New Orleans three days after the *Shotwell*, intending to beat the *Shotwell's* time. She came close to doing it, but the *Shotwell* withstood the challenge, completing the course in 4 days, 9 hours, and 30 minutes—50 minutes better than the *Eclipse.*[4]

And then, in 1870, there came the race of the century—the fabled match between the *Natchez* and the *Robert E. Lee*—a twelve hundred-mile, no holds barred, side-by-side, all-out gallop from New Orleans to St. Louis. According to a contemporary paper, it came about in this manner:

> . . . A spirit of rivalry has for some months existed between the officers of both boats, and also between parties and places where the contracts for building these boats were fulfilled. Louisville claims the credit of launching the Lee and Cincinnati heralded to all the land that the Queen City gave the Natchez to the mighty Mississippi. The owners of each steamer claimed that their craft was the swiftest, and both sides had at various times given practical demonstrations that their boats were fully up to the highest degree of merit. Time wore on when at last the lightning flashed the intelligence that the Lee and Natchez were registered at New Orleans to start up the river at 5 P.M., June 30, 1870. This was enough. The news spread with wonderful rapidity, and in the quickest time imaginable, the people all along the Mississippi resolved themselves into one grand lookout committee.
>
> At New Orleans, Memphis, Louisville, Cincinnati, and St. Louis the great race became the principal topic of conversation. And not only were the rivermen in the towns and cities along the route enlisted in the contemplated race, but the people generally evinced an enthusiasm which plainly told of an approaching event of a wonderful and extraordinary character. Especially in the Crescent City, the Queen City, and the Falls City* did the excitement run high, and money was passed from the pockets of men to the hands of the stakeholders as freely as water runs down the stream on which the boats were to run their race. Memphis was also at fever heat in regard to the race, and increased the capital of the deposit banks there many thousands of dollars. The evening previous to the departure of the boats from Orleans, Hawkins' Club Room was besieged by crowds of boatmen and citizens generally all anxious to learn something and bet their bottom dollar.[5]

* New Orleans, Cincinnati, and Louisville.

The race came at the best of times and the worst of times for steam-boating. The War Between the States was over, commerce was brisk, and the boats were bigger, better, and more reliable than ever before. But the railroads had seized an opportunity; their lines paralleled every major river and extended from coast to coast. They were faster, more convenient, and generally impervious to the seasons. Slowly, methodically, they were killing the steamboat business. Only a gimmick, a spectacle of major proportions, could stem the loss of business on the river. It came to pass through the intense rivalry and personal animosity between two captains: John W. Cannon of the *Lee*, and Thomas P. Leathers of the *Natchez*.

> *Only a gimmick, a spectacle of major proportions, could stem the loss of [steamboat] business on the river.*

Self-made, self-reliant, experienced, mature, wealthy—these terms applied equally to both men. Both had gone to the river in their teens, Cannon as a cub pilot, and Leathers as a deckhand. Both rose through the ranks to become captains and owners of their boats. Then came the war, and their fortunes changed. Leathers placed his boat in the service of the Confederacy; in 1863 his vessel was burned to prevent capture by the Yankees. Cannon, on the other hand, was lukewarm to the Southern cause and hid his boat away on Red River until the Union took control of the Mississippi; then he placed his vessel in cotton trade with the North. By war's end Cannon had made a small fortune and Leathers was left to start anew. In 1866, John Cannon placed an order at New Albany, Indiana, for construction of the *Robert E. Lee*. He planned to operate the steamer on the Lower Mississippi, and chose the name not so much out of reverence for the Confederate general, but rather to attract the business of Southern shippers. Leathers worked his way back by borrowing money and chartering boats. In 1868 he was operating a boat owned in part by Captain Cannon. The two men came to a disagreement over the terms of the charter and it resulted in a tavern brawl between them. Leathers went on to build the *Natchez* in 1869.

Captain G. L. Nourse, the New Orleans harbor master in 1870, described the contrasts in the personalities of Cannon and Leathers:

> *. . . I became well acquainted with both of these prominent men*
> *and found there was as much difference in their temperaments as*

there is between a lion and a lamb. Captain Cannon was a mild-
mannered, extremely polite person, approachable at all times and
never happier than when exploiting all the good qualities of the Lee,
which was his idol. He held at that time no prejudices against his fellow citizens.

Captain Thomas P. Leathers, his competitor in the Vicksburg trade,
had one of the most commanding presences possible. He was over six
feet tall, a giant in stature, wore a ruffled shirt with a large cluster
diamond pin and always dressed in Confederate gray. Woe be to him
who referred to the late unpleasantness, as Captain Leathers did not
recognize that the war was over, nor did he ever lose sight of the fact
that I was a government official and therefore a carpetbagger. The
decided differences of temperament in these two equally eminent
men caused them to have admirers temperamentally constituted as
they were, so that Captain Cannon's friends were largely of those
who accepted Reconstruction gracefully, while Captain Leathers had
a following that died hard as it were.[6]

Both Cannon's Lee and Leathers' *Natchez* had arrived in port at New
Orleans late in June. On her previous up trip, the *Natchez* had beaten the
J. M. White's long-standing record run between New Orleans and St. Louis,
yet many rivermen claimed that the *Lee* was faster still. A steamboat
designer in Cincinnati posited his reasons for favoring the *Lee:*

The boilers of the Lee are considerably larger in diameter than
those of the Natchez, and being made of lighter iron, are not calculated to carry the steam pressure usual with boats of her class. I have
been informed that her usual working pressure does not exceed one
hundred or one hundred and twenty pounds per square inch. Her
cylinders have each a diameter of forty inches, and are the largest
high-pressure engines ever used on Western steamers. The Lee was
constructed with the view of working a moderate steam pressure on
a large piston.

The Natchez' boilers are of a lesser diameter than those on the
Lee, and made of heavier iron. Her cylinders each have a diameter
of thirty-four inches, with a working steam pressure, as allowed by
law, of one hundred and thirty-nine pounds per square inch, her

proportions of power being such as to enable her at all times to maintain that pressure. Assuming that both boats, when racing, would use all the steam they could generate, the limited diameter of the Natchez' cylinders would soon attain their maximum, while the six inches excessive diameter of the Lee's cylinders would be able to work to advantage all the steam she could take.

I am of the opinion that the wheels of the Natchez are too large for her cylinders. They are forty-four feet in diameter, with twenty-two arms, working fifteen and a half foot buckets, thirty inches in width, and were calculated to make seventeen revolutions per minute—but, I have been informed, have never done so, some fifteen revolutions being the excess.

The R. E. Lee's wheel is six feet less in diameter, with twelve inches more in length and two inches less in middle of bucket, consequently she should make a greater number of revolutions per minute.[7]

The time had come to settle the issue. Several newspapers carried the story of the race, though none better than the St. Louis daily, the *Missouri Republican*. With reporters on board both boats and correspondents at all of the major river towns along the route, the *Republican* kept its readers on the edge of their seats during five days of coverage. It is a classic work of river literature, and deserves resurrection from its moldering tomb of obscurity:

THE BOAT RACE
Steam Duel on the River
A Course 1,200 Miles Long
The Grandest Race on Record
Steamboats Dash at Railroad Time
Great Revival of River Interest
The Iron Horse Looking out for His Laurels
Immense Popular Interest

New Orleans, June 30. This afternoon, at the published time for the departure of the steamboats R. E. Lee and Natchez, the levee in the vicinity where these boats lay was entirely blocked with masses of people, viewing as best they could the preparations for the race. While the multitude were waiting on shore, preparations were going on qui-etly and almost noiselessly on board both steamers. Captain Cannon of the Lee *seemed in excellent spirits and evidently very confident, yet omitting nothing calculated to increase the speed of his boat. He was in occasional communication with the first engineer and pilot, who both appeared to realize that much was expected of them. Captain Leathers of the* Natchez *looked the triumphant veteran all over. Some of his friends think he has been altogether too confident, while oth-ers say that no one knows what he has been doing, and what his arrangements are about fuel, landings, &c.*

The Lee *is three years older than the* Natchez. *The* Natchez *is more than seven feet longer than the* Lee. *The latter, however, has a greater breadth of beam, by about three feet. The* Lee *is certainly in some respects in better trim than the* Natchez. *Neither takes any freight except pine knots. While it is given out that the* Natchez *will land six times between here and Cairo, it is declared that the* Lee *will go through without touching shore, getting her fuel from steamers under way.*

The friends of each steamer scrutinized closely the preparations being made by the private boats for the race. Every load of pinewood that crossed the levee was noted with the exactness that a bookkeeper watches his balance sheet. In fact every movement in connection with the preparation of each for the race was discussed apparently as learnedly as a presiding doctor gives his last lecture to the graduating class. One fact was soon revealed, and that was that the officers of the Lee *were as determined as desperadoes that the trip of their boat was to be run in every sense of the word a race and nothing but a race. Everything that could be spared from the* Lee *was left at the mouth of the Ohio on her last down trip from Louisville, and as soon as her cargo was on shore the carpenters went to work to remove other mate-rial that might impede her progress. No chicken fighter ever took more pains to trim and condition his game rooster for a battle royal than Captain Cannon took to prepare his boat for the race. The great-est clearing was aft of her wheels. Here everything was removed that could possibly check the flow of water from the paddles. Even the sash of the pilothouse, against which comes a strong current of air when under fast run, was taken out.*

Captain Leathers was advised of the means being used to beat the Natchez. His friends insisted on his making the same preparations, but he would not hear of it. He said he intended to run the Natchez according to the rules of legitimate and practical steamboating. He declared his purpose to go to St. Louis with the whole of his boat, and that the steam power of no boat should be credited with helping to propel the Natchez, unless she broke her machinery and had to be towed to save the boat and the lives of her passengers.

No such excitement has existed in New Orleans for a long time as the prospect of this race has created. Money has piled up "mountains high" at Hawkins' Club Room, and every man and boy in the streets talks of nothing but the contest between the two boats. The Lee is the favorite on short odds on account of being better prepared, but Captain Leathers can, if necessary improve the condition of the Natchez on the run. The friends of each steamer are jubilant and await the time of three dinners on board to decide which is fleetest.

The scene at Canal Street when the boats pushed out was exciting beyond description. My hand trembles writing this dispatch, from the nervousness it produced. The crowd swayed and sweated, straining necks and opening wide their eyes. The pilots were aloft sometime before the departure. Engineers below continued to look after nuts and bolts, and to find new places for oil. The hoarse voices of the mates were mellowed somewhat in giving orders to the crews. In the furnaces the fires cracked and rumbled, and from the chimney-tops rolled dense volumes of black smoke. The wheels dashed and splattered in the water like the hoofs of horses impatient to be off. On the hurricane decks paced the anxious captains, neither of whom could now conceal a spice of that excitement that was visible everywhere ashore. There was more nervousness shown aboard of the Lee than on the Natchez. The taps of the bell that indicated she was about to [depart] were followed by swift movements on the part of the Negro deckhands. The fastenings were quickly unloosed, the pilot spoke through the trumpet to the engineer, there was a tingling of bells, the great wheels revolved, and at precisely two minutes before 5 o'clock the steamer R. E. Lee started on her journey amidst the most deafening and prolonged cheering ever heard at this wharf.

The *Robert E. Lee* at New Orleans, from a painting by John Stobart. Built in 1866 at New Albany, Indiana, and completed at Louisville, Kentucky, the *Lee* enjoyed a ten-year career before being dismantled. Her hull was used as a wharfboat at Memphis. (Illustration courtesy of Murphy Library, University of Wisconsin-La Crosse.)

Scarcely was the Lee *fairly in the stream before another shout rent the air, and "Look! Look there!" was heard on all sides, and every eye was directed to where the* Natchez, *the movements on board which had been quieter, was gliding from her dock. Now again arose vociferous, tremendous, thunderous plaudits, in which it seemed that every voice in the whole vast multitude joined, and it was not for some moments that the hurrahing ceased.*

The progress of the boats was watched as long as the racers could be seen and then the throngs on the levee gradually dispersed, and formed knots upon the sidewalks and streets to discuss the event of the day.

At the start the Lee *was three minutes ahead; at Carrollton, 3 minutes 45 seconds ahead; at the nineteen miles point, 4 minutes 45 seconds ahead.*

ON BOARD STEAMER R. E. LEE

Natchez, Miss., July 1. We shall make Natchez between 10 and 11 o'clock this morning, Captain Cannon expecting to beat the best time ever before made. The scene from time of departure till dark last evening baffles description. As we steamed along the watery race-

track the whole country on both sides of the river seemed alive with a strange excitement expressed in a variety of gestures, the waving of handkerchiefs, hats, running along the river shore as if to encourage the panting steamer, and now and then far off shouts came cheeringly over the water, and were plainly heard above the roaring of the fires, the clatter of machinery, the dashing of the waters, and the rushing of steam. All the life in the vicinity of the river appeared to be thoroughly aroused into unusual activity by this struggle of two steamboats for the palm of speed. The settlements and plantations along the coast as we passed, turned out their whole forces, and seemed to have taken a holiday in honor of our flying trip.

Up and beyond Plaquemine the men and boys in skiffs came out almost in our track to hail us with warm welcome, and get a word if possible with one of the officers of the crew. This is but a moment. They are struck by the swells, and dashed and rocked away off toward the shore far off in our wake. As long as they are in sight they wave us adieu. The inhabitants all appear to live out of doors, or are crowded in the windows, or on the housetops as we approach. The most lively interest is depicted in every countenance, and is uttered in every voice.

At Baton Rouge, which we reached about one o'clock this morning, there were still people on the wharf, but silence had nearly been restored on shore, and during the rest of the night nothing was to be noted but the still, anxious groups on board.

We reached Stamps' Landing several minutes ahead of the time of the Princess, which is the standard of fast time. In a few minutes we will be opposite Natchez. The morning is beautiful, and everything is lovely.

Vicksburg, Miss., July 1. We lost five minutes at Natchez in taking fuel. The Natchez was in sight, but Captain Cannon was by no means uneasy. Our time was 17 hours and 11 minutes, which is about twenty minutes ahead of the Princess' time, and wins many thousand dollars on the first big point. Great crowds [gathered] on the wharf, and when we left the wildest shouts went up. Every heart on board was touched with excitement. The tension of the nerves is continual and almost painful at times. Truly is the Lee a thing of life.

FROM THE STEAMER NATCHEZ

Vicksburg, July 1st. The run to Plaquemine, in seven hours and twelve minutes, was without further incident than the general excitement on board. There was not much conversation. Captain Leathers remained but a short time on the roof and then sat on the boiler deck absorbed in thought. The engineers watched carefully every movement, the firemen worked like Trojans, and looked like demons in the red glare of the furnaces.

Thus we go cleaving the river wide open and making Baton Rouge in eight hours and thirty-one minutes, Bayou Sara in ten hours and thirty-eight minutes, and the mouth of Red River in thirteen hours.

Heavy swells from the Lee are still striking the shores and, to confess it, impeding our progress. But the Natchez still plows on her way, puffing white clouds and streaming a myriad of sparks from her chimneys. A wide breadth of the river is lighted up in front of the boat.

Stamps' Landing was passed at 7 o'clock, about fourteen hours out, which is the exact time of the Princess. In two hours and thirty-seven minutes afterwards we glided by Ashley, and the next point is Natchez where we land for fuel, some ten minutes behind the Lee. Thus both boats beat the fastest time ever before made. And if the time has been correctly kept, the Lee has gained on us four minutes since leaving New Orleans.

In effecting a landing we lost some eight minutes at Natchez.

The scenes on board as we witness the crowds and hear the shouting cannot be portrayed. At this hour we are approaching Vicksburg, the Lee being still considerably ahead. But we are surely though slowly lessening the distance.

Sometimes in a long stretch of clear river she is plainly in sight, then a bend shuts her out—all but her smoke which hangs away off northward like a dense cloud; then an island or a sudden projection of woodland hides all traces of our lively rival from our view. We feel safe but keep wonderfully busy, because we know she is there going like lightning. There is life and wakefulness and speed and determination in the swiftly following vessel which will give us the victory before we are done with her. These occasional glimpses of the Lee seem to give the Natchez more muscle and force her to her very best.

FROM POINTS ASHORE

Memphis, July 1. The city is wild tonight with excitement with regard to the race between the Lee and Natchez. Bets are freely made. Parties offer largely on the Lee to this point, and on the Natchez to St. Louis. The bulletin boards are watched by eager crowds, and the levee is lined by disputants who are debating the chances and offering all sorts of wagers on time, etc.

Betters in Cincinnati. Cincinnati, July 1. Over two hundred thousand dollars have been staked here today on the result of the race between the Lee and the Natchez. Such excitement has never been seen here on any like occasion.

In the City. [St. Louis, July 1.] The dispatches published in the Republican *announced that the race had begun. The boats were both coming up at a great rate of speed. The greatest eagerness and anxiety to obtain the very latest intelligence by telegraph was manifested. So great was the public thirst for the latest news from the rival boats, that the most weighty matters of business could not be considered, and the almost universal inquiry was, "What about the race? Have you had any news from the Lee and the Natchez?"*

The excitement in the city was very great. Merchants turned away from customers to inquire about the race. Steamboatmen forgot to inquire about freights. Commission merchants forgot the orders of their patrons. At the Union Merchants' Exchange the dispatches were posted on the bulletin boards. Groups of men gathered about on the floor of the hall; but not to talk about corn, oats, hay, flour, and bacon. These were subjects ignored. No one seemed to care whether the stocks on hand were light, or heavy.

Among the betting clan of our citizens, much excitement prevailed. The Lee seemed to be favored with the largest number, but the friends of the Natchez were neither few, nor cautious, in offering to back up their opinions of the running capacity of their favorite packet. Bets were freely made during the morning with odds against the Natchez at the rate of $100 to $75.

On the levee business was almost entirely suspended. The Natchez and Lee, the race, the probabilities of the one or the other gaining the victory, according to the bias or opinion of the different individuals who discussed the matter was the universal topic of conversation. Speculations and conjectures, reasons, pro and con, why this or that boat would win at last were freely given, each one offering to back up his judgment by a small or large bet according to the depth of conviction of the correctness of his opinions. Main and Second Street merchants called to any acquaintance or friend who might be passing to inquire, "What of the race? Have you heard of anything later from the Lee and the Natchez?"

Toward evening the anxiety to hear from the rival boats at Vicksburg was intense. The newspaper offices were besieged by a numerous throng anxiously inquiring: "What's the news from the Lee and Natchez at Vicksburg?" The wharfboats, steamboat agents' offices, hotels, club rooms, and other places of frequent resort by steamboatmen, were thronged by people representing all classes of citizens. There is no way of accounting for the universal excitement pervading this community in consequence of a trial of speed between two steamboats, unless we accept the fact that a larger proportion of our citizens are interested in the navigation of our rivers than in any other city on the continent.

The sun went down, the shadows of night gathered thick and dark, but far into the night the newspaper offices and other centers of news were visited by many desirous of knowing how the race progressed. And the stillness of the midnight hour was broken by the click of the telegraph conveying intelligence of the great race.

Helena, Ark., July 2. *The entire population of the bluffs in this region has been gathered by the riverside since noon, watching for the upward bound boats Lee and Natchez. At exactly half-past four the indigenous effervescence found free course in cheering the Lee, which moved between heaven and the muddy deep like some . . . bird of passage. With window blinds tightly closed, wheelhouse stripped (for fuel?) and whistle screaming, she swept by before the onlooking crowds had fairly collected their wits. Such a roar as followed in her wake you never did hear.*

Her time, from New Orleans to this place, twenty-four minutes less than two days, is the shortest on record, and is more than six hours less than that made by the White. *The* Lee *had no time to stop, and held no communication whatever with the shore.*

The Natchez *steamed by this landing at twenty-four minutes past five, just fifty-four minutes behind the* Lee. *Her time from New Orleans is two days and thirty-four minutes, which is an hour and a half less than on her last upward trip. She sent off dispatches by a small steamer which went out to meet her.*

FROM THE STEAMER LEE

On Board the Steamer R. E. Lee. July 2, 1870, 6 P.M. *Nothing has occurred on board our vessel since leaving Natchez worthy of special note. We have certainly been making very fast time, and we are certainly beating Captain Leathers most beautifully. Yet our gallant commander persists he is not running a race. He thinks the* Natchez *not so fast a boat as this, and supposes by the time we reach Cairo that fact shall be known to all; but he is taking no extraordinary risks.*

Everybody on board and notably the firemen seem hard to convince that we are not having a race. The machinery works most beautifully and uniformly, and we are gliding over the water like a thing of life, sure enough. Excitement on board is still at fever pitch, and sleep has visited our eyelids only to be driven off.

FROM THE STEAMER NATCHEZ
LEE LOSES ALL BETS ABOVE VICKSBURG

On Board the Natchez. **Near Helena, July 2, 1870.** *We broke our pump in the night, and tied up to the shore for repairs, losing 36 minutes. The* Natchez *is now in splendid condition, as trim and tidy as a new baby; and she will make a clear stretch through, stopping only at Memphis and Cairo.*

The Natchez *stopped at Greenville for passengers; but she will now stop only at Memphis and Cairo. Captain Leathers has run his boat in a practical business manner and order all the way, and has a sure thing.*

The steamer [Frank] Pargoud gave the Lee *100 cords of pinewood, and aided the* Lee *with all the steam power she could put on, accompanying her for many miles of the way above Vicksburg.*

Steamboat *Frank Pargoud* taking on freight, circa 1870. Bearing a slight resemblance to the *Robert E. Lee*, the *Pargoud* was a smaller boat, but still among the larger class of packets when compared to the boats moored behind her. (Photo courtesy Murphy Library, University of Wisconsin-La Crosse.)

The Lee won all her bets up to the time when the Pargoud improperly and unfairly aided her by making use of her own propelling power while transferring a heavy lot of pine fuel. The propelling power being thus divided from another boat, loses the race for the Lee and all bets, notwithstanding she is in the lead. Hurrah for the Natchez!

Everything goes lovely just now, and the goose hangs a trifle high; but Captain Leathers has a fearfully long reach, and aside from the question of the bets (which the Lee has forfeited) the Natchez has a good show to make the best time. We are making a fair, open business trip, although not attempting to do much business. But we are not making a run for a race, but to try and see what can be done . . . on a regular trip.

The Natchez will undoubtedly set a mark that will be the goal of other boats for years to come. If we had put her through without landing, taking our fuel from steamers with full head on, and for the sole purpose of racing, we could have made Helena at least an hour ago, which is the opinion of every man on board.

EXCITEMENT AT MEMPHIS

Memphis, July 2. *All day long the city has been greatly excited, and the excitement increased each hour. Anxious groups of people are collected on nearly every corner, and the great topic of all is the boat race. Many rumors have been flying about during the day, all false, but gaining credence so far as the feelings of the people led them to believe. Some were to the effect that the Lee had broken down and would be unable to continue the race; others that the larboard wheelhouse of the Natchez had been blown off and that the Lee was towing her. Others still said that the Natchez was gaining on the Lee, and that her captain was sanguine of success.*

The curiosity of the people to see the boats as they pass is intense. Many have been on the bluff all the forenoon, and since dark the crowd has increased till the whole bluff is now covered, and still people are coming in from all parts of the city.

Great preparations are being made for the reception of the boats. Tar barrels are placed ready to be fired as they approach, and a battery of artillery is in position ready to thunder forth a salute in honor of the victor. All seem wild with enthusiasm. Men, women, and children are striving for favorable positions to witness the race, and all seem animated with an intense desire to gain a good look at the boats as they pass the city.

Latest—10 P.M. *The boats are not in sight yet. The crowd on the bluff in front of the river is immense. Nothing like it has been seen in this city for many years. Seats have been appropriated for the ladies, and the whole front of the city looks like one vast amphitheater, and the utmost interest is manifested on all sides.*

Tugs have been stationed in the river with barges of coal ever since eight o'clock, but up to this hour nothing has been heard of either boat.

Eleven P.M. *A bright light is just coming into view around President's Island, six miles from this city. It is believed to be the Lee.*

11:04. *The Lee has just arrived and is taking coal barges in tow. Enthusiasm is immense. The crowd is cheering, cannon firing, and bonfires blazing.*

11:10. *The Lee has just left. Such an ovation has never been given* to any boat before. *The people are wild and bets are freely offered that she will beat the* Natchez *to Cairo one hour and fifteen minutes.*

12:13. *The* Natchez *has just passed; the crowd is fast dispersing and a day of great excitement is over.*

THE NATCHEZ AT MEMPHIS

On Board the Natchez *off Memphis, July 2.* Our time to Memphis is fifty-five hours and two minutes, which is five hours and six minutes less than the time made by the White, and two hours and forty minutes better than we ran last trip. The Lee is now one hour ahead.

The Lee gobbled the horns of the Princess' fast time to Natchez, but did not land to get them. They were [brought] to her through the dignified agency of a coal heaver on board a coal flat, which was shoved out in the stream to her. The Lee is trimmed down to all she will bear. All is stripped off her decks and out of her hold that could be removed, and her bulkheads were also cut loose to lighten her.

Shotwell's forty-eight hours' run was made by the Natchez in forty-four hours thirty-five minutes. Men who bet against the Lee to points above Vicksburg say they will not give up the money, because the Pargoud used all her steam power to propel the Lee, whilst giving her a load of pinewood. The Natchez will do her best all the way from here to St. Louis, and will be better prepared to get her fuel than she was coming here.

LEE STILL GAINING

Cairo [Illinois], Sunday, July 3. Orders were received here on Saturday to have two flats laden with coal at this point in readiness for the Lee, so as to make it unnecessary for her to cross the river to Cairo, which would break up her headway nearly a quarter of an hour. A similar order for two barges for the Natchez was not received till this morning. The fact shows, perhaps, a difference of forethought that has run through all the appointments for the race. The commander of the Natchez is undoubtedly one of the most skillful commanders in the West or South; but in the little details of management to avoid delay, it is said that up to this time Captain Cannon, of the Lee, has had the advantage.

The tug Montauk, *in which came over from Cairo Enoch King, the Lee's pilot from here to St. Louis, stood ready to adjust the boats as they arrived; but here again the* Lee *had a slight advantage. She was the first comer and, of course, took the two outside flats, leaving the* Natchez *to run in closer to shore and into shoaler water to get the other two. There were but few persons gathered at this point to see the boats; but Cairo, with its multitude of spectators, is in plain view, and as the hour for the arrival of the* Lee *drew near we could see the assembled spectators in the city and along the neighboring shores turn their faces down the river to the point where the first indication of her approach was to be looked for. They had not long to wait. In a short time a faint smoke made its way above the distant southern horizon, announcing that a boat was approaching. Gradually, this faint smoke thickened into a strong dense cloud, and the eyes of the expectant gazers were now intently fixed on the point to catch the first glimpse of the object for which all were waiting. The scene at this time from above the point where the barges were lying, was most interesting. Before us was a long spit of sand, from the extreme point of which stretches back a line of boys and men to the distance of five hundred yards. Back of them on the higher bank of the point were other groups of sightseers, all dressed in Sunday attire, some on horseback, some in buggies, but the greater number sitting on the bank or under the trees. Still behind those was Cairo with its larger crowds gathered on the wharfboat and on the levee, or clinging to balconies, or merged in front windows, watching for the* Lee *to appear in sight. It was a picture of expectation. Even . . . the cottonwood forests that looked into the river seemed to stand like expectant sentries, waiting the appearance of some stately monarch of the waters. A little before six the boys on the point of the sand-spot raised a cry, the groups behind them caught it up and sent it over to Cairo, and the crowd in the streets of the city caught it up in turn and echoed it over the broad water to the Missouri shore where we were waiting. We knew what it meant. The* Lee *was coming. The* Rubicon

Even . . . the cottonwood forests that looked into the river seemed to stand like expectant sentries, waiting the appearance of some stately monarch of the waters.

had backed up from Cairo and straightened herself downstream to continue her voyage; but when the expected steamer hove into view, she backed her wheels and stood in the middle of the harbor, to wait for the monarch to pass.

Up to this time we could not see the Lee from the Missouri shore above the point; but directly a jackstaff glided past the point, then the bow, the glistening chimneys, and the huge wheelhouse, and the Lee was in full view from where we stood, and not more than three-quarters of a mile distant. She looked, every inch of her, the monarch of the rivers as, turning her head up the Mississippi, she spurred the smooth water in two deep furrows from her cleaving prow and sent a stream spurting six feet high from the groove of her iron cutwater. The great breadth of her guards gave her the aspect of bulkiness, but beneath them was as clean and symmetrical a model as was ever launched. Notwithstanding her great size, she was drawing only six feet, and her guards stood so high up that we could see clear under them, and observe the strokes of her wheels as they barely dipped their paddles in their rapid revolutions. When immediately opposite Cairo, she tapped her bell to score the thousandth mile in the race, at three days, one hour, and as she did so a gun that had been firing on the Cairo levee in honor of her arrival returned the salute with the loudest and heaviest report. The swift steamer Idlewild, the crack boat of the Lower Ohio River, went alongside of the Lee to obtain passengers, and although the Idlewild was at her greatest speed, the Lee was passing her so rapidly as to render it impossible to make a rope fast to the Idlewild until the Lee stopped her engines.

Our little tug had grappled the outside coal barge and stood with it out in the stream that the monarch might run between it and the next one and take them in tow. Enoch King, the pilot who had come down to meet the Lee at Cairo and take her over the worst part of her race from that point to St. Louis, stood on the gunwale of the larboard barge and waved his handkerchief to direct his charge where to come; the little black tug whistled fiercely by way of letting people know that it was not to be sneezed at, and the great steamer responded to the call of her noisy little friend with the deep hoarse voice of her own whistle.

In a few moments the Lee was between the barges and they were made fast to her sides, the tug snorted a fierce adieu and turned back to Cairo, and the monarch, without having come to a full halt, and without losing more than three minutes in her headway, was steaming up the river. In just twenty-four minutes by the watch the larboard was cleared, and in one minute more the one on the starboard was cleared also, and fifteen hundred bushels of coal had been transferred to the broad guards of the Lee. The cables were unlashed and, with a shout from the bargemen to the noble steamer, the detached flats whirled away from her sides on the deep swells she threw from her bow, and the unclogged vessel shot through the water with her accustomed speed.

The Lee ran under the disadvantage of a broken supply pump from a point thirty miles above New Orleans, and was compelled to keep two men constantly at work to keep the leak from becoming too large to allow a full supply of water to the boilers. The leak in the pipe is so great that bilge pumps are compelled to run to free the hull from water.

She also lost some time on the way by a rivet in the steam drum leaking badly, and was compelled to allow the steam to go down to ninety pounds pressure to repair. The Natchez lost considerable time also with her pump, but I could obtain no definite information of how much.

The race is considered virtually ended, without an accident between here and St. Louis to delay the Lee till the Natchez can overhaul her. But she is not content with simple victory. She has spent much labor and sacrificed much money to prepare for this race, and is determined to set her peg where it will not be pulled up soon. The J. M. White's time remained untouched for twenty-six years. Captain Cannon wants his boat's time to remain untouched to the end of the present century.

ON BOARD THE LEE

When the Lee left Cairo, the smoke of the Natchez could be seen hanging on the horizon in the rear, and apparently about twenty miles away. The Lee lost sight of her antagonist at Vicksburg, . . . but up to 12 o'clock Sunday night she did not, for one hour, lose sight of that pursuing black cloud, which told where our great rival was when she could not be seen. Sometimes it seemed to approach nearer, and then it appeared to recede farther off, but all the time, day and night, it followed like the breath of an avenging fiend on the track of the Lee.

The Sunday sunset on the river was a lovely scene. The sky was perfectly clear, the air bright and pure, the stillness Sabbath-like in its sweetness, and the western horizon, after the sun had dropped below the green fringe of cottonwood that bound the stream, was one glow of rosy splendor; but as twilight came on the air grew chilly. The temperature continued to descend as the night advanced, and when about thirty miles below Grand Tower, the condensed moisture of the atmosphere began to send in ominous drifts just over the surface of the water, and athwart the bow of the boat. King and [Jesse] Jameson, the pilots, grew uneasy, and "the old man," as they called Captain Cannon, didn't half like the prospect. At eleven o'clock there was perceptible fog on the river; at 12 o'clock it had thickened so as to shut the more distant bank of the river out of view, and an hour later it had grown so heavy that a landsman could scarcely see the nearest bank only a hundred yards distant. It seemed certain that the boat would be compelled to halt in the middle of the home-stretch and lay by till morning, with the prospect of not getting under way till the Fourth of July sun had risen high enough to lift the fog. What the Natchez would be doing all this time, no one could tell. She might lay by, too; but she might not, and the bare possibility of having her creep up in the mist and get ahead of the Lee was something unendurable to contemplate. The boat was therefore kept to her work, fog or no fog, and the pilots managed to hold her pretty well in the channel when the fog was so dense that an inexperienced eye could not distinguish a mark on the river. It was slow work, however. Once she struck the shore, and at another time soundings were taken, and the water dwindled from "mark twain" to seven feet. There was a constant jingling of the bells in the engineer's department, accompanied by the stopping of the wheels, backing, and the swinging of the boat towards the adjacent shore. In spite of all this, however, she kept laboring forward, because she wanted not only to beat the Natchez, but to beat the Natchez' time to St. Louis, without which a victory would be indecisive.

[ON BOARD THE NATCHEZ]

. . . *Before the Natchez was fairly above Cairo on the Illinois shore, the helmsman got off his guard and came near getting the Natchez high up on a sandy foundation. This stroke of ill luck threw a damper on every soul on board. There we were again backing towards Orleans to take a fresh start, and a company of darkies on shore laughing and yelling that just ahead there was not water enough to swim a goose. The Natchez was delayed by this backward move several minutes. The same sort of delay occurred also at Dog Tooth Bend, and at Hacker's Bend we struck bottom and took towards New Orleans for about the thirteenth time since leaving for St. Louis. We were now losing several minutes every two or three miles, with a fair prospect of seeing the Lee on her down trip from St. Louis. Our progress was "all-fired" slow, and as regards the race with the Lee it was now virtually ended unless the pilots of the latter vessel should go crazy and jump overboard. . . .*

It was now two hours and forty-four minutes since we left Cairo, and the distance to that place only 22 miles. At length after leaving Hacker's Bend where the ringing of the [engine] bells was so frequent that it really seemed we were engaged in a sleighing excursion instead of a steamboat race, we came along finally until we reached Old Satan's Island. Here we got into a devil of a fix, for the fog gathered so thick around us that it was impossible to tell whether the river was flowing up or down stream except from memory. At twenty-five minutes to one the bank lays claim to us, and the Natchez put out her line and tied to it. Just before five o'clock the fog showed signs of clearing away, and we started out, but soon were forced to the shore again by the low-hanging vapors. . . . At 6:30 it cleared away and all came on without further delay from the fog, having lost five hours and fifty-five minutes altogether.

ON BOARD THE LEE

About half-past one in the morning the fog began to be shattered by a gentle breeze, and in three-quarters of an hour afterwards it had almost entirely disappeared. The boat then resumed her usual rate of speed, and maintained it without further obstruction.

At Carondelet, the iron furnaces turned their whistles loose to salute us, and the inhabitants of the ancient burg congregated on the heights around the town [and] waved green branches at the imperial steamer. Opposite the workhouse, three quarry blasts were fired in honor of the Lee and the Fourth together, which made very loud reports and sent the shattered rocks flying through the air as if from a volcanic eruption.

All this time the Negro deckhands of the victorious steamer, collected round the jackstaff, were chanting their wild, barbaric song of victory, the choir being led by an improvisataire *mounted on the crosstrees, who made up the song as he went along, and his companions repeating the chorus with deep, melodious voices that were heard above all the din on the boat and on shore.*

[St. Louis, July 4, 1870.] *The morning of the Fourth was bright and beautiful, and promised not too hot a day for comfort out of doors, so the people seemed to prepare with one accord for a grand entertainment in the open air. As the day advanced occasional light clouds curtained off the sun and made the prospect inviting, even in the broad exposure of the landing. The river and land excursions usually incident to the national holiday had been entirely forgotten in the culminating interest of a steamboat race. The particular significance of the Fourth of July was lost. The close of the contest between the* Robert E. Lee *and the* Natchez *was the all-absorbing topic and the special business of the day. The results will certainly never be disputed on account of a lack of witnesses.*

The first shout which announced the near approach of the Lee *came from the housetops. It is lustily echoed by the larger audience in the pit of the street and so passed along from block to block till the exciting intelligence is communicated to all. There is restlessness and anxiety on the front seats, and a general movement of expectancy down the levee is instantaneous and irresistible. All eyes are strained to pierce the smoky haze through which the champion of the Southern waters will soon burst in all her glory. The suspense is not of long duration. Great volumes of black smoke which roll away to the east assure the gazers that she is there rapidly breasting the opposing current. Now came the chimneys which, with the expanding smoke above them, look like the funnel of a whirlwind, and now dashes out from the lessening obscurity into full view the steamboat* Robert E. Lee. *A cannon stationed at the foot of Walnut Street booms her a peaceful welcome. As she passes up the landing the shouts roll like billows before her, and the gun continues to greet her with its louder thunder. She herself responds to the latter with a report as she reaches Walnut Street, at 11 o'clock and 25 minutes, and passes on up as far as there are any people to cheer her with their voices. As she goes she draws the multitudes after her. The vehicles and pedestrians swayed by the magnetism of victory, dash along the levee with the vigor of a triumphant charge in battle, and the driving dust they raise and the quality of fireworks and small arms they discharge completes the picture.*

It had been arranged that the Lee *should land at the New Orleans wharfboat and the space in front of it was kept clear, but as the* Lee *shot past it, assembled thousands became perplexed with doubt and dashed up the levee in a vain effort to keep pace with the champion boat. There was in fact a repetition of that wild scamper seen so often on that memorable morning. All along from the Arsenal, when the* Lee *had passed any point, the dense mass of spectators on foot and in all kinds of vehicles rushed madly after the* Lee *as if pursued by demons. The clouds of dust in which they were almost hidden and the clatter of horses' hoofs together with the confused noise of thousands of stentorian voices foretold their approach, and the excitement spread at every block when it was found that the* Lee, *after steaming near to Cherry Street, was swinging round in stream; a backward movement was made, and the throng headed for the wharfboat. The* Lee *touched this at last but before she did so scores leaped on to her decks and, by the time the staging had been pushed from the boat, egress was practically impossible. The crowd boarded her from the bow to the wheelhouse and soon covered every part of the decks. The police made an ineffectual attempt to prevent the people from going up the stairway to the cabin, but gave it up. The excitement was tremendous, and it is a wonder that no one was trampled upon. The boilers and engines chiefly attracted attention and they were never before subjected to* such an inspection. *Every part of the boat except the staterooms was invaded.*

Everyone who had been employed on the boat, from the roustabouts to the captain, felt proud of the achievement which had been attained. Cheers were given for the boat and the captain, and all abandoned themselves to a general rejoicing.

The most forward object on the great steamer was a little white flag a foot square, with the name Lee rudely printed on it, which one of the deckhands had tied to a rod, and stuck in front of her bow. Just above this, was a painted tin mule, with the words, "Shoo fly, don't bother me," on his side. It was a device of the lower deck to express disdain of their antagonist.

[Six hours and twenty-seven minutes later:] *The greeting the* Natchez *received as she neared St. Louis was thankfully acknowledged. The boats lying below the city blew their whistles and rang their bells. Picnic parties and crowds of people, gathered on the hills and balconies of the houses, cheered and waved flags and handkerchiefs to the* Natchez. *The iron furnaces, too, gave the boat a welcome and blew their whistles in rapid succession as she passed along. [A number of steamers] rang their bells rapidly, and the crowds gathered on them shouted joyfully to the steamer that had made the two quickest successive trips between New Orleans and St. Louis ever made, or in all probability would ever be made again in all time to come.*

The great steamboat race which has engrossed the attention of almost the whole South and West for the last three or four days is over, and we place the result before the readers. Whatever may be the merits of the trial of speed between the steamers Robert E. Lee *and* Natchez, *one thing is quite certain: the contest was regarded with unexampled interest by all classes of people throughout a large extent of the Mississippi Valley. There was never an event of like character anywhere in which so many people, covering such a length and breadth of territory, were so completely absorbed. If, therefore, interest be taken as a criterion of merit, the boats above named have done the greatest and best thing that has ever been recorded of a steam vessel, either river or ocean. They have, moreover, both shown how quick a passage can be made between New Orleans and St. Louis in these days when many old portions of the river route have deserted steam-boats for railroads. Such a result may have the effect to call the wanderers back to the bosom of their first love, and thus encourage the builders of more first-class river steamers, especially for the accommodation of travelers.*[8]

1   Grandfort, pp. 79-81.

2   "Stopping to 'Wood,'" *Weekly Reveille* 2, no. 10 (15 September 1845): 493.

3   Thorpe, "Remembrances of the Mississippi," pp. 40-41.

4   The times are derived from tables in Twain, *Life on the Mississippi,* pp. 150-51; see also entries under the various boat names in Way.

5   "The Boat Race: Steam Duel on the River," *Daily Missouri Republican,* 6 July 1870.

6   Quoted in Way, pp. 395-96.

7   Letter to the editor of the Cincinnati *Commercial,* 2 July 1870, quoted in the *Daily Missouri Republican,* 6 July 1870.

8   This account is a shortened and rearranged compilation of the following series of articles that appeared in the *Daily Missouri Republican:* "Pine Knot! *Natchez* vs. *R. E. Lee,*" 1 July 1870; "The Great Race: Unexampled Speed," 2 July 1870; "The Great Race: *Lee* Runs at Last!" 3 July 1870; "The Great Race: *Lee* Still Gaining," 4 July 1870; "The Boat Race: Steam Duel on the River," 6 July 1870. Pages in the *Republican* are not numbered.

The River Claims Its Victims

The *New Orleans*, first of the Mississippi steamboats, caught fire on its maiden trip in 1811. The cabin was ruined. Only luck and quick action by the crew kept the fire from consuming the entire vessel. Three years later the *New Orleans* hit a stump and sank. Her successor, the *Vesuvius*, burned and sank in 1816. Prior to that *Vesuvius* had spent much of her brief career stranded on a sandbar. Also in 1816 the boilers on Henry Shreve's otherwise successful steamer, the *Washington*, burst without warning and killed ten of her passengers and crew. The first three river steamers thus established an unenviable tradition of danger, a tradition that was reinforced time and again throughout the nineteenth century.

Running Aground

Over the years steamboat accidents fell into specific, even predictable, categories. First and most frequent were the groundings. Most instances of running aground were minor, unless the bottom was uneven and the boat hard aground—the combination might cause the hull to sag and break in two. Next in frequency were collisions with submerged objects. Snags, rocks, and even sunken wrecks claimed dozens of boats each year; as long as hulls were made of wood they would be susceptible to punctures. Then, there was fire. Steamboat superstructures were built of light pine and covered with linseed oil-based paint; with fires in the boilers, stoves, and lamps, it took only a careless moment or a hard jolt to set off a raging conflagration.* Boiler explosions were only slightly farther down on the list of potential disasters. Crude and imprecise methods of determining boiler water level and steam pressure resulted in many ghastly "burst ups," as the papers sometimes termed them. Explosions caused the highest number of fatalities, and often touched off fires on the disabled wrecks. Additional hazards to steamboats included collisions with other vessels and with bridge piers, and destruction from the ravages of windstorms.

We will ease into the harrowing realm of steamboat accidents with the following short reminiscence of an inexperienced passenger. It is not the account of a serious event, yet there is enough in it to see how panic might have broken out if something dreadful had developed. It comes from 1844:

> It was a foggy, wretched night. Our bell was kept tolling to warn other boats of our whereabouts or to entreat direction to a landing by a fire on the shore. Suddenly a most tremendous concussion, as if all-powerful Nature had shut his hand upon us, and crushed us all to atoms, upset our cards and calculations, and a general rush was made, over chairs and tables, towards the doors. The cabin was entirely cleared or, rather, all the passengers were huddled together at the entrances, with the exception of one of the poker players, quietly shuffling and cutting the poker deck for his own amusement. In less time than I am telling it, the swarm came laughing back, with broken sentences of what they thought had happened, in which snags, sawyers, bolts blown out, and boilers burst were most conspicuous. But all the harm the fracas caused was fright; the boat, in rounding to a woodpile, had run on the point of an island, and was high and dry among the first year's growth of cottonwood.[1]

A shallow place in the river easily could claim more than one boat. Indeed, the passengers of a stranded vessel found devilish delight in watching other

---

* The tall chimneys so prominent on steamboats served a dual purpose. Besides increasing the furnace draft, they were meant also to carry off the smoldering embers rising from the firebox. Hurricane decks often were sanded as an additional fire-retardant precaution.

boats fall prey to the same predicament. The danger here was not so much to the hull of the boat as it was to the good temperament and future plans of the passengers. A travel account from 1845 tells a typical story:

> *"Yes, gentlemen, off this evening, positively, the water's falling above, and I'm* bound *to go!"*
>
> *This is the* hourly *reply for something less than a week, which the gathering passengers receive on the lighter class of Ohio riverboats, during the fall, or low water season. The channel is daily lessening, the draft is daily deepening till, at length, the steam hive swarms alive to thrice its capacity, at trebled prices. The "Cap'n" rings the last bell, actually, and starts, say—for St. Louis, the mouth, or, in other words,* as far as he can get, *and that generally means Flint Island, of shoal celebrity.*
>
> *One day [out], and no stick! Matters begin to assume a shape, and the prospect is mighty fair for a trip. The gentlemen have got the hang of the ladies—that is, they have ascertained their precise number and calculated how many chairs it is necessary to leave vacant at meals, thus avoiding the mortification of having to get up again; the blacklegs are recognized by a sort of mesmeric sympathy, or repulsion, as the case may be; the "judges" and "colonels" discuss politics on the boiler deck, and the junior generation the varied mixtures of the bar. Things look "mighty fair for a trip," and, with the word, there comes a* bang! *[followed immediately by] a universal shudder of the timbers, a ringing of the engineers' bells, a rush out to the guards or boiler deck, and a let-off of steam that would seem to rend the iron throat of the monster! She has only struck a log; a few licks back sets her free again; all return to their busy idling, and the mighty fair chance is as good as ever.*
>
> *Thumps and bumps succeed each other rapidly during the next day, merely exciting the remark, "Oh, it's only a log!" The partial delays are uncomplained of; a six hours lay-up, during the night, on account of fog, is uninquired about when, during dinner, the forward end of the table gracefully elevates itself, the sitters oscillate for a moment in their chairs, there comes the same ringing of bells and let-off of steam, and the boat is "fast on a bar!"*

Under a full head of steam, the engine works as if demon driven; the [steam] escape pipe roars with fury; the momentary let-off, to prevent bursting, is a sudden abrupt shriek of iron agony, whilst every joint of the racked craft shivers as if the destruction of her frame must follow! This first effort in vain, the nervous are further alarmed by the plunging into the water of some dozen deckhands, who, instead of disappearing under the surface, however, immediately begin wading about, knee deep, hunting for the channel, and sticking their hands under the bottom of the boat to see "how far she's on." Another tremendous effort follows; another and another; at length night falls, and, perhaps, . . . the morning fog brings its further detention. By the aid of enormous spars and the windlass, the boat, as upon crutches, is lifted across into deep water.

By the aid of enormous spars and the windlass, the boat, as upon crutches, is lifted across into deep water.

Onward once more, and hope is strong again. Another day and night of rubbing, bumping, backing, and fog. But one more bad place remains—Flint Island bar. "Only one! Well, then, we'll be all right!" exclaim the greenhorns; the experienced, however, calculate the probable chances of a "rise out of the Wabash," the exact draft of the boat, and remember the depth of water on the last bar rubbed against. Thus it goes until the critical spot is neared, [when we] sweep around the bend and—startling intimation—a dozen boats are beheld "stuck fast," and in exceedingly picturesque groups, choking up the river.

One stroke of the bell: "Starboard lead."*

The boiler deck is thronged, the wheels revolve with caution. "Three feet large" lessens into "two feet scant," the stranded boats are neared, each one presenting its swarm of imprisoned victims waiting for—in fact, wishing for—the moment when another swarm shall be involved in their dilemma.

"The pilot is sure of the channel?" hesitatingly inquire some anxious voices. To be sure he's sure of it, he is at this moment scanning it, and two full-sized boats, also, which lie directly across it! Yet he

* The "lead" was the lead-weighted rope thrown out on either side of the bow to measure the depth of the water.

goes on "a-screwin' of her up," as the Yankee said. He stops her, goes ahead—starboard lead, larboard lead—he is drawing but twenty inches and may get over the edge of the bar. The excitement becomes intense. Among the myriad watchers—twenty yards more—she touches—"rush her over!" The engine works like mad, but—she sticks! The weight of the current swings her quarter around, and bang she goes, her bow fixed, and her stern riveted into the wheel-house of her obstructor!

"Oh!"

"That makes it bad!"

"Too damn bad!"

A thousand groans are heard on board, while a general laugh from the myriad neighbors is the welcome to a week's acquaintance! Now comes a rush of visitors! Friends, who had parted a thousand miles away, here unite again! The other bars, too, are exhausted, and the newly arrived is a godsend in the way of ice and liquors! Mad spirits, reckless laughter, a hundred schemes of frolic and depredation upon the adjacent shores are concocted and, in the general whirl, we shall leave the crowd—too glad to escape the weary, stale, flat, and unprofitable term which must elapse before the smallest possible boat, charging the highest possible price, takes the tallest possible number to the sweetest possible place—Cairo—for further transport![2]

Hitting Snags

Year in and year out, scarcely a week went by without a boat somewhere on the river system hitting a snag. The stricken boats did not always sink; bilge pumps and hemp packing kept many of them afloat until they could go in for repairs. When they did sink, passengers and crew needed only to ascend to the roof as the boat settled; the water seldom rose above the cabin. But there was always then the danger of a break-up. It happened aboard the *James Watson*, descending the Mississippi River on the stormy night of March 2, 1865. The *Watson* carried both civilians and Union soldiers bound for New Orleans; among the latter was Private John F. M. Fortney, of an Illinois regiment. Fortney and his compatriots were asleep in the main cabin of the boat when she struck a snag. We take up Fortney's eyewitness account of the subsequent events:

. . . Crash *went the steamer against some object which shook her from stem to stern, and which brought everyone in my presence to their feet. Perfect silence ensued for about a minute. After that time some began to lay down and some to dress themselves. Immediately upon hearing the noise made by the vessel, I jumped up and hastily pulled on my boots, and seizing my hat and coat I at once started to go below, to find out the cause of the crashing noise we had heard. I had just got to the cabin door, when I felt the boat settling down upon her right side. The captain at the same time rushed frantically past me exclaiming, "My God boys, we are lost. The boat is sinking!" He then rushed up to the hurricane deck. I followed him.*

When I got up the boat had sunk her main deck entirely, and one half of her boiler deck was also completely submerged. By the time the boys below had got up, the boat had turned upon her side, so much that the water upon the side of the hurricane deck on which I was standing, was up to my knees and fast rising. I knew that I would soon be lost if I maintained my position here, but how to get upon the other side was the question. I saw many boys attempt to climb on the texas (a row of staterooms upon the hurricane deck), and saw them fail to get up. But I concluded to make the effort, and watched my chance to make the jump which would either take me out of the water, or which would plunge me into the river, perhaps into eternity. A flash of lightning revealed to me an open space upon the texas, and I made a desperate leap, and succeeded in catching hold of the cornice around its outer edge.

Fifteen minutes had not elapsed since the snagging of the boat and the time I got upon the texas, but in that time two-thirds of the boat was under water, and the remaining third, containing all who had escaped immediate death, fast sinking into the depths of the murky Mississippi. I will not attempt to describe to you my feelings at this time. You must endeavor to imagine them. I had no hopes of being saved, had made my mind to drown, and with the brief ejaculation, "God, have mercy upon my soul," I seated myself upon the narrow deck of the texas and complacently awaited the fast approaching fate of the doomed Watson. *From this time forward I was per-*

fectly composed, completely self-possessed, and preserved throughout complete presence of mind.

I suppose I had been upon the deck of the texas perhaps ten minutes when I heard another crashing sound which almost froze the blood in our veins. The smokestacks had given way, and were fast falling into the water, threatening to tear away the delicately constructed deck upon which I was seated. I made haste to abandon my seat, and concluded to jump down upon the upper side of the hurricane deck. I did so, and so did nearly one-half who were up there. We had not been down over five minutes till the smokestacks went overboard, and down came the texas and pilothouse, a heap of broken rubbish. How many were precipitated into the river I am unable to say, and how many were then drowned we will never know. After the breaking away of the cumbrous smokestacks and the falling down of the pilothouse, the steamer righted herself so much that the right side of the hurricane deck was entirely out of the water. This circumstance revealed the fact to all who were not scared out of their wits, and who were noticing such things, that the boat was not sinking any farther, but that she was slowly drifting in the current. This gave me the only hope I had yet entertained of our ultimate deliverance. I knew that if she kept in the deep waters of the main channel, that we could probably hold on till morning when some passing steamer would rescue us.

While indulging in the pleasures of hope, listening to the piteous groans of the men, and the more piteous cries of the ladies, I quietly occupied a recumbent position near the stern of the hurricane deck. As I told you before, this entire deck was now for the first time above water, but I could reach over the side and feel the water with my hand. I was aroused at length from my reveries by a loud and prolonged shout from the men, who seemed to be determined to drown the reverberating echoes of the terrible thunder. I got up and, looking ahead of the boat, I espied a light, and readily attributed the joyous outburst to this hope-inspiring object. It was impossible to tell how far distant the light was whose faint glimmerings were scarcely visible through the torrents of rain, descending upon our devoted heads. But we knew it proceeded from a steamer. And now if you could only have heard the one prolonged—I might say continual—shout from the mouths of these hopeful men, you would have thought that all animated nature were together in one assembled group, shouting, yelling, whooping, and crying, all at the same time. In vain the captain importuned, commanded them to be silent. In vain he told them that such discordant shouting and yelling would avail them not. But they continued to halloo at the top of their voices, some one thing and some another, and thus they hallooed till our boat drifted opposite the light, which proved indeed to proceed from a steamer at anchor, at a short distance from us.

> ∞
>
> *Here I again*
> *gave up to drown.*
>
> ∞

No recognition of our signal, if signal it may be called, was seen or heard. The result was just as the captain had foretold. We were conceived to be guerrillas, on the Arkansas shore, and no attention was paid to our uproarious shouts. We soon passed the light, and as its faint twinklings receded in the distant past, hope again went out in the hearts of many.

I had again laid down, and this time I found that the water was again upon the hurricane deck. I was endeavoring to find a cause for this, other than a sinking condition, when her bow struck something which shook her almost to pieces. I looked across her right side and could see the timber on the Arkansas shore. All on the wreck were now in a dreadful tumult, rushing first to her bow, then to her stern, first upon one side, then upon the other, some jumping overboard and saving themselves by swimming ashore, others perhaps to sink into a watery grave.

Here I again gave up to drown. I knew that she could not stand together as she was but . . . would go to pieces and the most of us inevitably drown. But I saw that her stern was swinging around, and I had hopes that she would again float off without receiving further injury.

This she did. Just as her stern had swung around so as to bring her sides at right angles with the course of the river, she let go her hold and again we were adrift upon the rapidly rolling waters of the Mississippi. Her striking caused a momentary lull in the cries and prayers of the men, but no sooner had she resumed her downward progress than had the men resumed their upward flight. All again was a tumultuous, heart-rending, and head-distracting noise. I suppose we had proceeded in this way for an hour perhaps, when again the joyful exclamation of, "A light! A boat!" was heard from the lips of the entire crowd. And such unearthly hallooing as immediately ensued, was never heard by me before; one shout after another might have been heard for at least an hour. Still no answer was given from the vessel which was now nearly opposite. Indeed no sound could have been heard by any of us, so deafening was the tumult around us. The captain again tried to still the men, but they would listen to no arguments, no appeals, no commands nor threats. We drifted by again, and gradually the light began to fade from our sight, when the boat struck once more and seemed as if she was being lifted out of the waters. She rocked from one side to the other, and threatened momentarily to go to pieces. I was upon her stern, the waters were rolling over her decks sweeping all the loose timbers away.

Now I was sure my time had come. I caught a cabin door that was floating by me, pulled off my boots and coat, threw my hat into the river, and resolved when the worst came to the worst, to make a desperate effort to make the shore, which was not more than 200 yards off. I held on to my coat and boots up to this time, but a sudden plunge of the boat threw me flat upon my back into the water. I saw my coat and boots float away but I could not save them. I held to my door however, and soon got up to find the deck high and dry. I walked to the bow, and looking over I saw that she was raised at least ten feet out of the water. The captain announced that the boat was fast upon a sandbar, and that the probability was we would all be saved if we would keep our places till morning, but that any swimming around would be likely to careen the boat upon one side or the other, and in this case he could not see how escape could be possible. After some silence had been secured, he also told us that the light of the boat we had just passed was still within hailing distance, if they would all keep perfectly still and allow but one man to halloo at a time we might succeed in making known our condition to them. This was agreed to, a man elected to give the signal who hallooed till he could halloo no longer, then another relieved him, and so on, till at least a dozen *men with stentorian voices had been worn out. Still no answer had been elicited.*

Fortunately some fellow found the bell which everyone supposed had gone overboard. When its deep ringing tones went out upon the dark expanse of muddy waters, 'twas accompanied with such a tremendous shout of heartfelt joy as was seldom heard by mortal ears before. The captain directed it to be struck five consecutive strokes, then an interval of a minute, then five more, and so on, till a reply was heard. Oh, how eagerly was every ear adjusted to catch the answering signal. How awfully still and silent were the men during the interval between the ringing of the bell. At last the eagerly expected signal was heard, as it floated musically upon the boisterous waters what hopes were excited within the bosoms that had long been filled with despair.

Soon a yawl was sent to ascertain our condition. When within speaking distance they hailed us, we made known our condition, they pulled up to us, left one of their men on board with us, while they returned to hurry up preparations for our rescue.[3]

In 1845, manufacturers and businessmen from the South and West gathered in Memphis to discuss ways of improving their regional economy. Many of those attending felt that steamboat commerce could stand to gain from a concerted effort to rid the river of snags. The lesson was driven home even as some of the delegates traveled to the convention: one boat containing a delegate and his family hit a snag and sank. There were some 800 steamboats operating on the Western Rivers in 1845, but only two or three government snagboats. And these snagboats operated without the benefit of assigned districts or central dispatching. Little wonder, remarked a Memphis delegate, that in one year, 1839, forty boats were sunk by snags.[4]

The newspapers of the day treated snag sinkings in prosaic style; they were far too common to sensationalize. An example comes from the St. Louis *Weekly Reveille* of 1846:

STEAMERS SUNK. By the steamer Mendota, *in yesterday evening from Cairo, we learn that the steamer* Wiota, *from this port for New Orleans, struck a snag near Neelys' Landing, about 11 o'clock on the morning of the 24th instant, and sunk almost immediately, in from nine to ten feet [of] water. The greater portion of the machinery and furniture will probably be saved, but the boat and cargo will be a total loss. The* Wiota *was a new boat, and made her first trip late in the past season; we understand she was fully insured.*

By the Mendota *we likewise learn that the steamer* Nebraska *is sunk, about twenty miles below Vicksburg, and will prove a total loss. Her machinery and furniture had been saved and sent to Vicksburg. She was from this port to New Orleans, being on her first trip, having arrived here from Pittsburgh, where she was built, just before the recent suspension of navigation.*[5]

During prolonged seasons of low water the number of sinkings rose like an epidemic and the papers devoted entire columns to a single recurring theme. From the *Missouri Republican,* December 5, 1842:

ANOTHER BOAT SUNK. The steamboat Boston, *from Cincinnati for this port, with a valuable cargo, struck a snag in the Mississippi, a short distance above the mouth of the Ohio, by which a hole was knocked into her bow forward of the bulkhead. This they succeeded in stopping. She again struck upon the Grand Chain, but not to seriously injure it. At the foot of Devil's Island, three miles above Cape Girardeau, on Thursday last, about eleven o'clock, she struck another snag which entered the breach formerly made and passed through her after bulwarks. She hung upon this snag and sank immediately in water from twenty to twenty-five feet deep. As soon as she began to sink, the passengers gathered with their baggage on the hurricane deck. As she filled, she careened over, by which a number of the trunks were thrown overboard and lost. With the exception of the trunks lost in this way, the passengers saved their baggage. The boat's papers were also saved. No lives were lost. The boat and cargo is considered a total loss. She lies with her bow sunk, her stern resting on the snag out of the water. Her upper works, which were out of the water, have been cleared away in the attempt to get at her furniture, etc.*

STILL ANOTHER STEAMBOAT SUNK. The steamer Juniata, *from Nashville, . . . reports the* Iris *sunk at Eddyville [Kentucky], on* the Cumberland. She had on board 100 bales of cotton for the Covington, Kentucky, factory. She was taking out her engine when the Juniata passed. Of course, the hull is a total loss. We presume the cotton was saved, probably in a damaged state.

YET ANOTHER STEAMBOAT SUNK. The Patrick Henry, bound upward with a cargo of sugar, etc., struck a snag on the morning of the 24th ultimo, six miles above Memphis, and sunk to her guards. She was run into shoal water and it is expected she will be raised, but her cargo will be lost, very much injured. We believe she was freighted for the Ohio.

AGAIN ANOTHER STEAMBOAT ACCIDENT. We are told that the Tioga, on her passage down, struck a snag and knocked a hole in her hull. When met, she had all her pumps going, by which means she was able to go on.

ANOTHER BOAT SNAGGED. The Fame, six miles below Cape Girardeau, struck a rock and knocked a hole in her. The crew, keeping the pumps going, were able to keep her up. She returned to the Cape and landed her passengers and cargo, and left for the Ohio to repair.[6]

Fires

Even had it been possible to remove every snag and deepen each shoal, steamboating still would have been a dangerous venture. The boats themselves posed as many hazards as the rivers, and when something went wrong with a boat the lives of the passengers were immediately at risk.

During 1842, the steamer *General Pratte* plied the Mississippi between St. Louis and New Orleans. There was nothing distinctive about the *Pratte;* she was just one of many packets in the trade. She was based in St. Louis and every few weeks she announced for departure in the Gateway City's papers:

FOR NEW ORLEANS. The splendid passenger steamer Gen. Pratte, T. J. Casey, master, will leave for the above and intermediate landings, this day, the 2d instant, at 10 o'clock A.M., positively.[7]

And that was all—routine business, with no hint of trouble on the horizon. But in November, as the *Pratte* worked her way up the Mississippi, fate asserted itself into the lives of her passengers and crew. The story unraveled slowly in the newspaper, beginning with the unexpected arrival in St. Louis of the boat's clerk:

> *Mr. Papin, clerk of the* Gen. Pratte, *arrived here this morning; from him we learn the following painful particulars:*
>
> *On Thursday morning, the 24th ultimo, about 2 o'clock, when about 12 miles above Memphis, the steamboat* Gen. Pratte *was discovered to be on fire, between the wheelhouse and privy. The fire originated from the [chimney] sparks. The wind was blowing very strong at the time. Captain Casey, clerk, mate, and carpenter, were all up at the time. An effort was made to extinguish it by water from buckets, but it soon became apparent that this was impossible.*
>
> *The captain then ordered her to be run ashore, and the passengers to be awakened. So rapidly did the flames spread, that there was hardly time to arouse the passengers before she was a complete sheet of flames. Fortunately, the pilot and engineer retained their presence of mind, and stuck to their posts. One wheel was unshipped, and she was run on to the foot of Beef Island. It so happened that she had a long flat in tow at the time, which lay in between the boat and the shore, and to this is ascribed the preservation of the lives of the passengers.*
>
> *The* Pratte *had on board about twenty cabin and about five hundred deck passengers. It was with great difficulty that numbers of them, especially the children, were aroused in time to save them, and it is believed that if the captain and his officers had not exerted themselves at the risk of their own lives, many of them would have perished. As it was, every one on board, it was believed, is saved. A few of the passengers got out their trunks and a little baggage, but by far the greater number saved nothing at all.*
>
> *The deck passengers were all German emigrants, who came over*

> ⌒
>
> *It was with great difficulty that numbers of them, especially the children, were aroused in time to save them, and it is believed that if the captain and his officers had not exerted themselves at the risk of their own lives, many of them would have perished.*
>
> ⌒

in the ships Indiana, Columbus, *and a vessel whose name is not remembered. The weather was extremely cold.*

There was on board about 175 tons of freight, consisting of dry goods and groceries, for this port, all of which was lost. The books, papers, and money of the boat, and the letters on board, were lost; consequently, there is no means of arriving at the owners of the goods.

The captain and some of the passengers returned to Memphis—a portion of the passengers came up on the Walnut Hills *to the mouth of the Ohio—the residue were on the island when the clerk left.*

The destitute condition of most of the emigrants appeals loudly for sympathy and some immediate relief. Several families have not even clothing suitable for the season.

It is due to the pilot, Samuel Donnel, and to the engineer, Oliver Fairchild, that their steady, composed, and heroic conduct should be remembered. Both, though surrounded by the flames and in imminent danger all the time, remained firm and unwavering, and to them is due the credit of having brought the boat safely into shore. When they had fully discharged the responsibilities of their respective places, and not until then, did they leave the wreck.

Captain Casey several times rushed through the flames to rescue children who had been overlooked. He saved two young ladies who were asleep, after the boat had been abandoned by the passengers.

The entire hull of the boat was burnt out. She broke in two and sunk in about fifteen feet [of] water.

The boat was owned by P. Chouteau, Jr., & Co., Berthold, Tesson & Co., Chas. Mulliken, Pratte & Cabanne, and Captain Casey. The two first insured, the others not.[8]

Two days later, more information came to light:

EMIGRANTS ON THE GEN. PRATTE. We learn that the Meteor *brought up, from Memphis to Cairo, about sixty of the passengers of the* Gen. Pratte. *They are represented as in a very destitute and even suffering condition—being without much clothing and destitute of means to purchase provisions. Captain Dunnica, of the* Meteor, *at his own expense, had procured them a house at Cairo, and*

had purchased them a beef and some corn, &c. A small sum has also
been raised for them on board of some of the Ohio [River] boats.
The Meteor was hailed by those on Beef Island, but from her crowded
condition, she was unable to take any of them on board. There was
an Ohio boat behind the Meteor, which probably brought them into
Cairo.[9]

For their heroic conduct during the burning of the *Pratte,* Captain Casey,
Pilot Donnel, and Engineer Fairchild were awarded gold medals by the
St. Louis Insurance Company. It would have been fitting, indeed, had they
thought also to cite Captain Dunnica of the *Meteor* for his humanitarian
assistance.[10]

Boiler Explosions

As devastating and frightening as a steamboat fire may have been, there
was yet a more dreaded catastrophe—boiler explosion. Most boats were
powered by two to eight boilers; and those boilers typically measured
twenty-four feet in length, with diameters of thirty-six inches. Some were
considerably larger. They operated at steam pressures in excess of 100
pounds per square inch. Metallurgical testing was virtually unheard of; a
boat engineer's common sense carried more weight. But what the engineer did not know, or did not concern himself with, could prove fatal.
Cast iron boiler heads, cracked rivet holes, encrustation, clogging, defor-
mation, superheating—anything could go wrong in the blink of an eye.
And when a component failed, there was no warning—only concussion,
scalding water, and searing steam.

The public was neither unaware nor indifferent to the tragedy of boiler
explosions. Those familiar with steam machinery aired their opinions in
public forums of the day. An editorial writer in 1845 pointed out that the
current trend of rolling boiler iron to one-quarter- or five-sixteenths-inch
thickness was not sufficient—one-half- or five-eighths-inch would be better—and that blowers could be used "to overcome the increased difficulty
of generating steam in thick boilers." The same writer suggested that boilers undergo a static test of at least twice their ordinary steam pressure. He
opined that a boat thus tested "would be sought and waited for by passengers."[11] Perhaps; but the typical steamboat owner or captain was not

convinced. And he had powerful allies. A journal devoted to the mechanical applications of the day, *The Manufacturer and Builder,* dismissed static boiler testing as pointless. A boiler, it stated, might pass a high-pressure static test at cooler temperatures, yet explode at a lesser pressure when heated in actual service.

The Manufacturer and Builder asserted that boiler explosions resulted from a well-known scenario—one that was avoidable if the engineer remained alert:

> *The only reasonable theory which accounts for sudden increase in pressure is the low water theory, and this has been agreed to by theoretical as well as practical men. When certain parts of the boiler exposed to fire have no water touching it on the inside, they may become red hot; and when water is suddenly thrown on this red hot surface, it may so quickly flash into steam as to cause an excess of pressure over the amount the boiler is calculated to resist. This sudden contact of water with such a red hot surface may be produced either by injecting water, or by starting the engine when standing still, or by opening the safety valve. . . .*[12]

At the heart of the matter was money. Thicker boiler iron, blowers, and static tests were expensive fixes. Steamboating was a business—a cutthroat business; if any changes were to be made they had to be changes that would reduce the operating costs, not increase them. Even captains who had survived previous explosions were remarkably unconcerned about their chances of encountering another such disaster. The river was no place for the faint of heart.

The Pennsylvania *Tragedy*

The explosion of the *Pennsylvania* in 1858, one of three such disasters that year, probably resulted from hidden flaws in the boiler. The incident took the life of Henry Clemens, the younger brother of Sam Clemens. A few days before the disaster Sam and Henry had passed a pleasant evening engaged in conversation at the New Orleans levee. Motivated by an unrecognized premonition, the brothers had talked about steamboat disasters. "We decided that if a disaster ever fell within our experience we would at least stick to the boat, and give such minor service as chance might throw

Passenger ticket for the steamer *James Robb,* circa 1853. The fine print informs passengers that she is equipped with all the latest boiler safety devices, and that the doors and blinds "can be unhooked instantly, and used as floats in case of accident." She also features "Bathing Rooms for Ladies and Gentlemen." (Courtesy Battle of Lexington State Historic Site—Missouri.)

in the way," wrote the elder Clemens.[8] Writing as Mark Twain some fifteen years later, he devoted a chapter of his book *Life on the Mississippi* to the circumstances of his brother's death. But Sam did not witness the tragedy. Word of it came to him in fragments as his boat, the *Alfred T. Lacy,* followed two days behind the *Pennsylvania.* The selection that follows, a newspaper article, tells more fully the story of the *Pennsylvania*'s destruction and the plight of her passengers:

> *Memphis, June 14 [1858]*
>
> The Railroad Steam Packet Pennsylvania *exploded her boiler Sunday morning at six o'clock, at Ship Island, seventy miles below Memphis, and burned to the water's edge.*
>
> *There were about 350 passengers on board, and it is believed that a hundred of them are killed and missing. The steamers* Diana, Imperial, *and* Frisbee *picked up all they could find in the water and took them ashore.*
>
> The Pennsylvania *was on her way from New Orleans to St. Louis, and was owned by Captain [John] Klinefelter, George Black & Co., and the two engineers. The boat and cargo are a total loss.*

STATEMENT OF MR. W. G. MEPHAM.

The steamer Pennsylvania *left New Orleans on the* 9th *instant with one hundred and twenty-five cabin passengers and one hundred and fifty-eight deckers. She afterwards took on board, at Baton Rouge, Natchez, and Vicksburg, 62 passengers and at Napoleon, ten. There were 40 deckhands and firemen; 24 of the steward's crew, and 16 officers—making in all 450 souls.*

Out of this number, 182 were rescued by a wood-boat, and about 70 others escaped in various ways. These numbers include the wounded and scalded. About 200 are lost and missing.

At about 6 o'clock on the morning of the 13th instant, when the boat was about 70 miles below Memphis, she exploded four of her boilers, while under way. At the time of the explosion, she was near 300 yards from shore. The cabin was torn to pieces forward of her wheelhouses. Very few of the passengers were out of their staterooms at the time. The passengers in the after part of the cabin—men, women, and children—rushed out, and the utmost confusion ensued them, all supposing the boat was on fire, from the smoke and steam which came rushing through the cabin. After close examination it was ascertained that the boat was not on fire, and the excitement was in some degree quelled. After the explosion the boat commenced drifting down with the current, and an anchor was thrown overboard for the purpose of checking the boat, for at that time we were of the opinion that we could prevent the boat from taking fire. But the water being so deep and the current so swift, the anchor dragged and the boat continued to drift down. As quickly as possible Captain Klinefelter and two or three of his men made an attempt to carry a line ashore by the yawl, but from the line being too short, or some other cause, they did not succeed. Without losing a moment's time the captain ordered the yawl turned downstream to a Mr. Harris' woodyard, for the purpose of bringing an empty wood-boat, which was lying there, to the rescue. This boat was not supplied with oars, and it was an exceedingly difficult matter to accomplish this purpose, but by dint of skill and hard labor the captain succeeded in getting it alongside.

In from three to five minutes from the time the wood-boat touched the steamer it was discovered that the Pennsylvania *was on fire.*

The fire appeared to issue from about the after end of the boilers, and in one minute from the time of the alarm, the boat was wrapped in flames. Passengers and crew immediately rushed from the burning boat upon the wood-boat, and filled it as full as they could stand. Captain Klinefelter was the last man that jumped from the steamer to the wood-boat, as it was being pushed off, with its living freight, from the burning boat.

The most intense excitement prevailed on board the wood-boat, as we endeavored to propel it from the burning mass—as we had only a few boards, in place of oars, and the crowd rendered it almost impossible to work them with success. But we finally succeeded in getting her bow turned out, so that the current struck her stern and swung the wood-boat around, and by that means we cleared the burning boat, and she drifted by, but not until many of the passengers were severely scorched. By turning our backs, and with the aid of a few counterpanes and quilts which were saved, we screened ourselves from the heat, as much as possible, and finally succeeded, after drifting one mile, in reaching an island or tow-head, called Ship Island, where the wood-boat was made fast to some trees.

After shoving the wood-boat from the steamer there were a good many deck passengers seen rushing out with their trunks, boxes, &c., in the hope of saving their little stock of plunder, and by trying to save their effects, they lost their lives, for it was impossible for us to render them any assistance. I remember seeing one man and woman, who, from their appearance, were German emigrants, hanging to a line from the stern of the boat—the man holding the line with one hand and his chest with the other, and as the boat swing around they disappeared from view. They, doubtless, remained in this position until they were compelled, by the heat of the flames, to loose their hold, and drown. The cabin passengers, with the exception of one or two, behaved with great coolness and decision, and rendered one another every assistance in their power, but among the deck passengers the greatest excitement prevailed. It seemed that all they cared for was to save their plunder, throwing it over the guards into the wood-boat not heeding where it fell. A number of the passengers in the wood-boat were bruised and injured by the falling of the trunks and boxes into the boat. From this disposition to save baggage, many of the deckers were lost, who would otherwise have saved their lives.

About twenty-five of the wounded escaped on the wood-boat, amongst them were the first mate, second engineer, two Frenchmen late of the Theatre d'Orleans, *Colonel Harris of Arkansas, badly scalded, and others very badly cut and bruised*—mostly deck passengers. They suffered very much in consequence of there being no medical attendance to dress their wounds, and no means of procuring any for the space of two hours. But at length neighboring planters, from the Arkansas shore, brought some linseed oil and liniment which, with the aid of cotton taken from the quilts, gave some relief to the wounded. The scalded victims suffered much from the heat of the sun, as the whole country was overflowed, and we could not succeed in getting the boat to the main land, and in this condition we were obliged to remain under a broiling sun for fully eight hours. The women and children who were unhurt also suffered excessively from the heat of the sun and hunger. After remaining on the island eight hours the steamer Imperial, bound down, came to our relief, and after giving us a good dinner, put us on board of the Kate Frisbee and Diana, bound up. Too much praise cannot be given to the officers of these boats for the kindness they extended to us.

The Diana being crowded with passengers, very few of us came on her, the greater portion of our company going on the Frisbee, which the Diana left behind. It was the intention of the captain of the Frisbee when we left, to try and save all he could, and pick up scattering passengers along the shore. The Diana brought up fifteen of the wounded to Memphis to be taken to the hospital. The passengers on the Diana raised a subscription of between two and three hundred dollars towards defraying the expenses of the sufferers in Memphis. They also made up several purses for destitute women who were aboard. Altogether, they acted very magnanimously in the way of supplying the women and children, who were scantily dressed with garments.

Mrs. Witt of St. Louis, who was lost, occupied with her daughter, Mrs. Fulton, room number 8, in the gentlemen's cabin. Mrs. Witt was taken from the ruins just as the fire broke out, perfectly blind, and in a dying condition; by that time the wood-boat had left the steamer, and a young man, who was endeavoring to rescue her, was compelled to jump overboard, and swim to the wood-boat to save his life.* Mrs. Fulton was not seen after the explosion. There was a man buried in the wreck who, from his expressions, must have been either a sugar or cotton planter—as in his despair he said he had money, Negroes, a plantation, and would give all to save his life. He was covered deeply in the ruins and the fire coming on so rapidly it was impossible to rescue him.

A gentleman passenger had gone to the boiler deck just before the explosion, and the next thing he recollected was being precipitated to the main deck amongst fragments of the boat, and pinioned to the deck by the boat's bell, which in falling, caught him around the neck, which, together with other fragments, rendered it impossible for him to move. By the timely aid of the passengers he was rescued from his perilous position and escaped without much damage.

At the time of the explosion, Captain Klinefelter was in the barbershop being shaved, and at the explosion the barber says the captain exclaimed, "Oh, my God! What is that?" He hurried out through the back door and climbed upon the hurricane roof, as all the forward part of the boat was blown to pieces. Too much credit cannot be awarded to Captain Klinefelter for his daring and gallant conduct in endeavoring to save both life and property.

Nearly all the deckhands were either killed or missing—first and second mates so badly injured as to render them helpless. First clerk, Mr. Black, and Mr. Brown, pilot, both missing, the captain had to assume the whole charge of the boat, under the trying circumstances. Of the firemen on watch at the time of the explosion, only one was saved, and he stated to me that they had just hauled the coals from the ash pan, and had neglected in some measure to replenish the fire. At that time the engi-

> *There was a man buried in the wreck who, from his expressions, must have been either a sugar or cotton planter—as in his despair he said he had money, Negroes, a plantation, and would give all to save his life. He was covered deeply in the ruins and the fire coming on so rapidly it was impossible to rescue him.*

---

* This young man may have been Henry Clemens. The explosion blew Henry into the water; he then swam back to the boat to assist in the rescue of those on board. His actions after that are unknown.

neer came around, and called on them saying, "Shove her up boys, for we are scarcely stemming the current," and he states that they had scarcely put any wood into the fire doors before the explosion occurred. By some miracle this man escaped with a slight scald in the back.

From the report of those engaged in trying to keep down the fire, barrels of turpentine or some other combustible liquid must have taken fire in the hold from the rapidity with which the flames enveloped the whole boat, so soon after the alarm of fire. If not for the timely aid of the wood-boat, or if it had been delayed five minutes, there would not have been fifty of us left to tell the tale.

A number of passengers were saved by the skiffs of the neighboring woodmen, who acted very promptly and gallantly in coming to the rescue and picking up those adrift on pieces of the wreck, planks, &c.

One of the wounded musicians states that he had 20,000 francs on board, which were lost. Of course, all the boat's money, books, and papers were lost.

A Mr. A. L. Bartlett, of New York, had $800 in gold in a small box in his trunk, but in the confusion the money was forgotten. Not a trunk or piece of clothing, save what they had on, was saved by any cabin passenger, and most of them were left without funds. Those who had money divided with those who had none, and all seemed perfectly satisfied to have escaped with their lives.

The wreck floated down about two and a half miles, and landed on the point of a towhead, where it burned to the water's edge. All that could be seen of it when we left were some portions of the machinery and one of the boilers. When the river falls, the wreck will be left high and dry.

Captain Klinefelter remarked to me before I left on the Diana that he would stay by the wreck and save all he could, both of life and property, until he could be of no further service.

The cook of the boat tells us that he and five others were in the cookhouse at the time of the explosion, but all escaped without injury.

One of the female passengers informed us that she escaped with the loss of two trunks and all her wardrobe except the clothing she wore. She represented that all the passengers found it impossible to save anything—they barely escaped with their lives.[14]

The Sultana *Disaster*

Early in the morning of April 27, 1865, the grossly overloaded steamer *Sultana* exploded near Memphis and brought new meaning to the term "maritime disaster." One thousand, five hundred forty-seven died—some 1,100 of them were Union army veterans, including former prisoners, returning home at war's end. Rumors later spread that the vessel had been sabotaged by Confederates, that they had placed an explosive charge in a lump of coal; but this was xenophobic nonsense. The captain of the *Sultana* had displayed little regard for the safety of his passengers and the operating limitations of his boat. The vessel was licensed to carry a maximum of 376 passengers and crew, and already had a large manifest of civilian passengers on board when she took on 1,886 soldiers at Vicksburg. There were other steamers available, but four years of war had fostered an attitude of risk-taking on the river. The *Sultana*'s captain, J. Cass Mason, insisted on taking all the troops in order to boost his revenue.

The *Sultana*'s boilers were of a different design than those used on most steamboats. They were called fire-tube boilers. Somewhat more compact than conventional return-flue types, each of the four boilers was pierced by twenty-four five-inch hot air flues. This design was more efficient in transferring heat from the firebox to the boiler and had seen general acceptance in railroad locomotive applications. But one of *Sultana*'s boilers had leaked so badly on the trip up from New Orleans that it required a patch—a very imperfect patch placed over a bulged portion of the boiler shell. At the moment of the explosion the *Sultana* was in a crossing and many of her passengers who were still awake had shifted from one side to the other to get a better view of the approaching shore, creating a list in the boat. The list may have uncovered water from fire-tubes in one of the boilers.[15] But we will never know the exact cause, we can only stand aghast at the results. An accurate eyewitness account of the explosion comes in a letter from a soldier, Alonzo Van Vlack, written at Memphis, April 28, 1865:

> Dear Father and Mother,
>   It is with pleasure that I take my pen in hand to write you a few lines to let you know that I am alive and getting along very well. But it is almost a miracle that I am here. We left Vicksburg on Monday on the steamer Sultana. There was nearly two thousand soldiers on

board and nearly 200 citizens. Everything went off well until we arrived at Memphis. There we took off 200 hogsheads of sugar and took on coal. It was then near one o'clock A.M. We had all gone to bed and the boat had gone some 8 or 10 miles up the river when she exploded.

> *There was over 1,000 drowned, it was an awful sight. Some was praying and some screaming. There was some ladies on board and small children. They was nearly all drowned.*

The river at that place was 1½ miles wide and very swift current. The pilothouse and smokestacks were all blown away and hundreds of men blown overboard and a great many scalded to death. The wreck immediately took fire; it was an awful scene. Hundreds crowded on the part not yet in flames but all had to leave her or be burnt.

At the time of the explosion I was asleep on the top of the cookhouse forward of the wheelhouse. A piece of the falling deck struck me and knocked me senseless for about 5 minutes. I collected myself and started to find a board, but did not. I then climbed down on the lower deck and got behind the [paddle] wheel and made a leap (a leap for life). I then swam off and on my way saw a great many going down to rise no more. I succeeded in finding a board about 4 inches wide and 12 feet long, then tried to make the Tennessee shore but the water drawed me toward the other side. I then made for the Arkansas side and landed 6 miles below the wreck on some flood wood on a cottonwood swamp. Was picked up next morning half froze.

There was over 1,000 drowned, it was an awful sight. Some was praying and some screaming. There was some ladies on board and small children. They was nearly all drowned. I am now in Adams Hospital. I received a small bruise on the top of my head, but not serious. Do not know how long I will stay here. You will see the account of the accident in the papers by the time you receive this. Some that got ashore are [so] badly scalded that the hide all come off of them and their toenails.

It is an awful thing to think of. I will write again soon if I stay here long. Give my best respects and wishes to all. Good bye.[16]

The Explosion of the Glencoe

Steam vessels were especially vulnerable to the possibility of a boiler explosion when they maneuvered into a landing. It might develop that a clog obstructed the feedwater check valve, or perhaps the "doctor" engine briefly ceased operating; in either case the water level would drop, unnoticed by the engineer who was otherwise engaged in answering the engine bells. If the clog then opened or the pump suddenly resumed operation, water would rush over the red-hot boiler flues with predictable and sudden consequences.

The explosion of the *Glencoe* probably resulted from those circumstances. It took place at the crowded St. Louis waterfront on April 3, 1852. Reporters from the *Missouri Republican* covered the catastrophe in depth. For sheer horror and morbidity the story has few equals:

> The steamer Glencoe *had just arrived, on Saturday evening, between seven and eight o'clock, from New Orleans, heavily laden, and was endeavoring to effect a landing between Pine and Chestnut Streets. The steamers* Aleck Scott, Georgia, Cataract, *and* Western World *were lying one beside the other at that point, and the* Glencoe *was attempting an entrance between the* Cataract *and* Georgia. *She lay with her bows a little above the stern of the* Georgia, *when two or more of her boilers exploded, spreading death and destruction in every direction about her.*
>
> From a young gentleman who, during the upward trip of the Glencoe, *acted as her assistant clerk, we learn that she carried eighty deck passengers, more or less, and from twenty to twenty-five cabin passengers. The boat had touched at several adjacent steamers a sufficiently long time to allow many persons from shore to board her, swelling her numbers considerably.*
>
> The explosion was, as we have intimated, a tremendous one. The entire upper works of the Glencoe, *forward of the pilothouse—unfortunately the part where the majority of the passengers had gathered to witness the landing—were torn away. Chimneys, boilers, timbers, and freight were scattered about, with many human beings, in every direction.*
>
> The work of destruction was not confined to the Glencoe. *The after upper works of the* Cataract, *which lay close by, taking in the*

whole of the ladies' cabin, was destroyed. Other boats nearby were visited, but to a lesser extent, by the calamity.

Shortly after the explosion, the boat was discovered to be on fire, and simultaneously with the discovery commenced floating down. The full extent of ruin presented itself as she passed down.

The cabin forward of the wheelhouse was gone. A portion of it had been thrown on the freight piled at the forecastle, this mass rising as high as the after hurricane deck. The flames were burning fiercely about where the boilers had been, and spreading rapidly to all sides. From the shore many human beings, men and women, could be descried hurrying from one side to the other, desperately seeking someplace of escape.

One or two poor fellows who had been scalded and afterwards caught in the falling timbers, were seen motioning and heard crying wildly for assistance, as the flames reached and enveloped them. The scene was a most horrible one. As the boat continued to glide down, her yawl became filled with surviving passengers. The yawls of some other boats also were pushed out and succeeded in saving others. We can make no correct estimate of the number of persons lost by scalding and drowning. It is supposed that from sixty to seventy were saved. Allowing this estimate to be correct, from thirty to forty, or even more, lives have been lost.

The scene witnessed immediately after the occurrence of the catastrophe are of the most heart-rending description. We noticed several men, their faces blackened, their clothes wet and soiled with ashes, hurrying along the levee and crying for relief. One body on the Cataract had the head blown entirely off. We saw, also, the legs of a boy or girl, the body having lodged in some other direction. A number of physicians were in attendance and rendered every service which lay in their power.

The body of a lady, so horribly mangled that it scarcely held together, was taken from the ruins of the Cataract's ladies' cabin. She was not, of course, identified. It was thought that she had been blown from the ill-fated Glencoe. A little girl, aged about thirteen, was also picked up on the Cataract, and it was for a while believed that she could be saved. But a closer examination by the physicians revealed one or two fatal wounds, which induced the opinion that she would not survive until morning.

The burning Glencoe lodged at first about the foot of Spruce Street, where some of the survivors who had not escaped by the yawls succeeded in gaining the wood-boats and thence reaching shore. Afterward, she swung around and floated until within a few blocks of the gas works, where she permanently lodged and burned to the water's edge. The fire was communicated to the wood-boats she had passed, seven of which that were fully freighted were destroyed.

Five other empty wood-boats were also consumed. The flames spread next to the corded wood on shore. It is estimated that from 250 to 300 cords of this wood were consumed. Fortunately the fire did not spread to the buildings on the levee.

In our statement of the injuries to the steamers lying near the Glencoe when she exploded, we failed to give all the particulars. One of her chimneys, we are informed, struck the after cabin of the steamer Georgia, demolishing it completely. The starboard forward guard of the Cataract was greatly damaged. Some slabs from the table of the Glencoe fell on the hurricane roof of the Aleck Scott, penetrating it in several places. One of the escape pipes entered the texas of the Western World, demolishing several staterooms. Flattened sheets of the Glencoe's boiler lodged on the decks of the adjacent steamers. One of her flues was driven in the ladies' cabin of the Cataract. Timbers were strewn on shore, and bricks from the works about the boilers passed a considerable distance.

We went into the Health Officer's room Saturday night, where a portion of the dead of the ill-fated Glencoe were collected, and examined particularly the bodies; those who have never had the painful task of witnessing death in this form can but faintly imagine the ghastly and horrible appearances which a steam explosion produces. In addition to wounds and bruises, and the attendant violent disfigurements, there is a pallor and peculiar effect upon the body, the result of scalding water and steam, which almost obliterates the natural features, and renders it exceedingly difficult to recognize even an intimate acquaintance. The bodies, with two exceptions, were horribly mutilated. The limbs seemed all to be broken—literally crushed—and in *several instances many of them were separated from the trunks.*

But one female was in the group. Her face and bust were apparently but slightly injured, and we judged her to be about twenty or twenty-five years of age. She bore the appearance of respectability, and was more than likely an emigrant. Two boys were among the number; one, the captain's son (at least recognized to be such by his clothing, for the body was in pieces) aged ten years, and the other, an emigrant's child, we should suppose, a few years older. The latter was not badly disfigured, and while we were present, we noticed a gentleman endeavoring to ascertain if he had not yet some life in him. Mr. John Denny, the clerk of the boat, was among the number. The rest, judging from their clothes, were deckhands, firemen, or it may be, passengers.

> *The catastrophe is one of those which, from their disastrous and general effects, blot out all means of ascertaining the number and the names of the sufferers.*

The majority of these persons must have occupied exposed situations. With two or three exceptions the bodies seemed to be literally crushed, and in two instances they are torn almost into fragments, portions of them not yet having been obtained. The group formed a horrible spectacle. Hushed in the silence of death, they lay mutilated and parboiled, while the living were examining them, with the help of candles, to recognize if possible some lineament of countenance, some peculiarity of ornament or dress. With the exception of Captain Lee's little son, and Mr. Denny, the clerk, no recognition was made of the bodies.

The catastrophe is one of those which, from their disastrous and general effects, blot out all means of ascertaining the number and the names of the sufferers. The book containing the passenger list is gone, with everything else in the clerk's office, except the freight record—the clerks themselves are dead—the comparatively few bodies recovered are unrecognizable, and its seems impossible that even the loss of life will be correctly ascertained.

The escape of Captain John Lee, and a portion of his family, is deemed almost providential. When the explosion took place the deckhands were engaged on the capstan, a line having been taken ashore, and the captain stood on the forward extremity of the hurricane deck superintending their operations. At the same instant that he became aware of the explosion, the cabin behind him was shattered to atoms and he felt the portion of the deck on which he stood give way, listing as it went, to one side. He fell a distance of probably twenty or twenty-five feet, catching as he went at the object nearest to him, and being violently struck several times by the falling timbers. Preserving his consciousness, so soon as he could extricate himself from the surrounding timbers, he began to re-ascend. Attaining the cabin floor he hurried back to the ladies' cabin, whence, finding nothing at that advanced stage of the disaster to do, he proceeded to the steamer Cataract.

The greater number of passengers in the cabin of the Glencoe were embraced in a party consisting of Mrs. John Lee and servant, Miss Jane Lee, Mrs. John Finney, and two children of Mrs. Lee. Fortunately, no heavy missile took the direction of that portion of the boat. The concussion which followed the explosion was, however, so great as to extinguish every light, to smash the lamps, etc. The ladies in time groped their way to the larboard guard. Mrs. John Lee and servant, with Miss Jane Lee, stepped on the Cataract, and Mrs. Finney, who alone of the party retained her full presence of mind, returned to the cabin in quest of the children of Mrs. Lee, who in the prevailing confusion had been forgotten. Feeling her way to the proper stateroom, she entered and found the younger child still lying securely in its berth. She carried it to the parent, and then returned for the other. Failing in the object, she carried to the guard of the Cataract several boxes and packages, the property of various members of the party.

Mrs. Finney, believing that the full extent of the mischief had been consummated with the explosion, was not aware that the ill-fated craft had caught fire, and been cast loose. She continued courageously to exert herself in attempts to save the lives and property of her fellow passengers, and had returned again to the cabin in search of the other missing son of Mrs. Lee. The darkness was such that she failed to discern often the objects nearest to her. Added to this, large volumes of steam which poured into the apartment rendered respiration very difficult. On several occasions she called loudly for assistance, but received no reply, although she believes she heard the *frequent sounds of footsteps as of persons hurrying rapidly to and fro. Going out again on the guards she discovered that the boat was much below the point where she previously lay, and was being carried rapidly down the stream. She became at the same time aware of the existence of the fire and perceived that the flames were spreading in every direction. From the guard, by means of one of the stanchions, she reached the deck below. Some four persons, to wit: Mrs. Finney, and another lady passenger whose name we do not know, a colored man servant of Mrs. Lee, and a colored servant of Mrs. Finney, stood here as the last boat load of deck passengers pushed away from the burning steamer. The yawl lay down to her gunwale in the water, so heavily had she become laden. Another yawl was fastened to the boat and the party, fearing the sinking of the former, prepared to avail themselves of this. Some gentleman, unknown, joined them here and rendered valuable assistance. They got into this boat and shoved off. They had gone a short distance when the burning wreck, which drifted faster, overtook them and the yawl commenced to pass underneath her guard. At this time Mrs. Finney received a severe blow on the forehead from the boat's guard which prostrated her for a few moments, senseless, to the bottom of the yawl.*

The steamer, as we have said, was heavily laden, and her guard in some places almost touched the water. The yawl continued to hug and glide along her hull—the tenants of the former stooping low as they passed—and at last, where the guard was nearer the water, she became fast, and the two pursued their fearful course together. The feeling of the inmates may be conceived. Owing to the projection of the flooring overhead, they were enveloped in complete darkness, and thus while the roar of the flames and the cracking of the timbers above advised them of the full horrible peril of their position, they were prevented by the guard from even rising to a sitting posture to attempt an escape. At last the steamer stuck violently against the shore. Persons on the adjacent wood-boat discovered the party in the yawl.

The fire above had made considerable progress when Mrs. Finney discovered a means of escape by the light which gleamed to the after part of the yawl. Creeping to that point she found the aperture sufficiently large to pass out. Some wood-boats were hard by, on which, after a few moments, herself and her companions succeeded to find security. The trial was a great one, but equaled by the admirable presence of mind and courage of a lady on whom it might well have proven most overwhelming.

We mention above that the missing son of Captain Lee was killed. The unfortunate boy was blown into fragments. On Saturday night last the pieces were identified by parts of garments found hanging to them. A moment before the explosion, he was seen standing in the social hall. After it, his trunk was found lying on the hurricane deck, and his legs on the guard of the lower deck. His remains were conveyed to the residence of Mr. Finney, on Franklin Avenue, thence to that of his parents, on Morgan Street. They were accompanied, yesterday afternoon, by a large number of the friends of the family, to the Wesleyan Cemetery, where they were interred.

The steamer Glencoe, as well as we can learn, was built at New Albany [Indiana] in 1846. She had four boilers which, report says, had served several years on other boats. At various periods she was run in different trades, and passed into different hands. Captain Lee became possessed of her this season, and had made four or five trips. Recently she went into [dry] docks, where she was repaired under the superintendence of Captain Sparhawk. Her boilers were lately inspected by Mr. Hall, and a certificate of serviceability was given to her owners. [17]

Licensing and Inspection

Steamboat licensing and inspection did not begin until 1838, and even then it was little more than a formality to satisfy an otherwise weak law. Indeed, the Steamboat Act of 1838 was more remarkable for its omissions than its stipulations. It did not establish maximum boiler pressures, nor did it require a test of boiler strength. No provision was made for lifeboats or flotation devices. The law did not address the then-common use of combustible tiller ropes, nor did it oblige the installation of safety devices to release boiler pressure or dampen the furnace fires.

Apologists for the steamboat concerns found any kind of regulation grating, and they argued that most ideas and devices aimed at the reduction of accidents or deaths were unworkable and unreliable. Nevertheless, the passage of time brought new inventions and innovations that did work—if not perfectly then at least with some degree of benefit. When steamboat owners applied these improvements it was usually done to satisfy insurance underwriters.

In the meantime, steamboat death tolls climbed until over 1,200 people had died in an eighteen-month stretch during 1850-1852. That was enough. In 1852 Congress enacted a new law that corrected most of the earlier oversights and greatly strengthened the anemic Steamboat Inspection Service. Under the new law, the inspectors were more competent, aggressive, and better organized. And they were quite up to suspending licenses and issuing fines. Writing many years later, Captain Beck Jolly recalled a long-ago trip with a leaking, patched boiler on the steamer *Die Vernon*. In light of the much more stringent inspection laws, he surmised, "such things would nowadays bring someone trouble." The old *laissez faire* game on the river was over.[18]

One way of judging the scope of the Steamboat Act of 1852 and its amendments is to examine the inspection certificate required of all steamboats that operated under its provisions. In 1867, the following documentation hung on the pilothouse wall of the steamboat *Evening Star*:

PASSENGER STEAMER, INSPECTORS' CERTIFICATE
Steamship Evening Star

Application having been made in writing to the subscribers, inspectors for this district, to inspect the steamer Evening Star *of St. Louis in the State of Missouri, whereof H. S. Bryan and others are owners, and H. S. Bryan is Master, and having performed that service, now, on this 2d day of October, A.D. 1867, do certify, that she was built at Wellsville, in the State of Ohio, in the year 1864; is of 432 6/100 tons burthen, and is in all respects stanch, seaworthy, and in good condition for navigation, having suitable means of escape, in case of accident, from the main to upper deck. That she is provided with 24 state-rooms, and a total of 48 berths for cabin passengers.*

That she is permitted to carry not exceeding 100 deck or steerage passengers.

That she is provided with three high-pressure boilers, 26 feet long, and 38 inches diameter, (of cylindrical form, two 13½ inch return flues each) constructed of C.H. No. 1 iron of $^{13}/_{48}$ *of an inch in thickness and made in* A.D. *1864; iron manufactured by and stamped Shoenberger & Co. C.H. No. 1, and are in all respects conformable to law. That said boilers have been subjected to a hydrostatic pressure of 198 pounds to the square inch, and the maximum working power allowed was 132 pounds to the square inch, and left in charge of the Engineer; and 1 locked safety valve of* $2^{21}/_{40}$ *inches diameter loaded to 134 pounds pressure per square inch. And has 2 supply pipes of* $2^{3}/_{8}$ *inch diameter, and has sufficient means to keep the water, at all times and under all circumstances, up to four inches over the flues. Has 2 steam pipes of* $4^{1}/_{2}$ *inches in diameter. Has 2 high-pressure engines of 18 inches in diameter of cylinder, and 5 feet stroke. Has 2 feed pumps of* $4^{1}/_{2}$ *inches plunge, with 10 inches stroke, worked by auxiliary engine. Has no independent steam feed pump. Has 8 gauge cocks in the after end of boilers. Has 3 water gauges and 1 steam gauge all properly secured and arranged. Has alloyed metal on the flues in accordance with the Act of Congress approved July 25th, 1866. Has 2 fire pumps, viz: forward pump* $4^{1}/_{2}$ *inches diameter and 6 inches stroke, worked by hand; midship pump 5 inches diameter, 10 inches stroke, worked by steam; all double acting; and has 150 feet of hose, 20 buckets, and 5 axes. Has 1 metallic life-boat in good order, yawl and stage floats containing 160 superficial feet. Has 48 life preservers, viz: of block cork, 2 kept in each state-room. Has wire steering ropes, and additional steering apparatus, independent of the steering wheel.*

And we further certify that said vessel is run only within the following lines, to wit: on Mississippi River and its tributaries.[19]

Although unprecedented events, such as the *Sultana* disaster, occasionally would mar the record, the chances of death attributable to boiler explosion on the river diminished five-fold after the implementation of the Steamboat Act of 1852.

Collisions

Still, there were risks that could not be legislated away. One was the danger of collision. A landsman might have found the possibility absurd;

after all, the boats moved slowly, they stood out like snow-capped mountains, and the Ohio and Mississippi Rivers were as wide as a farm. But boat traffic grew heavy at times, the channel was narrow, and down bound boats were only nominally under control as the current pushed them along.

The death rate from steamboat collisions usually was not high unless the collision set off an explosion or a fire. One of the worst collisions involved the steamers *United States* and *America*, in 1868. Both boats were owned by the same packet company; both boats plied the Ohio River between Louisville and Cincinnati. The packet line held a mail contract, so the two steamers kept to a regular schedule while working in opposite directions. They normally passed each other, larboard to larboard, near Warsaw, Kentucky. As prescribed by law, the signal for a larboard-side pass was one blow of the whistle. On the night of December 4, a substitute pilot was at the helm of the upward bound *America*, and on seeing the approach of the *United States*, he blew for a starboard-side pass—two whistles. The pilot of the *United States* did not hear the second whistle, and both boats steered for the same line. The collision stove in the larboard side of the *United States;* both steamers caught fire and sank. Sixty-three people died.[20]

The destruction of the *United States* and the *America* was attributed to piloting error and mistaken signals. The collision of the *Plymouth* and the *Lady Madison* came about from a more culpable cause. A newspaper edition from 1845 tells the story:

> *We are pained to announce a dreadful catastrophe, or rather a most negligent destruction of the steamer* Plymouth, *by the* Lady Madison, *with the loss of human life. The collision occurred on Monday night, the 27th [of October], at about 10 o'clock, at the head of Raleigh Bar, six miles above Shawneetown [Illinois], on the Ohio. The* Plymouth *sank in a few minutes, and the unfortunates who were drowned were deck passengers—German emigrants—who jumped overboard.*
>
> *The panic (says the extra of the* Illinois State Gazette*) was extreme and the cries of the unfortunate sufferers most horrific. Twenty-five or thirty are missing; one whole family is gone. One poor woman saved two other women and a child, but lost her own husband*

and one child; another lost all her family. The deck passengers who were saved lost all their property, many of them even barefooted. No cabin passengers were lost.

The Plymouth *was bound for St. Louis, with a full cargo, about two hundred and fifty tons of merchandise, some seventy deck passengers, and a large number in the cabin. The night was perfectly clear. An obliging correspondent at Shawneetown, one of the editors of the* Gazette, *writes us as follows:*

Shawneetown, Oct. 28, 1845

The pilot of the Madison *is severely censured on the ground of gross carelessness, or perhaps drunkeness. He ran on the rocks at this place yesterday morning, one hundred yards out of the channel, and nearly ran into the* Fulton *in the crossing just before he struck the* Plymouth.

The Plymouth *had stopped her engines some four hundred yards above, and allowed the* Madison *to take her choice of the channel coming up, and the river was more than a mile wide.*[21]

Windstorms

The closest thing to blameless steamboat accidents were those caused by high winds; the tall profile of most riverboats made them difficult to handle when the wind blew hard. The steamer *Lady Lee,* for example, sank in 1865 after hitting a snag; but she did not run into the snag, she was blown into it while backing out of a landing. The boat had lost headway, the engines took hold too slowly, and the helm was unresponsive.[22]

Windstorms came in all degrees of severity on the river. A hurricane moving inland in 1909 sank several boats and barges as far north as Vicksburg, and killer tornadoes swept away boats at Natchez in 1840 and at St. Louis in 1896. In the latter instance the vessels had been wrenched from their moorings and torn apart as the winds hurled them across the river.[23] This was bad enough, but imagine standing in the pilothouse of a steamboat, while in midstream, and watching as a tornado funnel dropped from the sky directly in the path of the boat. Grant Marsh discovered that "sinking" feeling in 1894. In those waning years of steamboating he was captain and first pilot of the towboat *Little Eagle No. 2:*

As usual, she was towing lumber barges from points below Cairo to St. Louis. On the morning of September 17th, a day when the sky was cloudy above and the river oily beneath, the Little Eagle *swung out from the St. Louis levee for a daylight run downriver. She was pushing one barge ahead, neither barge nor steamer carrying any cargo. At about eleven o'clock in the morning, when some seventy miles below St. Louis and just above the point where the Okaw River comes in on the Illinois side, the captain, who was in the pilothouse, steering, glanced to starboard. The air was perfectly still, oppressively so, and in the western sky he noticed an ominous cloud rapidly gathering. His practiced eye instantly comprehended that it was a cyclone. Turning to the speaking-tube, he shouted down to Charlie DeWitt, the engineer on duty, that a bad storm was coming but he would try to make a landing before the boat should be struck.*

But in less than thirty seconds the storm was upon them. Under the terrific force of the wind the Little Eagle *began to careen. Captain Marsh, standing by the wheel, again shouted to DeWitt for all hands to run for the barge. The men obeyed, but none too soon, for they had scarcely reached it when the capsizing steamer careened so far that the boilers broke loose from their fastenings and slid off into the river. The instant they struck the water, they exploded with tremendous force, shattering the forward hull and deck and tearing loose the hawsers which held the barge to the steamer.*

The captain, still in the pilothouse, was now cut off from the barge and his only hope for life was to get aft and there seek some means of escape. Fortunately the furious wind had driven the scalding steam and the flying wreckage of the exploded boilers away from him, so that he was not injured. He climbed through the pilothouse window and, as the boat continued to careen, scrambled upward toward the highest point until in a moment the hull was on edge, with the captain clinging to the upturned side. A second later, with a great splash, the Little Eagle *"turned turtle" completely, and the captain walked out on her flat bottom, dry-shod and unharmed.*

The barge with the crew on board was drifting off downstream and presently the wind drove it into the bank at Fort Gage, just above Chester, Illinois, where all hands landed safely. The Little Eagle, with her single passenger, floated downriver for some distance, then some of her submerged upper works caught in the bottom and she grounded in the channel. The short-lived "twister" had now passed, and presently the towboat Sidney Dillon, Captain Nick Beaver, hove in sight, downward bound. She rescued Captain Marsh from his improvised raft and landed him at Chester where he rejoined his crew.

All of the captain's possessions on board the Little Eagle, as well as those of his men, were, of course, lost, and the captain was even obliged to borrow money from John and Bill Rollins, the pilots of the Sidney Dillon, to take his crew back to St. Louis. It is said, and probably no one will arise to dispute the statement, that this is the only instance on record of a man walking from the pilothouse to the keel of a vessel without even getting his feet wet.[24]

1   Cowell, p. 95.
2   "Fast on a Bar," *Weekly Reveille* 2, no. 9 (8 September 1845): 481.
3   Letter, John F.M. Fortney to "Dear Sir," 4 March 1865, in the Illinois State Historical Library, Springfield.
4   "Editorial Correspondence," *Weekly Reveille* 2, no. 19 (17 November 1845): 651.
5   *Weekly Reveille* 2, no. 30 (2 February 1846): 740.
6   *Daily Missouri Republican*, 5 December 1842.
7   *Daily Missouri Republican*, 2 July 1842.
8   "Another Terrible Steam Boat Accident," *ibid.*, 2 December 1842.
9   *Ibid.*, 5 December 1842.
10   *Ibid.*, 9 December 1842.
11   *Weekly Reveille* 2, no. 8 (1 September 1845): 475.
12   "On Boiler Explosions," *The Manufacturer and Builder* 1, no. 5 (May 1869): 132.
13   Twain, *Life on the Mississippi*, p.178.
14   "Explosion of the Steamer *Pennsylvania*," *Daily Missouri Republican*, 15 June 1858; and "Additional Particulars of the Explosion and Burning of the *Pennsylvania*!" *ibid.*, 16 June 1858.
15   For more discussion of the possible causes, see Nicholas F. Starace II, "America's Worst Maritime Disaster: The Ill-fated Sidewheeler *Sultana*," *Sea History* 92 (Spring 2000): 33-35.
16   Letter, Alonzo Van Vlack to "Dear Father and Mother," Memphis, Tennessee, 28 April 1865, in the Michigan Historical Collections, Bentley Historical Library, University of Michigan, Ann Arbor.

17 "Dreadful Explosion and Loss of Life!" *Daily Missouri Republican*, 5 April 1862.

18 Ruth Ferris, ed. "Captain Jolly in the Civil War," *Missouri Historical Society Bulletin* 22, no. 1 (October 1965), p. 19; see Hunter, *Steamboats on the Western Rivers*, pp. 520-46, for a detailed treatment of steamboat regulations.

19 E. B. Trail Collection, folder 38a.

20 Way, pp. 19-20, 464.

21 "Steamboat Collision," *Weekly Reveille* 2, no. 17 (3 November 1845): 635.

22 W. J. McDonald, "The Missouri River and Its Victims," *Missouri Historical Review* 21 (1926-27): 473.

23 Wayman, p. 261.

24 Hanson, pp. 422-24.

Tales of the War

During the War Between the States, which lasted from 1861 to 1865, six major battles were fought on the Mississippi—four of them involved fleet actions between vessels of the Union and the Confederacy, the other two pitted gunboats against land fortifications. Six more battles of consequence raged on tributary waters, and dozens of lesser engagements took place at widely scattered points on the lower rivers. Most of the fighting was done with heavy cannon fired from odd-looking utilitarian craft. The river war also revived an ancient mode of naval warfare: the use of ramming vessels. It was a most peculiar sort of war.

River battles were spectacular in scope. Thundering volleys of cannon fire, burning vessels, intentional collisions, and desperate chases punctuated nearly every encounter. These obvious dangers seemed to attract the bold and the adventurous. The four stories that follow typify the excitement and terror that awaited all who dared fight on the river.

"We Were Now Surrounded"

In July of 1862 the Confederate river navy had lost most of its gunboats in battles above Memphis and below New Orleans. Now the Union navy, with some eighty vessels, took position off Vicksburg, Mississippi. The Yankees planned to bombard Vicksburg from the river and soften the defenses for a land assault. But the small army that accompanied the fleet was inadequate for the task. And the naval vessels—some of them deep-draft ocean warships that had ventured up the river from the Gulf of Mexico—could do little more than lob an occasional shell at Vicksburg and otherwise await developments.

The commander of the Federal fleet, Flag Officer David G. Farragut, had heard that the Confederates were building a gunboat of considerable size somewhere on the Yazoo River. The Yazoo flowed into the Mississippi twelve miles above Vicksburg. And in that twelve-mile stretch lay most of Farragut's fleet. So Farragut sent a patrol of three gunboats—the *Carondelet,* the *Tyler,* and the *Queen of the West*—up the Yazoo to find and destroy the Confederate boat. He didn't expect much of a problem. But Farragut had not counted on the likes of one very resourceful Confederate naval officer: Lieutenant Isaac Newton Brown.

Energetic, competent, and courageous, Newt Brown was the Confederacy's best man for the task at hand. He was a career naval officer who twice had sailed around the world. He would need all of that experience and more, for he was about to embark on the most one-sided naval battle of the war.

Two decades later, a New York publisher asked Brown to write the story of this incredible voyage—the voyage of the *C.S.S. Arkansas.* Brown, who had long since assumed the quiet life of a farmer, agreed to pen the article—not for the money or the prestige, but rather as a tribute to his crew:

> On the 28th of May, 1862, I received at Vicksburg a telegraphic order from the Navy Department at Richmond to "proceed to Greenwood, Miss., and assume command of the Confederate gunboat Arkansas, *and finish and equip that vessel without regard to expenditure of men or money." I knew that such a vessel had been under construction at Memphis, but I had not heard till then of her escape from the general wreck of our Mississippi River defenses. Greenwood is at the head of the Yazoo River, 160 miles by river from Yazoo City.*
>
> *It being the season of the overflow, I found my new command four miles from dry land. Her condition was not encouraging. The vessel was a mere hull, without armor; the engines were apart; guns without carriages were lying about the deck; a portion of the rail-*

Lieutenant Isaac Newton Brown, Confederate States Navy. The son of a Presbyterian minister, Brown had chosen the more exciting career of a naval officer. He sailed twice around the world, fought in two wars, and served on the staff of the Naval Observatory. But his greatest achievement would come as commander of the *C.S.S. Arkansas* on the Yazoo and Mississippi Rivers. (From Scharf, *History of the Confederate States Navy.*)

road iron intended as armor was at the bottom of the river, and the other and far greater part was to be sought for in the interior of the country. Taking a day to fish up the sunken iron, I had the Arkansas *towed to Yazoo City, where the hills reach the river. Here, though we were within fifty miles of the Union fleets, there was the possibility of equipment.*

Within a very short time after reaching Yazoo City we had two hundred men, chiefly from the nearest detachment of the army, at work on the deck's shield and hull, while fourteen blacksmith forges were drawn from the neighboring plantations and placed on the bank to hasten the iron-work. Extemporized drilling machines on the steamer Capitol *worked day and night fitting the railway iron for the bolts which were to fasten it as armor. This iron was brought from many points to the nearest railroad station and thence twenty-five miles by wagons. The trees were yet growing from which the gun carriages had to be made—the most difficult work of all, as such vehicles had never been built in Mississippi. I made a contract with two gentlemen of Jackson to pay each his own price for the full number of ten. The executive officer, Mr. [Henry K.] Stevens, gave the matter his particular attention, and in time, along with the general equipment, we obtained five good carriages from each contractor.*

This finishing, armoring, arming, and equipping of the Arkansas *within five weeks' working time under the hot summer sun, from which we were unsheltered, and under the depressing thought that there was a deep channel, of but six hours' steaming between us and the Federal fleet, whose guns were within hearing, was perhaps not inferior under all the circumstances to the renowned effort of Oliver Hazard Perry in cutting a fine ship from the forest in ninety days.*

We were not a day too soon, for the now rapid fall of the river rendered it necessary for us to assume the offensive without waiting for the apparatus to bend the railway iron to the curve of our quarter and stern, and to the angles of the pilothouse. Though there was little thought of showing the former, the weakest part, to the enemy, we tacked boiler plate iron over it for appearance's sake, and very imperfectly covered the pilothouse shield with a double thickness of one-inch bar iron. Our engines' two screws, one under each quarter, worked up to eight miles an hour in still water, which promised about half that speed when turned against the current of the main river. We had at first some trust in these, not having discovered the way they soon showed of stopping on the center at wrong times and places; and as they never both stopped of themselves at the same time, the effect was, when one did so, to turn the vessel round, despite the rudder. Once, in the presence of the enemy, we made a circle, while trying to make the automatic stopper keep time with its sister-screw.

The Arkansas *now appeared as if a small seagoing vessel had been cut down to the water's edge at both ends, leaving a box for guns amidships. The straight sides of the box, a foot in thickness, had over them one layer of railway iron; the ends closed by timber one foot square, planked across by six-inch strips of oak, were then covered by one course of railway iron laid up and down at an angle of thirty-five degrees. These ends deflected overhead all missiles striking at short range, but would have been of little security under a plunging fire. This shield, flat on top, covered with plank and half-inch iron, was pierced for ten guns—three in each broadside and two for-*

ward and aft. The large smokestack came through the top of the shield, and the pilothouse was raised about one foot above the shield level. Through the latter led a small tin tube by which to convey orders to the pilot.

We obtained over 100 good men from the naval vessels lately on the Mississippi, and about 60 Missourians from the command of General Jeff Thompson. These had never served at great guns, but on trial they exhibited in their new service the cool courage natural to them on land. On the 12th of July we sent our mechanics ashore, took our Missourians on board, and dropped below Satartia Bar, within five hours of the Mississippi. I now gave the executive officer a day to organize and exercise his men.

On Monday A.M., we started from Satartia. Fifteen miles below, at the mouth of Sunflower River, we found that the steam from our imperfect engines and boiler had penetrated our forward magazine and wet our powder so as to render it unfit for use. We were just opposite the site of an old sawmill, where the opening in the forest, dense everywhere else, admitted the sun's rays. The day was clear and very hot; we made fast to the bank, head downstream, landed our wet powder (expecting the enemy to heave in sight every moment), spread tarpaulins over the old sawdust and our powder over these. By constant shaking and turning we got it back to the point of ignition before the sun sank below the trees, when, gathering it up, we crowded all that we could of it into the after magazine and resumed our way, guns cast loose and men at quarters, expecting every moment to meet the enemy. I had some idea of their strength, General [Earl] Van Dorn, commanding our forces at Vicksburg, having written to me two days before that there were then, I think he said, thirty-seven men-of-war in sight and more up the river. Near dark we narrowly escaped the destruction of our smokestack from an immense over-hanging tree. From this disaster we were saved by young [Lieutenant John] Grimball, who sprang from the shield to another standing tree, with rope's end in hand, and made it fast. We anchored at Haynes' Bluff at midnight and rested till 3 A.M., when we got up anchor for the fleet, hoping to be with it at sunrise, but before it was light we ran ashore and lost an hour getting again afloat.

At sunrise we gained Old River—a lake caused by a "cut-off"
from the Mississippi; the Yazoo enters this at the north curve, and,
mingling its deep waters with the wider expanse of the lake, after a
union of ten miles, breaks through a narrow strip of land to lose itself
finally in the Mississippi twelve miles above Vicksburg. We were soon
to find the fleet midway between these points, but hid from both by
the curved and wooded eastern shore.

As the sun rose clear and fiery out of the lake on our left, we saw
a few miles ahead, under full steam, three Federal vessels in line
approaching. These, as we afterward discovered, were the ironclad
Carondelet, the wooden gunboat Tyler, and a ram, the Queen of
the West. * Directing our pilot to stand for the ironclad, the center
vessel of the three, I gave the order not to fire our bow guns, lest by
doing so we should diminish our speed, relying for the moment upon
our broadside guns to keep the ram and the Tyler from gaining our
quarter, which they seemed eager to do. I had determined, despite our
want of speed, to try the ram or iron prow upon the foe, who were gallantly approaching; but when less than half a mile separated us, the
Carondelet fired a wildly aimed bow gun, backed round, and went
from the Arkansas at a speed which at once perceptibly increased
the space between us. The Tyler and ram followed this movement of
the ironclad, and the stern guns of the Carondelet and the Tyler
were briskly served on us. Grimball and [Lieutenant George W.] Gift,
with their splendid sixty-fours, * * were now busy at their work, while
Barbot and Wharton watched for a chance shot abeam. [Lieutenant
Charles W.] Read chafed in silence at his rifles. The whole crew was
under the immediate direction of the first lieutenant, Henry Stevens,
a religious soldier, of the Stonewall Jackson type, who felt equally
safe at all times and places. I was on the shield directly over our bow
guns, and could see their shot on the way to the Carondelet, and with

---

*   Though the *Carondelet*, like the *Arkansas*, was built new as a gunboat, the *Tyler*
     and *Queen of the West* were converted Ohio River steamers.
* * Naval cannon were referenced by either the diameter of their bore measured in
     inches or, in this case, by the weight of their solid iron shot. Most were smooth-
     bore guns, but some cannon—called "rifles"—featured grooves within the bore
     that created higher accuracy and greater shot penetration of the target.

my glasses I thought that I could see the white wood under her armor. This was satisfactory, for I knew that no vessel afloat could long stand rapid raking by 8-inch shot at such short range.

We soon began to gain on the chase, yet from time to time I had to steer first to starboard, then to port, to keep the inquisitive consorts of the Carondelet from inspecting my boiler plate armor. This gave the nearer antagonist an advantage, but before he could improve it we would be again brought ahead. While our shot seemed always to hit his stern and disappear, his missiles, striking our inclined shield, were deflected over my head and lost in the air. I received a severe contusion on the head, but this gave me no concern after I had failed to find any brains mixed with the handful of clotted blood which I drew from the wound and examined. A moment later a shot from the Tyler struck at my feet, penetrated the pilothouse and, cutting off a section of the wheel, mortally hurt Chief Pilot Hodges and disabled our Yazoo River pilot, Shacklett, who was at the moment much needed, our Mississippi pilots knowing nothing of Old River. James Brady, a Missourian of nerve and equal to the duty, took the wheel, and I ordered him to "keep the ironclad ahead."

All was going well, with a near prospect of carrying out my first intention of using the ram, this time at a great advantage, for the stern of the Carondelet was now the objective point, and she seemed to be going slow and unsteady. Unfortunately the Tyler also slowed, so as to keep near his friend, and this brought us within easy range of his small arms. I saw with some concern, as I was the only visible target outside our shield, that they were firing by volleys. I was near the hatchway at the moment when a minie ball, striking over my left temple, tumbled me down among the guns. I awoke as if from sleep, to find kind hands helping me to a place among the killed and wounded. I soon regained my place on the shield. I found the Carondelet still ahead, but much nearer, and both vessels entering the willows, which grew out on the bar at the inner curve of the lake. To have run into the mud, we drawing thirteen feet (the Carondelet only six), would have ended the matter with the Arkansas. The Carondelet's position could only be accounted for by supposing the steering apparatus destroyed.

The deep water was on our starboard bow, where at some distance I saw the Tyler *and the ram, as if awaiting our further entanglement. I gave the order "hard a-port and depress port guns." So near were we to the chase that this action of the helm brought us alongside, and our broadside caused her to heel to port and then roll back so deeply as to take the water over her deck forward of the shield. Our crew, thinking her sinking, gave three hearty cheers. In swinging off we exposed our stern to the* Carondelet's *broadside, and gave Read at the same time a chance with his rifles. The* Carondelet *did not return this fire of our broadside and stern guns. Had she fired into our stern when we were so near, it would have destroyed or at least have disabled us.*

We neither saw nor felt the Carondelet *again, but turned toward the spiteful* Tyler *and the wary ram. As these were no longer a match for the* Arkansas, *they very properly took advantage of a speed double our own to gain the shelter of their fleet, the* Tyler *making good practice at us while in range with her pivot gun, and getting some attention in the same way from our bows. Under the ordinary circumstances of war we had just got through with a fair hour's work; but knowing what was ahead of us, we had to regard it in the same light as our Missouri militia did, as "a pretty smart skirmish."*

On gaining the Mississippi, we saw no vessels but the two we had driven before us. While following these in the direction of Vicksburg I had the opportunity of inspecting the engine and fire rooms, where I found engineers and firemen had been suffering under a temperature of 120° to 130°. The executive officer, while attending to every other duty during the recent firing, had organized a relief party from the men at the guns, who went down into the fire-room every fifteen minutes, the others coming up or being, in many instances, hauled up, exhausted in that time; in this way, by great care, steam was kept to service gauge.

Aided by the current of the Mississippi, we soon approached the Federal fleet—a forest of masts and smokestacks—ships, rams, ironclads, and other gunboats on the left side, and ordinary river steamers and bomb-vessels* along the right. To any one having a real ram at command the genius of havoc could not have offered a finer view,

---

* Mortar boats.

the panoramic effect of which was intensified by the city of men spread out with innumerable tents opposite on the right bank. We were not yet in sight of Vicksburg, but in every direction, except astern, our eyes rested on enemies. I had long known the most of these as valued friends, and if I now had any doubts of the success of the Arkansas they were inspired by this general knowledge rather than from any awe of a particular name. It seemed at a glance as if a whole navy had come to keep me away from the heroic city—six or seven rams, four or five ironclads, without including one accounted for an hour ago, and the fleet of Farragut generally, behind or inside of this fleet.

The rams seemed to have been held in reserve, to come out between the intervals. Seeing this, as we neared the head of the line I said to our pilot, "Brady, shave that line of men-of-war as close as you can, so that the rams will not have room to gather headway in coming out to strike us." In this way we ran so near to the wooden ships that each may have expected the blow which, if I could avoid it, I did not intend to deliver.

As we neared the head of the line our bow guns, trained on the Hartford, began this second fight of the morning, and within a few minutes, as the enemy was brought in range, every gun of the Arkansas was at its work. It was calm, and the smoke settling over the combatants, our men at times directed their guns at the flashes of those of their opponents. As we advanced, the line of fire seemed to grow into a circle constantly closing. The shock of missiles striking our sides was literally continuous, and as we were now surrounded, without room for anything but pushing ahead, and shrapnel shot were coming on our shield deck, twelve pounds at a time, I went below to see how our Missouri backwoodsmen were handling their 100-pounder Columbiads. At this moment I had the most lively realization of having steamed into a real volcano, the Arkansas from its center firing rapidly to every point of the circumference, without the fear of hitting a friend or missing an enemy. I got below in time to see Read and Scales with their rifled guns blow off the feeble attack of a ram on our stern. Another ram was across our way ahead. As I gave the order, "Go through him, Brady!" his steam went into the air, and his crew into the river. A shot from one of our bow guns had gone through his boiler and saved the collision. We passed by and through the brave fellows struggling in the water under a shower of missiles intended for us.

The connection between the furnaces and smokestack (technically called the breechings) were in this second conflict shot away, destroying the draft and letting the flames come out into the shield, raising the temperature there to 120°, while it had already risen to 130° in the fire-room. We went into action in Old River with 120 pounds of steam, and though every effort was made to keep it up, we came out with but 20 pounds, hardly enough to turn the engines. It was a little hot this morning all around; the enemy's shot frequently found weak places in our armor, and their shrapnel and minie balls also came through our port holes. Still, under a temperature of 120°, our people kept to their work, and as each one, acting under the steady eye of Stevens, seemed to think the result depended on himself, I sought a cooler atmosphere on the shield, to find, close ahead and across our way, a large ironclad displaying the square flag of an admiral. Though we had but little headway, his beam was exposed, and I ordered the pilot to strike him amidships. He avoided this by steaming ahead, and, passing under his stern, nearly touching, we gave him our starboard broadside, which probably went through him from rudder to prow. This was our last shot, and we received none in return.

We were now at the end of what had seemed the interminable line, and also past the outer rim of the volcano. I now called the officers up to take a look at what we had just come through and to get the fresh air; and as the little group of heroes closed around me with their friendly words of congratulation, a heavy rifle-shot passed close over our heads; it was the parting salutation, and if aimed two feet lower would have been to us the most injurious of the battle. We were not yet in sight of Vicksburg, but if any of the fleet followed us farther on our way I did not perceive it.

The Arkansas continued toward Vicksburg without further trouble. When within sight of the city, we saw another [enemy] fleet preparing to receive us or recede from us, below; one vessel of the fleet was aground and in flames. With our firemen exhausted, our *smokestack cut to pieces, and a section of our plating torn from the side, we were not in condition just then to begin a third battle; moreover humanity required the landing of our wounded—terribly torn by cannon shot—and of our dead. We were received at Vicksburg with enthusiastic cheers. Immediate measures were taken to repair damages and to recruit our crew, diminished to one-half their original number by casualties, by the expiration of service of those who had volunteered only for the trip to Vicksburg.*[1]

Over the next seven days, Union vessels twice attacked the *Arkansas* at her Vicksburg moorings. Each attack killed more crewmen and did more damage to the Confederate gunboat, but still she remained afloat and a menace. Her position there was a major factor in the Union fleet's withdrawal from Vicksburg waters by the end of July. For a while, at least, the Confederates regained a considerable stretch of the Lower Mississippi.

Brown was exhausted from his ordeal and took medical leave. In his absence Lieutenant Henry Stevens assumed command of the *Arkansas*. General Van Dorn ordered the boat to Baton Rouge to take part in an attack on Federal troops. It was an ill-advised order, for the *Arkansas* needed much repair before assuming the offensive. On August 6, 1862, while in sight of Baton Rouge, and in the presence of enemy gunboats, the *Arkansas'* engines broke irreparably, and Stevens had no choice but to destroy his vessel. Upon hearing the news, a Federal navy officer wrote: "Thank God, this terror of the river is no more."[2]

Unarmed and Unprotected

By mid-1863 the Union navy had destroyed nearly all the Confederate river fleet, and had "opened" the entire length of the Lower Mississippi. But opening the river was one thing; guaranteeing safe passage along this 1,200-mile watercourse was something else. Confederate sharpshooters and roving artillery batteries quickly learned that packet boats were easy targets. Nevertheless, the promise of substantial wartime profits lured a few steamboat owners to risk it. War correspondent Thomas Knox rode the steamer *Henry Von Phul* as it left New Orleans in December, 1863. *Von Phul's* captain, Patrick Gorman, was a charitable old man who at various times had used his vessel to transport wounded soldiers of both the Union and

Confederate armies.[3] If ever a captain and his boat deserved the protection afforded a neutral noncombatant, it was Gorman and the *Von Phul*. But as the steamer passed Bayou Sara, Louisiana, on December 8, she entered an area where no vessel was safe and no reputation sacred. Knox recorded the incident in a dispatch to the *New York Tribune*:

> I can hardly imagine a situation of greater helplessness than a place on board a Western passenger steamer under the guns of a hostile battery. A battlefield is no comparison. On solid earth the principal danger is from projectiles. You can fight, or, under some circumstances, can run away. On a Mississippi transport you are equally in danger of being shot. Added to this, you may be struck by splinters, scalded by steam, burned by fire, or drowned in the water. You cannot fight, you cannot run away, and you cannot find shelter. With no power for resistance or escape, the sense of danger and helplessness cannot be set aside.
>
> It was my fortune to be a passenger on the steamer Von Phul, which left New Orleans for St. Louis on the evening of December 7th, 1863. I had been for some time traveling up and down the Mississippi, and running the gauntlet between Rebel batteries, on either shore. There was some risk attending my travels, but up to that time I escaped unharmed.
>
> On the afternoon of the 8th, when the boat was about eight miles above Bayou Sara, I experienced a new sensation. Seated at a table in the cabin, and busily engaged in writing, I heard a heavy crash over my head, almost instantly followed by another. My first thought was that the chimneys or some part of the pilothouse had fallen, and I half looked to see the roof of the cabin tumbling in. I saw the passengers running from the cabin, and heard someone shout: "The guerrillas are firing on us!"
>
> I collected my writing materials and sought my stateroom, where I had left Mr. Colburn, my traveling companion, soundly asleep a few minutes before. He was sitting on the edge of his berth, and wondering what all the row was about. The crash that startled me had awakened him. He thought the occurrence was of little moment, and assented to my suggestion that we were just as safe there as anywhere else on the boat.

Gallantry prevented our remaining quiet. There were several ladies on board, and it behooved us to extend them what protection we could. We sought them, and "protected" them to the best of our united ability. Their place of refuge was between the cabin and the wheelhouse, opposite the battery's position. A sheet of wet paper would afford as much resistance to a paving stone as the walls of a steamboat cabin to a six-pound shot. As we stood among the ladies, two shells passed through the side of the cabin, within a few inches of our heads.

The shots grew fewer in number, and some of them dropped in the river behind us. Just as we thought all alarm was over, we saw smoke issuing from the cabin gangway. Then, someone shouted, "The boat is on fire!"

Dropping a lady who evinced a disposition to faint, I entered the cabin. A half-dozen men were there before and seeking the locality of the fire. I was first to discover it. A shell, in passing through a stateroom, entered a pillow, and scattered the feathers through the cabin. A considerable quantity of these feathers fell upon a hot stove, and the smoke and odor of their burning caused the alarm. The ladies concluded not to faint. Three minutes after the affair was over, they were as ever.

> *A sheet of wet paper would afford as much resistance to a paving stone as the walls of a steamboat cabin to a six-pound shot.*

The Rebels opened fire when we were abreast of their position, and did not cease until we were out of range. We were fifteen minutes within reach of their guns. Our wheels seemed to turn very slowly. No one can express in words the anxiety with which we listened, after each shot, for the puffing of the engines. So long as the machinery was uninjured, there was no danger of our falling into Rebel hands. But with our engines disabled, our chances would be very good.

As the last shot fell astern of the boat and sent up a column of spray, we looked about the cabin and saw that no one had been injured. A moment later came the announcement from the pilot-house: "Captain Gorman is killed!"

I ascended to the hurricane deck, and thence to the pilothouse. The pilot, with his hat thrown aside and his hair streaming in the wind, stood at his post, carefully guiding the boat on her course. The body of the captain was lying at his feet. Another man was dying, close by the opening in which the wheel revolved. The floor was covered with blood, splinters, glass, and the fragments of a shattered stove. One side of the little room was broken in, and the other side was perforated where the projectiles made their exit.

The first gun from the Rebels threw a shell which entered the side of the pilothouse and struck the captain, who was sitting just behind the pilot. Death must have been instantaneous. A moment later, a "spherical-case shot"* followed the shell. It exploded as it struck the woodwork, and a portion of the contents entered the side of the barkeeper of the boat. In falling to the floor he fell against the wheel. The pilot, steering the boat with one hand, pulled the dying man from the wheel with the other, and placed him by the side of the dead captain.

Though, apparently, the pilot was as cool and undisturbed as ever, his face was whiter than usual. He said the most trying moment of all was soon after the first shots were fired. Wishing to "round the bend" as speedily as possible, he rang the bell as a signal to the engineer to check the speed of one of the [paddle] wheels. The signal was not obeyed, the engineers having fled to places of safety. He rang the bell once more. He shouted down the speaking-tube, to enforce compliance with his order. There was no answer. The engines were caring for themselves. The boat must be controlled by the rudder alone. With a dead man and a dying man at his feet, with the Rebel shot and shell every moment perforating the boat or falling near it, and with no help from those who should control the machinery, he felt that his position was a painful one.

We were out of danger. An hour later we found the gunboat Neosho, *at anchor, eight miles farther up the stream. Thinking we might again be attacked, the commander of the* Neosho *offered to convoy us to Red River. We accepted his offer. As soon as the* Neosho *raised sufficient steam to enable her to move, we proceeded on our course.*

Order was restored on the Von Phul. *Most of the passengers gath-*

---

* An exploding cannon shell. The hollowed casing contained a charge of powder surrounded by a layer of musket balls.

ered in little groups, and talked about the recent occurrence. I returned to my writing, and Colburn gave his attention to a book. With the gunboat at our side, no one supposed there was any danger of another attack.

A half-hour after starting under convoy of the gunboat, the Rebels once more opened fire. They paid no attention to the Neosho, but threw all their projectiles at the Von Phul. The first shell passed through the cabin, wounding a person near me, and grazing a post against which Colburn and myself were resting our chairs. This shell was followed by others in quick succession, most of them passing through the cabin. One exploded under the portion of the cabin directly beneath my position. The explosion uplifted the boards with such force as to overturn my table and disturb the steadiness of my chair.

I dreaded splinters far more than I feared the pitiless iron. I left the cabin, through which the shells were pouring, and descended to the lower deck. It was no better there than above. We were increasing the distance between ourselves and the Rebels, and the shot began to strike lower down. Nearly every shot raked the lower deck. A loose plank on which I stood was split for more than half its length by a shot which struck my foot when its force was nearly spent. Though the skin was not abraded, and no bones were broken, I felt the effect of the blow for several weeks.

I lay down upon the deck. A moment after I had taken my horizontal position, two men who lay against me were mortally wounded by a shell. The right leg of one was completely severed below the knee. This shell was the last projectile that struck the forward portion of the boat.

With a handkerchief loosely tied and twisted with a stick, I endeavored to stop the flow of blood from the leg of the wounded man. I was partially successful, but the stoppage of blood could not save the man's life. He died within the hour.

Forty-two shot and shell struck the boat. The escape pipe was severed where it passed between two staterooms, and filled the cabin with steam. The safe in the captain's office was perforated as if it had been made of wood. A trunk was broken by a shell, and its contents were scattered upon the floor. Splinters had fallen in the cabin, *and were spread thickly upon the carpet. Every person who escaped uninjured had his own list of incidents to narrate.*

Out of about fifty persons on board the Von Phul *at the time of this occurrence, twelve were killed or wounded. One of the last projectiles that struck the boat injured a boiler sufficiently to allow the escape of steam. In ten minutes our engines moved very feebly. We were forced to "tie up" to the eastern bank of the river. We were by this time out of range of the Rebel battery. The* Neosho *had opened fire, and by the time we made fast to the bank, the Rebels were in retreat.*

The Neosho *ceased firing and moved to our relief. Before she reached us, the steamer* Atlantic *came in sight, descending the river. We hailed her, and she came alongside. Immediately on learning our condition, her captain offered to tow the* Von Phul *to Red River, twenty miles distant. There we could lie, under protection of the gunboats, and repair the damages to our machinery. We accepted his offer at once.*[4]

Trapped on a Falling River

In 1864 Admiral David D. Porter took his Mississippi squadron of United States gunboats up Red River in Louisiana to support an army invasion. Porter was less than enthusiastic about the venture; earlier experiences had sobered him to the thought of running his fleet up tributary waters. This campaign was to take Porter's boats far into enemy territory. It would leave him vulnerable if the army should pull back. And that's exactly what happened. Defeated on land, the supporting army was now withdrawing, and Porter faced a devilishly tricky task. It was not merely a matter of turning around his ten gunboats and two tugs in the relatively narrow river. That was the easy part. But Red River had dealt its own hand; it had fallen to the point that there was not enough water in the channel. What happened next is described in Porter's subsequent report to the Secretary of the Navy:

> *MISSISSIPPI SQUADRON, FLAGSHIP BLACK HAWK.*
> *Mouth Red River, May 16, 1864.*
> *Sir: The water had fallen so low that I had no hope or expectation of getting the vessels out this season, and as the army had made*

arrangements to evacuate the country, I saw nothing before me but the destruction of the best part of the Mississippi Squadron.

Lieutenant Colonel Joseph Bailey, acting engineer of the Nineteenth Army Corps, proposed a plan of building a series of dams across the rocks at the falls and raising the water high enough to let the vessels pass over. This proposition looked like madness, and the best engineers ridiculed it, but Colonel Bailey was so sanguine of success that I requested General Banks to have it done, and he entered heartily in the work. Provisions were short and forage was almost out, and the dam was promised to be finished in 10 days or the army would have to leave us. I was doubtful about the time, but had no doubt about the ultimate success if time would only permit. General Banks placed at the disposal of Colonel Bailey all the force he required, consisting of some 3,000 men and 200 or 300 wagons. All the neighboring steam mills were torn down for material, two or three regiments of Maine men were set to work felling trees and, on the second day after my arrival in Alexandria from Grand Ecore, the work had fairly begun.

Trees were falling with great rapidity, teams were moving in all directions bringing in brick and stone, quarries were opened, flat-boats were built to bring stone down from above, and every man seemed to be working with a vigor I have seldom seen equaled, while perhaps not one in fifty believed in the success of the undertaking. These falls are about a mile in length, filled with rugged rocks, over which at the present stage of water it seemed to be impossible to make a channel.

The work was commenced by running out from the left bank of the river a tree dam, made of the bodies of very large trees, brush, brick, and stone, cross tied with other heavy timber, and strengthened in every way which ingenuity could devise. This was run out about 300 feet into the river. Four large coal barges were then filled with brick and sunk at the end of it. From the right bank of the river, cribs filled with stone were built out to meet the barges, all of which was successfully accomplished, notwithstanding there was a current running of 9 miles an hour, which threatened to sweep everything before it. I will take too much time to enter into the details of this truly *wonderful work; suffice it so say that the dam had nearly reached completion in eight days' working time, and the water had risen sufficiently on the upper falls to allow the* Fort Hindman, Osage, *and* Neosho *to get down and be ready to pass the dam. In another day it would have been high enough to enable all the other vessels to pass the upper falls. Unfortunately, on the morning of the 9th [of May], the pressure of water became so great that it swept away two of the stone barges, which swung in below the dam on the opposite side. Seeing this unfortunate accident I jumped on a horse and rode up to where the upper vessels were anchored, and ordered the* Lexington *to pass the upper falls if possible, and immediately attempt to go through the dam. I thought I might be able to save the four vessels below, not knowing whether the persons employed on the work would ever have the heart to renew their enterprise.*

The Lexington *succeeded in getting over the upper falls just in time, the water rapidly falling as she was passing over. She then steered directly for the opening in the dam, through which the water was rushing so furiously that it seemed as if nothing but destruction awaited her. Thousands of beating hearts looked on anxious for the result; the silence was so great as the* Lexington *approached the dam that a pin might almost be heard to fall. She entered the gap with a full head of steam on, pitched down the roaring torrent, made two or three spasmodic rolls, hung for a moment on the rocks below, was then swept into deep water by the current, and rounded to, safely into the bank.*

Thirty thousand voices rose in one deafening cheer, and universal joy seemed to pervade the face of every man present.

The Neosho *followed next, all her hatches battened down and every precaution taken against accident. She did not fare as well as the* Lexington, *her pilot having become frightened as he approached the abyss, and stopped her engine, when I particularly ordered a full head of steam to be carried; the result was that for a moment her hull disappeared from sight under the water. Everyone thought she was lost. She rose, however, swept along over the rocks with the current, and fortunately escaped with only one hole in her bottom, which was stopped in the course of an hour. The* Hindman *and* Osage *both* came through beautifully without touching a thing, and I thought if I was only fortunate enough to get my large vessels as well over the falls, my fleet would once more do good service on the Mississippi.

The accident to the dam, instead of disheartening Colonel Bailey, only induced him to renew his exertions, after he had seen the success of getting four vessels through.

The noble-hearted soldiers, seeing their labor of the last eight days swept away in a moment, cheerfully went to work to repair damages, being confident now that all the gunboats would be finally brought over. These men had been working for eight days and nights up to their necks in water in the broiling sun, cutting trees and wheeling bricks, and nothing but good humor prevailed amongst them. On the whole, it was very fortunate the dam was carried away, as the two barges that were swept away from the center swung around against some rocks on the left and made a fine cushion for the vessels, and prevented them, as it afterwards appeared, from running on certain destruction.

The force of the water and the current being too great to construct a continuous dam of 600 feet across the river in so short a time, Colonel Bailey determined to leave a gap of 55 feet in the dam and build a series of wing dams on the upper falls. This was accomplished in three days' time and on the 11th instant the Mound City, Carondelet, and Pittsburgh came over the falls, a good deal of labor having been expended in hauling them through, the channel being very crooked, scarcely wide enough for them. Next day the Ozark, Louisville, Chillicothe, and two tugs also succeeded in crossing the upper falls.

Immediately afterwards the Mound City, Carondelet, and Pittsburgh started in succession to pass the dam, all their hatches battened down and every precaution taken to prevent accident.

The passage of these vessels was a most beautiful sight, only to be realized when seen. They passed over without an accident except the unshipping of one or two rudders. This was witnessed by all the troops, and the vessels were heartily cheered when they passed over. Next morning at 10 o'clock the Louisville, Chillicothe, Ozark, and two tugs passed over without any accident, except the loss of one man *who was swept off the deck of one of the tugs. By 3 o'clock that after-noon the vessels were all coaled, ammunition replaced, and all steamed down the river, with the convoy of transports in company. A good deal of difficulty was anticipated in getting over the bars in lower Red River, depth of water reported only five feet, gunboats were drawing six. Providentially we had a rise from the backwater of the Mississippi, that river being very high at the time, the backwater extending to Alexandria, 150 miles distant, enabling us to pass all the bars and obstructions with safety.*

Words are inadequate to express the admiration I feel for the abil-ities of Lieutenant Colonel Bailey. This is without doubt the best engi-neering feat ever performed. Under the best circumstances a private company would not have completed this work under one year, and to an ordinary mind the whole thing would have appeared an utter impossibility. Leaving out his abilities as an engineer, [and] the credit he has conferred upon the country, he has saved to the Union a valu-able fleet, worth nearly $2,000,000; more, he has deprived the enemy of a triumph which would have emboldened them to carry on this war a year or two longer, for the intended departure of the army was a fixed fact, and there was nothing left for me to do in case that event occurred but destroy every part of the vessels, so that the rebels could make nothing of them. The highest honors the government can bestow on Colonel Bailey can never repay him for the service he has ren-dered the country.[5]

For his skill and effort Joseph Bailey received a special citation from Congress and a promotion to brigadier general. After the war he became sheriff of Vernon County, Missouri. In 1867 he was killed by two men as he attempted to arrest them.[6]

"It's no use . . . blow her up"

The war on the river never went well for the Confederates; with singu-lar exceptions their gunboats and rams had done poorly. By 1865 all but two of them either were destroyed or captured. The two that remained—the unfinished *Missouri* and the swift ocean tug *William H. Webb*—lay up Red River, hiding as it were, for they had no hope of successfully engaging the

Federal navy. That is, until a Confederate buccaneer named Charles W. Read came along.

This was the same Lieutenant Read who so deftly handled the stern guns on the *Arkansas* in 1862. That one voyage might have been enough for any cautious man, but Read was an adventurer. After the *Arkansas'* battles, Read went to sea, and as captain of a privateer he wreaked havoc and fear on Yankee merchant ships all along the eastern seaboard. He was captured in 1863 while trying to steal a ship in the harbor of Portland, Maine. Released more than a year later, just as the Confederacy began to crumble, Read proposed to his government to run the *William H. Webb* out of Red River and down the Mississippi to the Gulf, where he might yet seriously impede the Union war effort.

The race between the *Natchez* and the *Robert E. Lee* may be the most famous on the river, but it pales when compared with the last run of the *William Webb*. The story is told in two parts. First, the preliminaries written by Lieutenant Read in a report to the Confederate Navy Department, followed by the recollections of crewman William Biggio:

> *C.S.S. WEBB*
>
> *Alexandria, Red River, April 22, 1865*
>
> *Sir: On assuming command I found the vessel totally unprepared for the service upon which I was ordered to take her, without a single gun on board, little or no crew, no fuel, and no small arms, save a few cutlasses, and as the vessel was some eighty miles below Shreveport on her way here, I was obliged to return to the first-named place, where I expected to obtain all my wants from General Kirby Smith, commanding this department.*
>
> *From him I procured one 30-pounder Parrott [rifled cannon] for a bow pivot, and two small iron 12-pounders, that may serve me in bringing to vessels, etc. Carpenters were obtained and hastened in their work, as the rapid fall in this river made me apprehensive of serious impediment to the future execution of my instructions. On returning down the river I filled up every available place in the ship with wood, not finding more than one day's coal, which, together with the wood, will give me fuel for about five days. I have likewise taken on board 190 bales of cotton, which serves as a very efficient shield*

to the machinery, backed, as it is, by 12 inches of pine bulkhead, entirely surrounding the engine room. The great amount of wood I have been obliged to stow, with the cotton, causes an average draft of 9½ feet—about 2 feet more than when light. This increase in depth immerses the buckets on the [paddle] wheel so much as to enforce the necessity of lifting much weight in the passage of the buckets from the water up, thus impeding the progress of the vessel.

I have but two engineers understanding the machinery of the vessel, and two young third assistants whom I cannot trust alone in the engine room for some time as yet; the two former will therefore be obliged to remain on watch whilst going out and whilst the double engines are unconnected, it not being advisable to work them connected when there exists a probability for rapid maneuvering.

Thus apprised of my condition, you will be enabled to better account for any accident that may result from the step I propose taking tonight, starting from this point down, so as to reach the mouth of the Red in time to commence the downward passage of the Mississippi tomorrow about 8 P.M .

Off the mouth of the Red lies the [U.S.S] Tennessee, Manhattan, and Lafayette, ironclads, and one boiler-iron plated gunboat, the Gazelle. The distance from the mouth of the Red to the mouth of the Mississippi is about 300 miles, and at regular distances in most of this length there are one or two of the enemy's gunboats. To be the first to notify these of my approach is my chief aim; toward effecting this I have arranged with General Thomas to cut the [telegraph] wires as far down as Plaquemine by 8 P.M. tomorrow. I shall myself cut the wires below that place, and shall take every precaution to prevent the forts (Jackson and St. Philip) from being informed of my movements, as these formidable fortifications will have to be passed in daylight.

As I will have to stake everything upon speed and time, I will not attack any vessel in the passage unless I perceive a possibility of her arresting my progress. In this event I am prepared with five torpedoes (100 pounds), one of which I hold shipped on its pole on the bows.[7]

William Biggio now picks up the story. Biggio was a quartermaster on the *Webb*. During this race down the river Biggio's duty station was in the pilothouse where he kept the log and helped steer the vessel:

After leaving Alexandria the Webb moved down the river about forty miles and then tied up. At this point a spar torpedo fastened to a 35-foot spar was attached to the bow of the boat. It was intended with this torpedo to blow up the Manhattan or one of the other large vessels lying at the mouth of Red River, provided it became necessary. After getting the spar satisfactorily arranged, the Webb moved again slowly down the river just after dark. This was accomplished, and so far all plans had worked well.

In front of the Webb, only a few hundred yards distant lay the Federal fleet of about six vessels. It was a little after eight o'clock in the evening on a starlit night in April when we first descried the enemy's vessels. All of our lights were concealed, and we were running very slowly in order not to make much noise. We approached close enough to distinguish every vessel, and were within five hundred yards of them before they discovered us. I was at the wheel, and we had slowed up the vessel as much as possible preparatory to making the final run of the gauntlet. The steam in the engines was very high, and the engineer called to the captain that he could not stand it much longer without blowing the vessel up. At this moment a rocket went up from the Federal fleet, and we knew that we had been discovered.

Captain Read then yelled, "Let her go!" and I rang the fast bell. The engineer threw the throttle wide open, and the Webb fairly leaped and trembled. "Keep her for the biggest opening between them," shouted the captain. I did as commanded. By this time every whistle of the fleet was screaming, drums were beating, rockets were going up, and it seemed as if the very devil was to pay. I kept the Webb straight on her course, however, headed for the biggest opening, and before a gun was fired we passed the blockade and had turned the bend and were making down the Mississippi River.

After passing Hog Point I looked back and saw two Federal gunboats following the Webb, but kept on her course soon left her pursuers in the distance. All the way from Red River to New Orleans Federal gunboats were supposed to be anchored in the river every five miles. As the Webb approached one of these boats she was signaled. The signal was answered by [Quartermaster James] Kelly, who remained on deck uncovering lights. When the Webb was nearly on the gunboat, Kelly would run up any kind of light, and the Webb would be past the Federal boat before the fraud could be detected. About fifteen miles below the mouth of Red River the Webb lowered a boat and sent a squad ashore to cut the telegraph wires. This operation was performed several times, and thus passed the first night after running the blockade at the mouth of Red River.

At daylight we were close to a gunboat lying in front of us at Donaldsonville. She ran up her signals and at the same time ran out her guns. We thought we were in for it, but fortunately it was nothing more than a drill, and the guns were run back in again.

The signals of the Federal boats were duly answered by the Webb, flags being used in the daytime in the manner that the lights were used at night. We could have destroyed millions of dollars of property on our trip, but our sole object was to run the blockade.

Determining to pass New Orleans as soon as possible, we made the best time we could down the river. About 1 P.M. we reached New Orleans and found the Federal fleet lying at St. Mary's Market. We were all feeling good, thinking that everything was all right and that we were not expected. We reckoned wrong, however, for just as we got abreast of the Lackawanna, a 24-gun ship, her captain received news of our coming. Before he could get all his men to their quarters, however, we were right on him; in fact, so close that a rock could have been thrown from one boat to the other. In less time than it takes to tell it, the Lackawanna gave a shot that went clear through the Webb abreast the forehatch four feet from the water's edge and landed in Algiers [the town across the river from New Orleans].

After the first shot Captain Read ordered Kelly to haul down the false colors and run up the colors of the Confederacy, as he expected to see the Webb sunk right there and he wanted her to go down with her own colors flying. After giving this order the captain walked to the side of the Webb nearest the firing and remained there until we passed. Pilot Jim West, an old Red River pilot, who was helping me handle the vessel, lay down on the deck and I was left alone at the wheel. The Lackawanna's first shot was followed by others. Her second shot was aimed at the pilothouse, but struck a bale of cotton and glanced up, passing over the pilothouse and doing no damage. The third shot went through the chimney guys of the Webb and did little harm. By this time we were turning the bend of the river just below New Orleans and the firing from the Lackawanna ceased, her captain discovering that her shots were going straight into Algiers and doing great damage there.

At the lower part of Algiers, and about the middle of the river, was a large vessel supposed to be the Federal gunboat Hartford. We tried to blow her up with our torpedo, but by some mistake the torpedo couldn't be fired in time; and the mistake, as it happened, was a fortunate one, for the vessel proved not to be the Hartford, but the Fear Not, loaded with fixed ammunition. Had we run into her with the torpedo as we intended, the chances are that no one on either vessel would have lived to tell the tale.

When we got alongside the Fear Not, an odd incident occurred. A Federal officer was standing on the deck of the Fear Not with a lady. Price, one of the pilots of the Webb, picked up a gun and was in the act of shooting the officer when Captain Read ordered him to desist. Price reluctantly obeyed, remarking as he laid down the gun that it was the first time he was ever ordered not to shoot a Yankee.

Seeing that the Fear Not would not molest us, our next thought was to get away, so down the river we went. Looking back, we saw the steamer Hollyhock coming after us. The Hollyhock was a low-bar towboat, fast and powerful, but not so large as the Webb. Our object was to keep ahead of her, and this we did with little trouble. She chased us thirty-two miles down the river from New Orleans, when all of a sudden we ran right on top of the war sloop Richmond, a 24-gun ship lying in the middle of the river. As we neared her we saw that she had both broadsides out.

The Webb was slowed up and Captain Read called all the officers in front of the pilothouse and addressed them: "It's no use; it's a failure. The Richmond will drown us all, and if she does not the forts below will, as they have a range of three miles each way up and down the river, and they know by this time that we are coming. Had we passed New Orleans without being discovered, I would have cut the wires below the city and we could have reached the Gulf with little *trouble. As it is, I think the only thing left for us to do is to set fire to the* Webb *and blow her up."*

When the captain finished talking not a word was spoken by any one, but every man bowed his head in respectful obedience. Captain Read then ordered the pilot and myself, who were at the wheel, to steer to the shore, and ordered the gunner to set the fires in all parts of the vessel with slow match and magazine. Hardly had the captain finished his order when we made for the east bank of the river. We struck bottom fifty yards from the shore, running the Webb's *nose out in four feet less water than she drew. Life lines were then thrown over the bow of the boat to get overboard by, and everybody commenced to get ashore like rats leaving a ship. As soon as we got ashore we struck out across a sugar plantation until we reached the back of it, where we hid from the enemy's view and yet could see the* Webb.

In the meantime the Hollyhock *steamed up to the* Webb *and tried to put out her fires with water hose. She also rescued a man named Preston and a boy named Hyner, who had remained on the* Webb *and had made no effort to escape. The* Hollyhock *took from the* Webb *her flags and small arms and backed away. It was now about three o'clock in the afternoon, and from our position at the back of the farm we watched the boat burn. At length her magazine was reached, and with an explosion that shook the waters far and near the Confederate ram* Webb *came to her tragic end.*[8]

1   Isaac N. Brown, "The Confederate Gun-Boat 'Arkansas,'" in *Battles and Leaders of the Civil War*, pp. 3:572-79.
2   Quoted in Michael L. Gillespie, "Legendary Wake of Terror," *Military History* 3, no. 3 (December 1986): 25.
3   Ferris, p. 26.
4   Knox, pp. 471-77.
5   *Official Records . . . Navies*, series I, 26:130-33.
6   *Historical Times Illustrated Encyclopedia of the Civil War*, s.v. "Bailey, Joseph," by Dean E. Smith.
7   *Official Records . . . Navies*, series I, 22:168-69.
8   Quoted in Clarence Jeffries, "Running the Blockade on the Mississippi," *Confederate Veteran* 22 (1914): 22-23; see also Michael L. Gillespie, "The Great Gunboat Chase," *Civil War Times Illustrated* 33, no. 3 (July-August, 1994): 30-37.

Epilogue

$\underset{\text{(ornament)}}{}$

One Last Trip

$\underset{\text{(ornament)}}{}$

The bold, brash days of packet steamboating lasted approximately sixty years. They died slowly in fits and spurts, sometimes rallying, only to sink farther back into oblivion. Steam packets were victims of war and economics, of railroads and barge lines, of speed and reliability.

Mark Twain pronounced the great era dead in 1882. Having by then gained notoriety as a lecturer and author, he came back to the Valley to see what had changed. He was not entirely prepared for what he saw—the bustling levees, the mile-long rows of moored packet steamers—they all were gone. In their stead were nothing more than towboats and barges; and puffing in the background was the great interloper—the railroad locomotive. Thus in these waning days of packet steamboating Twain came back, with traveling companions and a stenographer, to ride the boats that were left, renew old acquaintances, and restore to his mind the mood of those days he never had intended to leave. The notes of his journey would become the basis for his book *Life on the Mississippi*.

In St. Louis Clemens boarded the steamer *Gold Dust* and decided, at least for the time being, to travel incognito. In his book he gave an account of his return to the pilothouse and the fantastic yarns that the unabashed steersman unloaded on him. But as an old man, many years later, Clemens set forth a different version to his biographer, and it was taken down exactly as he told it. The episode serves well as a fitting conclusion to this journey down the river, a river that has vanished forever beyond the distant bend of time:

> *I did not write that story in the book quite as it happened. We went on board at night. Next morning I was up bright and early and out on deck to see if I could recognize any of the old landmarks. I could not remember any. I did not know where we were at all. It was a new river to me entirely. I climbed up in the pilothouse and there was a fellow of about forty at the wheel. I said, "Good morning." He answered pleasantly enough. His face was entirely strange to me. Then I sat down on the high seat back of the wheel and looked out at the river and began to ask a few questions, such as a landsman would ask. He began, in the old way, to fill me up with the old lies, and I enjoyed letting him do it.*
>
> *Then suddenly he turned round to me and said: "I want to get a cup of coffee. You hold her, will you, till I come back?" And before I could say a word he was out of the pilothouse door and down the steps. It all came so suddenly that I sprang to the wheel, of course, as I would have done twenty years before. Then in a moment I realized my position. Here I was with a great big steamboat in the middle of the Mississippi River, without any further knowledge than that fact, and the pilot out of sight. I settled my mind on three conclusions: first, that the pilot might be a lunatic; second, that he had recognized me and thought I knew the river; third, that we were in a perfectly safe place, where I could not possibly kill the steamboat. But that last conclusion, though the most comforting, was an extremely doubtful one. I knew perfectly well that no sane pilot would trust his steamboat for a single moment in the hands of a greenhorn unless he were standing by the greenhorn's side. Of course, by force of habit, when I grabbed the wheel, I had taken the steering marks ahead and astern, and I made up my mind to hold her on those marks to the hair; but I could feel myself getting old and gray. Then all at once I recognized where we were; we were in what is called the Grand Chain—a succession of hidden rocks, one of the most dangerous places on the river. There were two rocks there only about seventy feet apart, and you've*

got to go exactly between them or wreck the boat. There was a time when I could have done it without a tremor, but that time wasn't now. I would have given any reasonable sum to have been on shore just at that moment. I think I was about ready to drop dead when I heard a step on the pilothouse stair; then the door opened and the pilot came in, quietly picking his teeth, took the wheel, and I crawled weakly back to the seat.

He said: "You thought you were playing a nice joke on me, didn't you? You thought I didn't know who you were. Why, I recognized that drawl of yours as soon as you opened your mouth."

I said, "Who the hell are you? I don't remember you."

"Well," he said, "perhaps you don't, but I was a cub pilot on the river before the war, when you were a licensed pilot, and I couldn't get a license when I was qualified for one, because the Pilots' Association was so strong at that time that they could keep new pilots out if they wanted to, and the law was that I had to be examined by licensed pilots, and for a good while I could not get one to make that examination. But one day you and another pilot offered to do it, and you put me through a good, healthy examination and endorsed my application for a license. I had never seen you before, and I have never seen you since until now, but I recognized you."

"All right," I said. "But if I had gone half a mile farther with this steamboat we might have all been at the bottom of the river."

We got to be good friends, of course, and I spent most of my time up there with him. When we got down below Cairo, and there was a big, full river—for it was high-water season and there was no danger of the boat hitting anything so long as she kept in the river—I had her most of the time on his watch. He would lie down and sleep, and leave me there to dream that the years had not slipped away; that there had been no war, no mining days, no literary adventures; that I was still a pilot, happy and carefree as I had been twenty years before.[1]

---

1   Paine, pp. 2:736-38.

Selected Bibliography

Manuscript Collections

Audubon, John J., Letters. Special Collections Department, Smithsonian Institution Libraries. Washington, D.C.

Blossom, Henry Martyn, Journal, 1851-1853. Missouri Historical Society Collections. St. Louis.

Fortney, John F. M., Letters. Illinois State Historical Library. Springfield.

Foster, Walter B., Diary, 1840-1845. Missouri Historical Society Collections. St. Louis.

Gilman, William Henry, Diary, 1840-1858. Rare Books and Manuscripts Division. New York Public Library.

Hand Papers. Columbiana and Special Collections, Columbia University. New York.

Hinchy, William James, Diary. National Frontier Trails Center. Independence, Missouri.

Hobart, Nathanial, Manuscript Letter-Journal, 1837-1838. Western Americana Collection, Yale University Library. New Haven, Connecticut.

Miller, Captain William B., Letter, 1875. Inland Rivers Library, Rare Books and Special Collections. Public Library of Cincinnati and Hamilton County.

Peale, Titian Ramsay, Journals, 1819-1842. Library of Congress Manuscript Division. Washington, D.C.

Trail, E. B., Collection, 1858-1965. Joint Collection—Western Historical Manuscript Collection and State Historical Society of Missouri Manuscripts. Kansas City.

Van Vlack, Alonzo, Letter. Michigan Historical Collections, Bentley Historical Library, University of Michigan. Ann Arbor.

Government Documents

Annual Report of the Secretary of War, 1868.

U.S. Congress. House. Committee on Commerce. *Railroad Bridge Across the Mississippi River at Rock Island.* H. Rept. 250, 35th Cong., 1st sess., 1858.

U.S. Congress. House. Committee on the Post Office and Post Roads. *Minority Report.* H. Rept. 158, 32d Cong., 1st sess., 1852.

U.S. Congress. House. Committee on the Post Office and Post Roads. *Wheeling Bridge,* H. Rept. 158, 32d Cong., 1st sess., 1852.

U.S. Congress. House. Letter from the Secretary of War. *Survey of the Ohio River.* Ex. Doc. 72, 41st Cong., 3d sess., 1871.

Newspapers

Daily Missouri Republican, St. Louis, Missouri.

Globe-Democrat, St. Louis, Missouri.

Niles' Weekly Register, Baltimore, Maryland.

Quad City Times, Davenport, Iowa.

St. Joseph Gazette, St. Joseph, Missouri.
Weekly Reveille, St. Louis, Missouri.

Books and Articles

Account of an Expedition from Pittsburgh to the Rocky Mountains under the Command of Major Stephen H. Long. Introduction by Howard R. Lamar. Barre, Mass.: Imprint Society, 1972.

Audubon, Maria, R., ed. *Audubon and His Journals*. 2 vols. New York: Scribner's Sons, 1897.

Beveridge, Albert J. *Abraham Lincoln, 1809-1858*. Boston: Houghton Mifflin, 1928.

Brown, Isaac N. "The Confederate Gun-Boat 'Arkansas.'" In *Battles and Leaders of the Civil War*, 4 vols., pp. 3:572-79. Edited by Clarence C. Buel and Robert U. Johnson. New York: Century, 1884.

Burman, Ben L. *Big River to Cross: Mississippi Life Today*. New York: John Day Co., 1940.

Chittenden, Hiram M., *History of Early Steamboat Navigation on the Missouri River: Life and Times of Joseph LaBarge*. 2 vols. New York: Francis P. Harper, 1903; reprint ed., Minneapolis: Ross & Haines, 1962.

Costello, Mary. *Climbing the Mississippi River, Bridge by Bridge*. Davenport, Iowa: By the Author, 1995.

Cowell, Joseph L. *Thirty Years Passed Among the Players in England and America*. New York: Harper, 1844; reprint ed., Hamden, Connecticut: Archon Books, 1979.

Cramer, Zadoc. *The Navigator*. Pittsburgh: Cramer, Spear & Eichbaum, 1814.

Devol, George H. *Forty Years a Gambler on the Mississippi*. 2nd ed. New York: George H. Devol, 1892.

Dohan, Mary H. *Mr. Roosevelt's Steamboat*. New York: Dodd, Mead & Co., 1981.

Dorsey, Florence L. *Master of the Mississippi: Henry Shreve and the Conquest of the Mississippi*. Boston: Houghton Mifflin, 1941.

Eads, James B. "Recollections of Foote and the Gun-Boats." *In* Battles and Leaders of the Civil War, 4 vols., pp. 1:338-46. Edited by Clarence C. Buel and Robert U. Johnson. New York: Century, 1884.

Encyclopedia USA. S.v. "Barge Lines," and "Barges," by Michael Gillespie.

Ferris, Ruth, ed. "Captain Jolly in the Civil War." *Missouri Historical Society Bulletin* 22, no. 1 (October 1965): 14-31.

Gillespie, Michael L. "The Great Gunboat Chase," *Civil War Times Illustrated* 33, no. 3 (July-August 1994): 30-37.

_____. "Legendary Wake of Terror." *Military History* 3, no. 3 (December 1986): 21-25.

Glazier, Willard. *Down the Great River*. Philadelphia: Hubbard Brothers, 1892.

Gould, E. W. *Fifty Years on the Mississippi; or, Gould's History of River Navigation*. St. Louis: Nixon-Jones Printing Co., 1889; reprint ed., Columbus, Ohio: Long's College Book Co., 1951.

Grandfort, Marie Fontenay de. *The New World*. New Orleans: Sherman, Wharton & Co., 1855.

Hamilton, Thomas. *Men and Manners in America.* 2 vols. Edinburgh: William Blackwood, 1833; reprint ed., New York: A. M. Kelley, 1968.

Hanson, Joseph M. *The Conquest of the Missouri, Being the Story of the Life of Captain Grant Marsh.* N.p.: A. C. McClurg, 1909; reprint ed., New York: Murray Hill Books, 1946.

Havinghurst, Walter. *Voices on the River.* New York: Macmillan, 1964.

Heckmann, William L. *Steamboating: Sixty-Five Years on Missouri's Rivers.* Kansas City: Burton Publishing, 1950.

Historical Times Illustrated Encyclopedia of the Civil War. S.v. "Bailey, Joseph," by Dean E. Smith.

Hopkins, Arthur E. "Steamboats at Louisville and on the Ohio and Mississippi Rivers." *The Filson Club Historical Quarterly* 17 (July 1943): 143-62.

Humphreys, Andrew A. and Abbot, Henry L. *Report upon the Physics and Hydraulics of the Mississippi River.* Philadelphia: Lippincott, 1861.

Hunter, Louis C. *A History of Industrial Power in the United States, 1780-1930.* Vol. 2: *Steam Power.* Charlottesville: University Press of Virginia, 1985.

_____. *Steamboats on the Western Rivers: An Economic and Technological History.* Cambridge: Harvard University Press, 1949.

Jeffries, Clarence. "Running the Blockade on the Mississippi." *Confederate Veteran* 22 (1914): 22-23.

Journey to New Switzerland: Travel Account of the Koepfli and Suppiger Family to St. Louis on the Mississippi and the Founding of New Switzerland in the State of Illinois. Edited by John C. Abbott. Translated by Raymond J. Spahn. Carbondale: Southern Illinois University Press, 1987.

Knox, Thomas W. *Camp-fire and Cotton-field: Southern Adventure in Time of War.* New York: Blelock & Co., 1865; reprint ed., New York: DaCapo Press, 1969.

Latrobe, Charles J. *The Rambler in North America.* 2 vols. London: Seeley & Burnside, 1836.

McCall, Edith. *Conquering the Rivers: Henry Miller Shreve and the Navigation of America's Inland Waterways.* Baton Rouge: Louisiana State University Press, 1984.

McDonald, W.J. "The Missouri River and Its Victims." *Missouri Historical Review* 21 (1926-27): 215-42, 455-80, 581-607.

Merrick, George B. *Old Times on the Upper Mississippi: The Recollections of a Steamboat Pilot from 1854-1863.* Cleveland: Arthur H. Clark Co., 1909; reprint ed., St. Paul: Minnesota Historical Society Press, 1987.

Miller, Henry B. "Journal." *Missouri Historical Society Collections* 6 (1931): 242.

Mitchell, C. Bradford, ed. *Merchant Steam Vessels of the United States, 1790-1868.* Staten Island, New York: Steamship Historical Society, 1975.

Monette, John W. "The Progress of Navigation and Commerce on the Waters of the Mississippi River and the Great Lakes, A.D. 1700 to 1846." *Publications of the Mississippi Historical Society* 7 (1903): 479-518.

Murray, Charles A. *Travels in North America During the Years 1834, 1835, & 1836.* 2 vols. London: R. Bentley, 1839; reprint ed., New York: DaCapo Press, 1974.

Nichols, George W. "Down the Mississippi." *Harper's New Monthly Magazine* 41 (June-November 1870): 835-45.

Official Records of the Union and Confederate Navies in the War of the Rebellion. 30 vols. Washington: GPO, 1895-1925.

"On Boiler Explosions." *The Manufacturer and Builder* 1, no. 5 (May 1869): 132-34.

Paine, Albert B. *Mark Twain: A Biography.* 3 vols. New York: Harper & Brothers, 1912.

Petsche, Jerome E. *The Steamboat* Bertrand: *History, Excavation, and Architecture.* Washington: GPO, 1974.

Ralph, Julian. "The Old Way to Dixie." *Harper's New Monthly Magazine* 86, no. 512 (January 1893): 165-85.

Reardon, Mark. *Big Load Afloat: The History of the Barge and Towing Industry.* 2 vols. Arlington, Va.: The American Waterways Operators, 1981.

Skinner, Charles M. *American Myths and Legends.* 2 vols. Philadelphia: J.B. Lippincott, 1903.

Smith, Solomon F. "Bewailings of a Barge." *Weekly Reveille* 2, no. 10 (15 September 1845): 489.

————. *Theatrical Management in the West and South for Thirty Years.* New York: Harper's, 1868.

————. "Who's at the Wheel?" *Weekly Reveille* 2, no. 44 (11 May 1846): 852.

Starace, Nicholas F., II. "America's Worst Maritime Disaster: The Ill-fated Sidewheeler *Sultana.*" *Sea History* 92 (Spring 2000): 33-35.

Steele, Eliza R. *A Summer Journey in the West.* New York: J.S. Taylor & Co., 1841.

Thorpe, Thomas B. *The Mysteries of the Backwoods; or, Sketches of the Southwest.* Philadelphia: Carey & Hart, 1846.

————. "Remembrances of the Mississippi." *Harper's New Monthly Magazine* 12 (December 1855-May 1856): 25-41.

————. "The Little Steamboats of the Mississippi." [New York] *Spirit of the Times,* 9 March 1844, p. 19.

Thurston, Robert H. *A History of the Growth of the Steam-Engine.* New York: Appleton, 1878.

Travels on the Lower Mississippi, 1879-1880: A Memoir by Ernst von Hesse-Wartegg. Edited and translated by Frederic Trautmann. Columbia: University of Missouri Press, 1990.

Twain, Mark. "Old Times on the Mississippi, Part 2." *The Atlantic Monthly* 35, no. 208 (February 1875): 217-24.

————. *Life on the Mississippi.* Boston: Osgood & Co., 1883.

"Up the Mississippi." *Emerson's Magazine and Putnam's Monthly* 5, no. 40 (October 1857): 433-56.

Way, Frederick, Jr. *Way's Packet Directory, 1848-1994.* Revised ed. Athens: Ohio University Press, 1994.

Wayman, Norbury L. *Life on the River.* New York: Bonanza, 1971.

Glossary

balance rudder A rudder that extended both fore and aft of the rudder post. The balance rudder made steering easier and provided better response due to increased surface area of the rudder.

banking freight The act of taking off freight from a boat and placing it temporarily onshore in order to lessen the draft of the boat. Banking freight was necessary in some instances to set free a grounded boat.

bar A naturally occurring shallow area in or adjacent to the channel; composed of sand or sometimes gravel. In very low water, bars are exposed above the surface.

beam The widest cross-section of a boat's hull, measured internally. The term also was used to denote the mid-point of a hull's length.

bell ropes Also known as bell cords, they were wooden-handled or brass-ringed cords strung from the ceiling, floor, or wheel stand of the pilothouse. The pilot used them to signal the engineer to stop, come ahead, or reverse the engine. Sidewheel boats had two sets of bell ropes—one for each engine.

boiler The enclosed iron cylinder in which water was heated to create steam. A firebox, located beneath the boiler, heated the boiler water. Hot gases from the firebox additionally were vented through flues within the boiler. A siphon pump replaced the water as it steamed off. The water level within the boiler was critical and usually was the contributing factor in boiler explosions. The largest steamboats had as many as eight boilers.

boiler deck The second deck. The boiler deck was one deck above the boilers. The cabin and staterooms were located on the boiler deck.

bucket A wooden blade, or paddle, of a paddlewheel. On larger vessels a single bucket consisted of several heavy boards bolted together.

bulkhead A vertical wall or partition. Bulkheads within the hull helped distribute the weight of the boat along the keelson. (See *keel*.)

bustle stern A design adaptation found on many sternwheel boats equipped with balance rudders. The bustle was a bulge in the stern below the waterline that prevented driftwood from jamming the forward throw area of the rudder.

cabin An elongated, central room, running fore and aft, on the boiler deck. Also known as the main cabin, or parlor, it served as both the social hall and dining room for the cabin passengers. The cabin usually featured ornate carpentry work and a raised roof with skylights of colored glass. Doors to individual staterooms lined either side of the cabin. On larger boats, the barbershop, bar, and clerk's office were located in rooms at the forward end.

capstan A large winch, or windlass, mounted vertically on a boat's forecastle. Capstans were used for pulling in heavy lines. Early in the steamboat era they were turned by hand, but in later years most boats utilized steam-powered capstans.

channel The deepest part of the river bed. The channel is more or less continuous, but is difficult to perceive as it crosses from one side of the river to the other.

chute The non-channel watercourse around an island. Often no more than a bayou or creek, the chute delineated the "back side" of an island. Like cut-offs, chutes could be navigated in high water by up bound boats. This usually resulted in a shorter running distance compared to the channel side.

cordelling The process of towing a vessel, usually a keelboat, upstream from the bank. The cordelle was a heavy line attached to the boat's mast. It was hauled forward by men or draft animals on shore. The word is derived from the French *corde*, meaning "rope."

cut-off An alteration to the water course that occurred when the river cut through the narrow neck of a horseshoe-shaped bend. Natural cut-offs took place during flood stages when saturation and erosion weakened the banks, causing them to cave-in and give way to the force of the moving water. Man-made cut-offs were formed by the construction of a narrow ditch across the peninsula, leaving a temporary earthen plug at either end. When the plugs were removed, the river flowed in and widened the ditch by scouring action. Given time, the river would abandon the longer path around the bend in favor of the cut-off.

cylinder head The solid end block, or cap, of a steam piston cylinder. It was attached to the cylinder by a series of bolts and had to withstand maximum steam pressure within the cylinder without leaking or cracking.

deck passage Equivalent to steerage class on ocean steamers, deck passage entitled the traveler to occupy only the main deck during the voyage. Meals were not included, but could be purchased individually. Shelter was minimal and often consisted of nothing more than a wide shelf upon which to make one's berth.

displacement The weight of water moved aside, or displaced, by the hull of a boat. In order to remain buoyant, the weight of a boat could not exceed the weight of the displaced water.

doctor (engine) A steam operated pump. Its primary purpose was to feed water into the boiler.

double The act of making two trips past a given point, while carrying half the cargo load on each trip. This was made necessary where the current was too strong for the boat to gain headway with its full load of freight.

draft The depth of a boat's hull under the waterline. Draft was measured at the bow and stern, and could be manipulated by shifting the cargo load fore and aft.

escape pipes Steam venting chimneys. Escape pipes resembled small smokestacks. They protruded well above the hurricane deck, directly over each high-pressure engine. Often referred to as 'scape pipes.

flanking Lateral movement of a boat. Since steamboats had virtually flat bottoms with no discernible keel, unintentional flanking could occur in conditions of high crosswinds or crosscurrents. Flanking was desirable in some situations, and sternwheelers could intentionally flank by playing the paddlewheel and rudders against the current.

forecastle The portion of the main deck that extended forward of the superstructure. The forecastle was the area for the anchors, capstan, spars, stage plank, and hawsers. It was common also to find freight stored in this area.

flue One or more pipes that extended through the length of a boiler. The flue carried hot gases from the firebox to the breeching and aided in heating the water within the boiler. The flue could become red-hot when exposed by low water in the boiler. This often then led to a collapse of the flue and an explosion of the boiler.

guard That portion of the main deck that extended beyond the width of the hull. On larger boats the overhanging guards on either side increased the main deck area by several hundred square feet; this allowed a much greater cargo carrying capacity. The guards also helped deflect floating objects and fixed obstructions from the path of the side paddlewheels. It is from this function that they derived their name.

gunwale The upper edge of the sides of the hull. Sometimes phonetically spelled as gunnel.

hawser A heavy line, or rope. Used for mooring or towing a vessel.

hog chains A system of chains and rods meant to prevent the hull from sagging, or "hogging," under heavy loads. Hog chains extended from the forward hull, up over the hurricane deck, and back down to the stern. They could be tightened or loosened as needed by means of turnbuckles.

hogshead A wooden barrel with a liquid capacity of at least 63 gallons.

hurricane deck The uppermost deck of a steamboat. The name was derived from the ever-present breeze that made it a favorite viewing place on warm evenings. It was the location of the boat's large signal bell.

jackstaff A tall pole mounted on the bow. Though often depicted as a flagpole, the jackstaff served primarily as a vertical reference line to assist the pilot in aligning the bow with a point on shore. (See also *verge*.)

kedge The act of pulling a steamboat over a shoal or bar by means of a small anchor known as the kedge. Trailing a hawser, the kedge was carried by yawl to a point beyond the shoal; it was then dropped overboard with the other end of the hawser wound around the boat's capstan. When the capstan turned, the boat was winched forward.

keel The main structural member of the hull, running fore and aft, upon which additional framework was formed. The keel of sailing craft projected well below the lines of the hull, but it was less prominent on river steamboats. Eventually the evolution of riverboat designs led to the elimination of the protruding keel in favor of an internal longitudinal beam known as the keelson.

ladies' cabin The back, or after section, of the cabin. On some boats the ladies' cabin was partitioned off from the main cabin, on others it was delineated by the presence of fine carpeting. The ladies' cabin sometimes featured a piano and colored-glass windows facing rearward. While not the exclusive domain of women, social mores of the time dictated that a gentleman would not enter the ladies' cabin unless escorted or invited in by a woman. It also served as a family room.

larboard The left side of a boat. Now called the port side.

lead (line) A weighted rope with marked increments that was used to measure the river's depth. The lead line was thrown forward from near the bow and pulled taunt as the boat drew alongside. The leadsman sang out the depth in a voice loud enough to be heard in the pilothouse.

lighter A barge or old hull used to carry a portion of a steamboat's cargo. Most often a lighter was used in order to reduce the draft of the steamboat in shoal water. Usually the lighter was lashed alongside the steamboat.

lock and dam A structure that dammed the river during periods of low water to create an artificial pool upstream, combined with facilities for permitting the passage of a boat from one water level to the other.

main deck The lower deck of a steamboat. Most of the main deck was open space. It included areas for boilers, fuel bins, engine room, livestock pens, and freight. (See also *forecastle*.)

minie ball A conical, hollow-backed bullet used in military rifles of the Civil War era. The name is derived from Claude-Étienne Minié, one of the developers of the projectile.

mud clerk An assistant clerk of the boat. The name derived from the assistant clerk's responsibility of going ashore at every stop to deliver or receive bills of lading— whether that stop be a paved city wharf or a muddy plantation landing.

mud drum A cylinder-shaped sump, located beneath the boilers. The mud drum was meant to collect sediment from the boiler water.

packet A boat that carried both passengers and freight. A packet company, or packet line, consisted of mutually owned or affiliated steamboats that operated on a regular schedule.

pitman (rod) Made of thick, layered wood with iron reinforcements, it was the connecting link between the piston rod and the paddlewheel crank. Use of the direct-connecting pitman rod replaced the walking beam.

planter A submerged tree trunk with one end lodged in the river bottom and the upper end poised at or near the surface.

prow The foremost, angled portion of the bow.

reef A submerged ridge. Reefs usually angled downstream from a point of land or the head of an island. Typically, they took shape as a gradual slope that rose to within a few feet of the surface, followed by a sharp drop-off.

rounding-to The act of turning a boat into the current, or into the wind, in order to bring the vessel to a stop.

samson posts A series of heavy poles over which the hog chains were strung. Samson posts extended vertically or diagonally upward from the hull and distributed the load of the hog chains evenly throughout the length of the hull.

sawyer A submerged tree, nearly waterlogged, but with enough buoyancy to permit the upper branches to occasionally rise above the surface. The name was derived from its up and down motion.

sidewheeler A steamer with two paddlewheels, one on either side of the boat. In all but the smallest sidewheelers, the paddlewheel was enclosed in a housing to minimize spray.

snag An object embedded in the stream that created an obstruction or hazard to navigation. The term most especially applied to trees and limbs encountered singularly or in clusters.

snagboat A shallow-draft, double-hulled steamboat designed to remove snags from the river channel. Removal usually was accomplished by pulling or lifting the snag from its location and then cutting it into small sections.

sounding The act of measuring a river's depth, usually by means of a lead-weighted rope, or a pole. Depth was measured in feet up to nine feet; when deeper than nine feet the depth was hailed at intervals of quarter-fathoms ($1\frac{1}{2}$ feet per quarter-fathom; 6 feet per fathom).

spoonbill bow A well-rounded prow, resembling the bowl of a spoon, that enabled a steamboat to beach itself at a shallow landing. The slow turning of the paddlewheels would hold the boat in place while loading or unloading, after which the boat could then extract itself by reversing the engines. Spoonbill bows were seen on many upper river boats beginning in the mid-1860s.

stage (plank) The walkway, or gang plank, that extended from a boat's forecastle to the shore. Most boats carried a stage on either side. Stage planks were heavy and usually required the aid of a derrick and boom to place them in position.

stanchion A vertical, load bearing beam or post. Rising from the main deck, stanchions supported the greater length of the boiler deck and are prominent features in most steamboat photographs. Also known as stationaries.

starboard The right side of a boat. Derived from the Old English word *steorbord,* meaning "steering side."

staterooms Sleeping rooms located on either side of the cabin. Each stateroom had an inner door leading to the cabin, and a window and outer door opening up to the boiler deck balcony. Staterooms were small with nothing more in them than a bunk bed and a wash stand and chair. Some staterooms could be enlarged by removing an interior bulkhead. The term "stateroom" supposedly is derived from an early-day custom of naming each room after a state rather than assigning a number to it.

sternwheeler A steamer with one, large paddlewheel located at the stern.

texas A housing containing staterooms for officers of a boat. The texas was built upon the hurricane deck, and in appearance it took the shape of a long, narrow cabin. The texas consisted of a suite of rooms, connected by a central hallway, with the captain's cabin located at the forward end. The term "texas" came about because it was the largest suite of rooms on most boats.

tiller The pivoting control arm that connected to the rudder post.

transom The abrupt, transverse closing of the stern found on sternwheelers. The transom formed a vertical wall to which the rudder posts were attached. Transoms were uncommon on sidewheelers due to the rounded closure of their sterns.

towboat A powered craft designed to push barges. Steam era towboats were sternwheelers. Outwardly they differed in appearance from packet boats by their squared prow and towing knees (i.e., forward-facing bumpers). Internally, they were more powerful and did not carry passengers. Despite their name, towboats pushed barges, either ahead or alongside.

verge (-staff) A flagpole mounted on a boat's centerline near the stern. By sighting with the jackstaff on the bow, and the verge at the stern, a pilot could keep his boat aligned with points on shore.

walking beam A fulcrum-like apparatus that transferred the up and down movement of the piston stroke to the circular motion of the paddlewheel shaft. Also known as a working beam, it was seen only on the earliest river steamboats.

wharfboat A floating dock, usually built from the hull of a dismantled steamboat. They often were owned by packet lines or freight consignment companies. Nearly all of them featured warehouse storage space; some sported an upper deck with rooms for passengers awaiting a boat.

warping The act of pulling a boat over shoal water by means of running a hawser from the boat to a fixed object on shore. The boat was then reeled forward by wrapping the hawser around the captsan.

wooding The act of loading fuel wood onto a steamboat. Typically, wooding lasting about an hour and took place twice a day.

woodyards Independently owned refueling sites along the river. Anyone with riverside property and access to wood for fuel could operate a woodyard. The woodyard owner cut the wood and sold it by the cord (4-ft.x 4-ft. x 8-ft. sections) at whatever price the market would bear. Some woodyard entrepreneurs loaded the wood onto flatboats so that a passing steamer could take the flat in tow and unload without stopping. After the Civil War, steamboats gradually converted to coal and the once common woodyards disappeared from the rivers' shores.

yawl A rowboat that served as an auxiliary craft on nearly all steamboats.

Index

About the Author

Even in his school days, author Michael L. Gillespie felt an affinity for history. Much of it certainly came from the town in which he grew up—Independence, Missouri.

"My boyhood home was just a block away from the Santa Fe Trail," Mike recalls, "and scarcely more than a mile from the place where Jesse James robbed a train. An easy bike ride would get me to an old steamboat landing on the Missouri River—the very site, too, where Lewis and Clark once camped. Little wonder that history had such a hold on me."

After four years in the Army, Mike earned a degree in secondary education with an emphasis in history from the University of Missouri-Kansas City. While still in college he began writing historical pieces for magazines and journals. The topics ranged from the military to railroads, with frequent forays into river history. Over several years he collected a wealth of source material on river steamboating.

Come Hell or High Water is Mike's tribute to the majestic waterways of the Mississippi and Ohio Rivers—a collection of contemporary tales of steamboating as preserved in the diaries and memoirs of those who lived the adventure and share it with us in their own words.

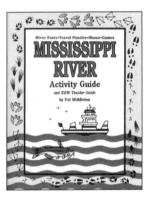

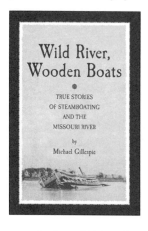
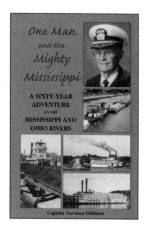